Guide to Modern Grammar and Exposition

Guide to Modern Grammar and Exposition

William Schwab

Professor of English
Oakland University
Rochester, Michigan

Harper & Row, Publishers · New York, Evanston, and London

Acknowledgments

The author expresses his gratitude to the following authors and publishers for use of materials from their works.

George Allen & Unwin, Ltd.: for a selection from *Essentials of English Grammar*, by Otto Jespersen, p. 17. Copyright 1933 by George Allen & Unwin, Ltd.

Appleton-Century-Crofts, Inc.: for a selection from *George Bernard Shaw: Man of the Century*, by Archibald Henderson, p. 732. Copyright 1956 by Appleton-Century-Crofts, Inc.

The Asia Magazine (Manila): for adaptations from "Do Asians Have an Inferiority Complex?" by Carmen Guerrero Napkil, September 1, 1963, p. 3.

The Atlantic Monthly: for a selection from "The Atlantic Report: Germany," December 1957, p. 14; "Discipline and Reward: A Writer's Life," by Catherine Drinker Bowen, December 1957, pp. 87, 88, 90; "What a Journalist Needs," by Louis Lyons, December 1957, pp. 151, 152; "The Undertaker's Racket," by Jessica Mitford, June 1963, p. 62; "What Makes News," by T. S. Matthews, December 1957, p. 81.

A. S. Barnes & Co., Inc.: for a selection from *The Tumult and the Shouting*, by Grantland Rice, p. 235. Copyright 1954 by A. S. Barnes & Co., Inc.

Thomas Y. Crowell Co.: for a selection from *Roget's International Thesaurus*, 3rd ed. Copyright © 1962 by Thomas Y. Crowell Company, publishers. By permission.

Dodd, Mead & Co.: for selections from *Sixteen Self Sketches*, by Bernard Shaw, pp. 113, 114. Copyright 1949 by Bernard Shaw.

Doubleday & Company, Inc.: for selections from *Eminent Victorians*, by Lytton Strachey, p. 135, n.d.; *Language and Society*, by Joseph Bram, pp. 10, 11, 16. Copyright 1955 by Doubleday & Company, Inc.; *Linguistics and Your Language*, by Robert A. Hall, Jr., p. 14. Copyright 1950 by Robert A. Hall, Jr.; *The Summing Up*, by Somerset Maugham, pp. 1, 30–31, 290, 293, 296. Copyright 1938 by Somerset Maugham.

E. P. Dutton & Co., Inc.: for selections from *Education and Freedom*, by H. G. Rickover, p. 151; Appendix 3, p. 4. A Dutton paperback. Copyright 1959 by H. G. Rickover.

Eyre & Spottiswoode Ltd.: for a selection from *The American People: Their Civilization and Character*, by Henry B. Parkes, p. 259. Copyright 1949 by Eyre & Spottiswoode Ltd.

Fawcett Publications, Inc.: for selections from *The Silent Language*, by Edward T. Hall, pp. 20, 132, 156. A Premier Book. Copyright 1959 by Edward T. Hall; *Mirror for Man*, by Clyde Kluckhohn, p. 186. A Premier Book. Copyright 1949 by McGraw-Hill Book Co., Inc.

Hamish Hamilton Ltd.: for a selection from *Here, There, and Everywhere*, by Eric Partridge, 2nd ed. rev., p. 50. Copyright 1950 by Eric Partridge.

Harcourt, Brace and World, Inc.: for selections from *Language and Language Teaching*, by Nelson Brooks, 2nd ed., pp. 1, 9. Copyright 1960, 1964, by Harcourt, Brace & World, Inc.; *Language in Thought and Action*, by S. I. Hayakawa, 2nd ed., p. 118, in consultation with Leo Hamalian and Geoffrey Wagner. Copyright 1939, 1940, by S. I. Hayakawa, and 1941, 1949, 1963, 1964, by Harcourt, Brace & World, Inc.; *The Miracle of Language*, by Charlton Laird, pp. 9, 109. Copyright 1953 by Charlton Laird; *Patterns of English*, by Paul Roberts, p. 1. Copyright 1956 by Harcourt, Brace & World, Inc.; *Language*, by Edward Sapir, p. 3, Harvest Book. Copyright 1921 by Harcourt, Brace & World, Inc., renewed 1949 by Jean V. Sapir.

Harper & Row, Publishers: for selections from *Only Yesterday*, by Frederick Lewis Allen, pp. 176–177, 190. Copyright 1931 by Frederick Lewis Allen, and 1951 by Harper & Row, Publishers. Reprinted by permission of Harper & Row, Publishers; *Who Killed Society*, by Cleveland Amory, p. 34. Copyright 1960 by Cleveland Amory; *Inside Africa*, by John Gunther, p. 465. Copyright 1953, 1954, 1955, by John Gunther; *Computers: The Machines We Think With*, by D. S. Halacy, Jr., p. 51. Copyright 1962 by Daniel S. Halacy, Jr.; *Profiles in Courage*, by John F.

Kennedy, pp. 19–20, 43. Copyright 1955, 1956, by John F. Kennedy; *This I Do Believe*, by David E. Lilienthal, pp. xiii, 65. Copyright 1949 by David E. Lilienthal; *What I Think*, by Adlai Stevenson, p. 159. Copyright 1954, 1955, 1956, by R. Keith Kane; "University Days," in *My Life and Hard Times*, by James Thurber, p. 110. Copyright © 1933, 1961, by James Thurber; "A Note at the End," in *My Life and Hard Times*, pp. 152–153. Copyright © 1933 by James Thurber; "The Secret Life of James Thurber," in *The Thurber Carnival*, by James Thurber, p. 45. Copyright © 1945 by James Thurber. Reprinted by permission of Mrs. James Thurber.

Harper's Magazine: for selections from "Letter to a Young Man About to Enter Publishing," Anon., October 1959, p. 26; "On Wisconsin," by David Boroff, October 1959, p. 36; "Why American Plays Are Not Literature," by Robert Brustein, October 1959, p. 167; "To Be a Bernhardt," by Henry Butler, August 1963, p. 56; "Japan Tries for a Second Miracle," by Peter F. Drucker, March 1963, p. 75; "Helping Hand for a Literary Upstart," by John Fischer, September 1963, p. 20; "How to Choose a College, If Any," by John W. Gardner, February 1958, p. 51; "Good Old London," by Martha Gellhorn, October 1959, p. 79; "On the Teaching of Writing," by Archibald MacLeish, October 1959, pp. 158, 161; "What Is Advertising Good For?" by Martin Mayer, February 1958, p. 26; "Newport Notes: The Kennedys and Other Salts," by George Plimpton, March 1963, p. 39; "Why Spoil the Adirondacks?" by Robert and Leona Rienow, October 1959, p. 74. By permission.

Holiday Magazine: for a selection from "Party of One," by Clifton Fadiman, February 1958, p. 9.

Holt, Rinehart & Winston, Inc.: for a selection from *Samuel Johnson*, by Joseph Wood Krutch, p. 116. Copyright 1944 by Holt, Rinehart & Winston, Inc.

Houghton Mifflin Co.: for selections from *The Affluent Society*, by John Kenneth Galbraith, pp. 181, 226. Copyright 1958 by John Kenneth Galbraith.

Alfred A. Knopf, Inc.: for selections from *The Declaration of Independence*, by Carl F. Becker, p. 3, a Vintage Book. Copyright 1922, 1942, by Carl Becker; *The American Character*, by D. W. Brogan, pp. 135, 136, 140, 141. Copyright 1944 by Dennis W. Brogan; *The Natural History of Nonsense*, by Bergen Evans, p. 16, a Vintage Book. Copyright 1948, 1958, by Bergen B. Evans; *Rendezvous with Destiny*, by Eric F. Goldman, p. 288. Copyright 1952; *Growing Up Absurd*, by Paul Goodman, p. 191. Copyright 1960 by Paul Goodman; *Hiroshima*, by John Hersey, pp. 5, 13, 70, 72. Copyright 1946 by John Hersey.

Little, Brown and Company: for selections from *Teacher in America*, by Jacques Barzun, pp. 48–49, 55–56. Copyright 1944, 1945, by Jacques Barzun; *The Years with Ross*, by James Thurber, pp. 96, 267, 268. Copyright 1957, 1958, 1959, by James Thurber.

The Macmillan Company: for selections from *The Cycle of American Literature*, by Robert E. Spiller, pp. 206, 275. Copyright 1955 by The Macmillan Company.

G. & C. Merriam Company: for a sample entry from *Webster's Dictionary of Synonyms*. Copyright 1951 by G. & C. Merriam Company, publishers of the Merriam-Webster Dictionaries. By permission.

Michigan State University Press: for use and adaptation of "Using the Dictionary," an unsigned article by William Schwab, pp. 23–24; and selected items from "Reference Books," pp. 109–115, in the *Communication Skills Syllabus*, 9th ed. Copyright 1956 by the Michigan State University Press. By permission.

The National Council of Teachers of English: for excerpts from "Linguistics and the Teaching of Composition," by Paul Roberts, in *The English Journal*, LII (May 1963), 332, 333; for use of items from "335 Real Spelling Demons for College Students," by Edna L. Furness and Gertrude A. Boyd, in *College English*, XLIII (March 1959), 292–295. Reprinted with the permission of The National Council of Teachers of English and Edna L. Furness and Gertrude A. Boyd.

The New York Times Company: for 37 sentences from *Background and Foreground: An Anthology of Articles from The New York Times Magazine*, ed. Lester Markel and published by Dell Publishing Co., Inc., 1965. © 1965 by The New York Times Company. Reprinted by permission; sample entry from *The New York Times Index* (1960). © 1960 by The New York Times Company. Reprinted by permission; selection from "Birthday (Natal Day, Jubilee)," by Charles Poore, January 17, 1954, p. 20.

The New Yorker Magazine, Inc.: for a selection from "Summer School," by Elizabeth Taylor, September 6, 1958, p. 27; "Intimations of Mortality," by Robert M. Coates, July 26, 1958, p. 58; "The Talk of the Town," March 10, 1962, p. 29; February 1, 1958, p. 23.

W. W. Norton & Company, Inc.: for selections from *The Greek Way*, by Edith Hamilton, pp. 106, 116–117, 170–171, 299, 336, 338. Reprinted by permission of W. W. Norton & Company, Inc. Copyright 1930, 1943, by

W. W. Norton & Company, Inc. Copyright renewed 1958 by Edith Hamilton; *The Ugly American*, by William J. Lederer and Eugene Burdick, p. 279. Copyright 1958 by William J. Lederer and Eugene Burdick; *A Nation of Sheep*, by William J. Lederer, pp. 151, 154. Copyright 1961 by William J. Lederer.

Oxford University Press: for a selection from *American English*, by Albert H. Marckwardt, p. 116. Copyright 1958 by Oxford University Press; *The Uses of the Past*, by Herbert J. Muller, p. 4. Copyright 1952 by Oxford University Press.

Kegan Paul, Trench, Trabner and Co. Ltd.: for a selection from *The Comforts of Unreason*, by Rupert Crawshay-Williams, p. 5. Copyright 1947 by Kegan Paul, Trench, Trabner and Co. Ltd.

Random House, Inc.: for a selection from *Lord Jim*, by Joseph Conrad, p. 304, Modern Library. Copyright 1899, 1900, by Joseph Conrad. Copyright 1921 by Doubleday, Doran and Co., Inc.; Introduction copyright 1931 by Modern Library, Inc.; *Personal History*, by Vincent Sheean, pp. 7, 336–337. Copyright 1934, 1935, by Vincent Sheean; Introduction copyright 1940 by Modern Library, Inc.

The Reporter: for a selection from "Revolt of the Brasses," by Fred Grunfeld, July 18, 1963, p. 50.

Saturday Review: for selections from "The Young Grandees on Tour," by Geoffrey Bocca, March 16, 1963, p. 59; "St. John's College," by David Boroff, March 23, 1963, pp. 58–59; "A Challenge to Our Assumptions," by Harry A. Bullis, October 13, 1962, p. 24; "While School Keeps," by James Cass, May 18, 1963, p. 76; "The Cosmos Is Still Friendly," by Norman Cousins, February 17, 1962, p. 34; "A Kingdom for Education," by Norman Cousins, January 20, 1962, p. 28; "Money Is Not Enough," by Claude M. Fuess, February 1, 1958, p. 10; "The Art of the Short Story," by Granville Hicks, April 13, 1963, p. 21; "A Free Trade in Ideas," by Robert Kennedy, February 16, 1963, p. 44; "The Human Situation," by U. Thant, March 23, 1963, p. 26; "The Threat and the Promise," by John F. Wharton, March 31, 1962, p. 12. By permission of *Saturday Review*.

Scott, Foresman & Company: for a selection from *Writer's Guide and Index to English*, by Porter G. Perrin, 2nd ed., p. 19. Copyright 1950 by Scott, Forseman & Company.

Martin Secker & Warburg Ltd.: for a selection from *An Assessment of Twentieth-Century Literature*, by J. Isaacs, p. 109. Copyright 1951 by Martin Secker & Warburg Ltd.

Simon & Schuster, Inc.: for selections from *Unpopular Essays*, by Bertrand Russell, pp. 14, 71, 83, 119. Copyright 1950 by Bertrand Russell; *The Public Arts*, by Gilbert Seldes, pp. 73, 231. Copyright 1956 by Gilbert Seldes.

Time, Inc.: for selections from *Time*, May 3, 1963, p. 105; March 2, 1962, p. 14.

D. Van Nostrand Co., Inc.: for adapted selections from Chapter 1 of *Southeast Asia and the World Today*, by Claude A. Buss. Copyright 1958 by D. Van Nostrand Co., Inc. By permission.

The Viking Press, Inc.: for a selection from *Philosopher's Holiday*, by Irwin Edman, Compass Book Edition 1956, p. 208. Copyright 1938 by Irwin Edman.

John Wiley & Sons, Inc.: for a selection from *Textbook in Organic Chemistry*, by Alexander Gero, pp. 156–157. Copyright 1963 by John Wiley & Sons, Inc.

The H. W. Wilson Company: for sample entries from *Essay and General Literature Index*, *Readers' Guide to Periodical Literature*, and *International Index*. Reproduced by permission of The H. W. Wilson Company.

Contents

III] Mechanics

Preface

The purpose of this book is to provide for the undergraduate student a concise, self-sufficient, and generously illustrated guide to expository writing and techniques of research, and to supply interesting and useful discussion questions, problems, and exercises for developing good habits of composition. The emphasis throughout is on writing, for an introductory text on exposition cannot simultaneously perform the function of courses in semantics, logic, or literature.

In its presentation of grammar, this book is guided by modern linguistics, especially transformational grammar. Grammatical analysis not directly applicable to student problems in writing, however, like the treatment of the auxiliary system in Chapter 2 or of negation, questions, and affirmation in Chapter 9, has been kept to a minimum. Attempts have been made throughout to relate the grammatical presentation to other parts of the text, particularly to those on punctuation and style. Nevertheless, it is hoped that both students and instructor will find the grammatical exposition exciting for its own sake, affording pleasurable insight into the miraculous ability of human beings to master a complex system of sounds and marks on paper for communicating with each other, and to understand and form sentences never before heard, spoken, or written. The knowledge gained by the student about the numerous kinds of arrangements and rearrangements of grammatical structures should make him aware of choices in conveying his meaning.

Each of the four main parts of the book focuses on one aspect of composition: Part I—the expansion and transformation of basic sentence types into complicated structures and their accommodation in larger units of discourse; Part II—the basic techniques of research and the efficient use of reference tools; Part III—the construction of correct sentences and the mechanics of punctuation and spelling; and Part IV—the cultivation of style. The opening chapter, "Language and Writing," introduces the concept of language as speech and its complex relationships to writing, for a clearer understanding of the unique problems facing the student writer.

The influence of linguistic scholars, whose names are well known, is evident in the point of view and the choice of materials that inform this book, and grateful acknowledgment is hereby made. Special debt to the works of Charles C. Fries is thankfully acknowledged. Particular thanks is expressed to Noam Chomsky, whose influence is apparent in Part I of this book. Others whose names must be mentioned in this connection include Zellig S. Harris, W. Nelson Francis, and Paul Roberts. The *Guide*, however, is not primarily intended as a grammar but as a book on expository writing. For whatever simplifications have been made and whatever violations of linguistic theory may have been committed, the author alone is responsible.

To publishers and authors who have given permission to use quotations, gratitude is acknowledged. To the Department of American Thought and Language, Michigan State University, the author is indebted for cooperation in getting this book under way; to Michigan State University, for faculty research grants to study problems of punctuation and syntax; and to the U.S. Educational Foundation in the Philippines, for cooperation in completing the manuscript.

A number of friends and colleagues have given helpful criticism and advice, and grateful acknowledgment is hereby made. Special thanks are due to Rev. Frank J. Dineen, S. J., Robert Gaylor, Edgar Sather, David Wilder, John N. Winburne, and Joe Palmer, who has assisted in gathering illustrations. Robert Hoopes, Barnet Kottler, Paul Roberts, and John C. Street have read the manuscript or portions of it and made searching comments and criticism. Robert Hoopes particularly offered many helpful suggestions. Finally, Marian Wilson and Jere Grant gave all manner of assistance, far beyond the call of duty. To them I am deeply grateful.

WILLIAM SCHWAB

Rochester, Michigan
September, 1966

Guide to Modern Grammar and Exposition

1) *Introduction: Language and Writing*

In order to study writing, we must know something about language,
but the reverse is not true.   LEONARD BLOOMFIELD

THE SUBSTANCE OF LANGUAGE

Language consists of noises—not any kinds of noises—but systematic noises. Most of us are unaware of the features of these noises, much as we may be of the parts of an automobile engine. To be sure, one does not have to be a mechanic to drive a car. Nor does one have to be a linguist to use English. But a knowledge of mechanics is useful in emergencies, especially if one is beyond reach of a telephone or a garage. A knowledge of how English operates can also be profitable as well as interesting. With some grasp of the complexity of the language, moreover, the beginning writer can approach his job with greater ease and confidence.

Fundamental to any language is a series of sound units which differentiate words having different meanings. The meanings of word-pairs like *large—larch, girls—curls, sell—sail*, for example, are distinguished solely by one sound unit in each group. This unit, or segment, called a **phoneme**, makes language a systematic, rather than a haphazard, grouping of sounds. English has thirty-three such segments, and in addition twelve units of pitch, stress, and juncture. Each native speaker learns these units automatically at an early age. Different languages use different sets of phonemes, usually between twenty and fifty, and no two sets are alike. Distinctions that a speaker of English ignores may be significant in another language. For example, we grasp the sounds represented by the letter *k* in *kill* and *skill* as "sames" and ignore their difference: the puff of air accompanying

1

the *k* sound in *kill* but not in *skill*. (The difference can be observed by holding the hand close to the mouth.) We pay no attention to this difference, because the presence or absence of this puff of air, or aspiration, is not used to separate words of different meaning in English. In Hindi, the national language of India, this same difference is significant: /khiil/ with the *k* sound of *kill* means "parched grain," and /kiil/ with the *k* sound of *skill* means "nail."[1] For a speaker of English this distinction is difficult to hear, because he never pronounces a *k* at the beginning of a word without aspiration. German never requires a speaker to put the tip of his tongue against his upper teeth, but in English such articulation is necessary to pronounce the sounds represented by *th* in *this* or *that*. Since subconscious habits are difficult to break, a German speaker learning English might conceivably go through life saying *I sink* instead of *I think*. But we are not concerned with learning foreign languages, and so long as we speak English, phonemes present no problem.

Writing is a different matter, since phonemes are inadequately represented by the letters of the alphabet. The English alphabet consists of twenty-six letters, but these twenty-six letters represent thirty-three phonemes. Some letters therefore represent more than one phoneme, and certain phonemes correlate with more than one letter of the alphabet. The letter *a*, for example, has distinctive sounds in *bat, bate, father, war*, and the phoneme /š/, represented by *sh* in *shame*, can be spelled *ss* (*assurance*), *sch* (*Schweppe's*), *ci* (*precious*), *ti* (*nation*), *x* (*complexion*), or *s* (*nausea*). A fundamental difference between English speech and writing then is the imperfect correlation between the spoken and written forms of the language. Certain spelling problems, taken up in Chapter 22, can be attributed to this unsatisfactory correlation.

ACQUISITION OF THE NATIVE LANGUAGE

Structure

Learning one's native language involves, first of all, complete control of its sound system. This means, as has already been pointed out, that we must learn those units, or phonemes, that make a difference

---

[1] H. A. Gleason, *An Introduction to Descriptive Linguistics*, rev. ed. (New York: Holt, Rinehart & Winston, 1961), p. 260. Phonemic transcriptions are enclosed throughout by slanted lines.

in meaning (*b*it, *p*it), and ignore all other differences (such as the aspiration of *p* in *pill* but not in *spill*). Language learning can be observed in children who speak "baby talk," an inability or refusal to make certain phonemic contrasts that results in substitutions like /d/ for /g/ as in *go* (*doe*) or /l/ for /r/ as in *mirror* (*miller*). Mastery of a sound system is naturally time consuming, but during months of effort and struggle, the child also learns to recognize and respond to other structural signals. If he is promised cookies as a reward for good behavior, he is disappointed with fewer than two. The reason? He has learned the grammatical signals distinguishing singular and plural number, and "cookies" means more than one. And if he says "mans" instead of "men," "the dog bited me" instead of "the dog bit me," he simply has not yet discovered all special instances of the major grammatical patterns.

At an early age a child can be said to have mastered the grammar of his language in the sense that he has an operational control of its major signaling devices. The English-speaking child intuitively learns to handle (1) **word order,** the arrangements and rearrangements of words in definite sequences, such as *nursing home, home nursing; the guests captivated the hostess, the hostess captivated the guests;* (2) **function words,** small sets of words that may signal major word classes like nouns, verbs, or adjectives, as in **the** *professor,* **might** *go, very late;* (3) **inflections,** suffixes that indicate grammatical features like number and tense, as in *book, book*s, *walk, walk*ed, and (4) **derivational forms,** prefixes and suffixes that usually, but not always, change the class membership of a word, as in *master, master***ful,** *master***y;** *friend,* **be***friend, friend***ly,** *friend***liness.** In addition to these four grammatical signaling devices, there is a fifth that applies exclusively to the spoken language: features of intonation, which are taken up later in the introduction. Grammatical constructions are treated in Part I.

Vocabulary

The grammatical devices of a language are finite, but a knowledge of these devices enables a speaker to recognize and produce an infinite number of sentences, even sentences he has never heard or specifically learned. The vocabulary of a living language is likewise open-ended. Merriam-Webster's *Third New International Dictionary* (1961) contains almost half a million entries (that is, listings of words, not including the definitions of each listing), yet the editors make no attempt to present all technical terms, the vast numbers of specialized vocabularies, or the varieties of slang and cant words. Many words, moreover, have a wide range of meanings. The *Oxford English Dictionary* for example, lists 69 numbered meanings for the verb *come*, 73 for *get*, 94 for *go*, 97 for *make*, 91 for *take*, and 58 for *will*.[2]

Meanings of words are in constant flux. A *knave*, for example, in Shakespeare's time "a serving boy," has slowly degenerated into "a rogue." In the King James rendering of the famous verse "And now abideth faith, hope, charity, these three; but the greatest of these *is* charity" (I Cor. 13:13), the word *charity* had a much wider range of meaning to the seventeenth-century reader than it now has. Indeed, modern biblical scholars have had to retranslate the Greek word ἀγάπη, for *charity* has so changed in meaning in three hundred years that its present sense of contributions to the poor completely misrepresents its seventeenth-century meaning of love. The difficulty in reading documents written after A.D. 1400 is due not so much to their grammatical structure as to the rapidly shifting meanings of words.

LANGUAGE AND SYMBOLIC BEHAVIOR

Few achievements in society can be considered more remarkable than mastery of a language, for language is a uniquely human achievement. Animals make meaningful sounds such as cries of pain, hunger, or danger, and some can even parrot language. But they do not have man's capacity to assign sounds to things arbitrarily. Perhaps equally important: they do not have phonemes.

The ability to manipulate these sounds in recurrent structural units constitutes symbolic behavior. Instead of howling or whining to indicate hunger, a human being can sit at a restaurant table and order *breakfast, Frühstück,* or *petit déjeuner,* depending on his language. The use of sounds for events is an efficient way of communicating that enables people to cooperate and not infrequently misunderstand each other. Words are tokens for events, but never the events themselves. One cannot eat the word *steak,* but it is possible to order a steak by making certain arbitrary noises. There is no mysterious relationship between a word and the event it denotes, though some people still

---

[2] Charles C. Fries and A. Aileen Traver, *English Word Lists* (Ann Arbor, Mich.: University of Michigan Press, 1950), p. 80.

believe a pig is called *pig* because it is dirty. Others may respond to the word magic of modern advertising and imagine they are buying social status, success, and happiness when they are actually incurring debt for a power boat or a ranch-style home. Some people prefer to say *final resting place*, *funeral director*, and *cemetery consultant*, instead of *cemetery*, *undertaker*, and *gravestone salesman*, if not to escape the reality of life, then at least to palliate it. Our Anglo-Saxon reluctance to refer to physical processes of elimination, and the substitution of euphemisms like *powder room*, *lounge*, or *restroom* for *toilet* are reflections of social attitudes rather than a sophisticated commentary on the intrinsic merits or imperfections of words. Meanings are socially determined, and the sophisticated speaker or writer is sensitive to this.

We control language only to the extent that we have experienced meaning. Unless we know Japanese, even the most simple conversation in that language sounds like gibberish and, being irrational sometimes, we tend to be suspicious of gibberish and of people who we think talk it. Our linguistic habits, moreover, are modified by the range and depth of our personal knowledge. In order to appreciate classical literature, we should have some acquaintance with Greek and Roman mythology, as well as with biblical history. Our diction is often indicative of attitude, and *egghead*, *intellectual*, and *scholar* can all refer to an able undergraduate. Dialectal variants may sometimes puzzle us, especially when a Midwesterner orders a tonic in a Boston cocktail lounge and winds up with a soft drink. American English abounds with slang, and a philatelist may find the jargon of a jazz addict a meaningless jumble of words. Words are substitutes for experience. They must be understood in context if they are to be useful. Memorizing words is not a key to a more powerful vocabulary.

Language gives unity to experience. It does more than that: it tends to structure the external world for us so imperceptibly that unless we can momentarily break away from our linguistic habits, we are likely to remain unaware that they *are* habits. As speakers of English we seldom complete an utterance without making some commitment to time or to singular or plural number. There is nothing universal about such a division of experience. A Chinese speaker is not required by his language to indicate either tense in verbs or number in nouns. Our classification of the colors of the spectrum into red, orange, yellow, green, blue, and purple strikes us as natural, but Bassa, a Liberian language, distinguishes only two primary categories, *hui* and *zīza*, which correspond to the botanist's color terms *cyanic* and *xanthic*. Speakers of Bassa have no visual defects, and their classification is not inferior to ours, but simply different. In fact, for botanical purposes Bassa may be superior to English, since its two categories correspond to the botanist's classification of yellows, oranges, and shades of red into xanthic, and blues, purples, and purplish reds into cyanic. What we often consider absolutes are simply linguistic categories through which we perceive the physical world.[3] As Sapir says, "We see and hear and otherwise experience very largely as we do because the language habits of our community predispose certain choices of interpretation."[4]

But neither English nor any other language constrains one's freedom of expression. On the contrary, each language serves the needs of its speakers equally well. If it lacks terms for modern scientific concepts, it can coin, borrow, or adapt them, as modern Hebrew or Thai have. Eskimos use many terms for snow, because snow is a vital element in Eskimo culture. Filipinos distinguish many types of palm trees, and every American boy knows the difference between a compact car, station wagon, and hard-top convertible. The more culturally pervasive an object, artifact, or concept, the more words there are likely to be for it. A craftsman can exploit language as a vehicle of practical communication, and a poet as an instrument of the most sublime vision. Whether one experiences a new poem or engages in chitchat over the telephone, the external world impinges continuously on each one of us through the language we speak.

SPEECH AND WRITING

By language, we mean its spoken form. Speech is basic, and writing an approximate, though systematic, representation of speech. In the history of mankind, writing is a relatively late invention. Man has lived on earth some quarter of a million years, but historical records have been available for little less than six thousand. It is perhaps not surprising therefore that even today only about half of the world's

---

[3] See Gleason, pp. 4–5.

[4] Edward Sapir, *Culture, Language, and Personality*, ed. David G. Mandelbaum, (Berkeley, Calif.: University of California Press, 1957), p. 69.

population can read and write. Hundreds of languages, moreover, still lack writing systems, and hundreds of others have existed and drifted into oblivion. Linguists are now devising writing systems for languages that lack them, to bring literacy to millions all over the world.

Learning to write means developing new habits and conventions, some of them different from those of speech. Perhaps one reason why students are reluctant to write is that they do not fully understand some of these conventions. As forms of communication, speech and writing naturally share many characteristics: unity and coherence, appropriateness of purpose, and effectiveness of presentation, provided speakers and writers give them these qualities. Yet each has unique features. One important difference has already been mentioned: the distinctiveness of the sound system in relation to the alphabet and the resulting problems in English spelling. In the remainder of this chapter other contrasts between speech and writing will be taken up.

An apparent difference between the two forms of communication is the transient quality of speech. An utterance is a momentary, unique event. If a listener does not grasp it, he can ask for repetition of the utterance, though he hardly ever gets an exact duplication of what was said before. Repeated utterances are almost always rephrased. Writing, on the other hand, can be read repeatedly. The mind can linger over written material, contemplate, examine, and challenge it at will. That is why the writer's commitment is at once sterner and more considered than the speaker's. He does not enjoy the speaker's privilege immediately to clarify or alter his statement in the light of criticism or objection.

Another difference between speech and writing is that speech implies one or more listeners. (We can ignore lyric outpourings and talking to oneself.) Speech involves the transmission of sound waves and the eliciting of responses from another individual. These responses may consist of carrying out a request, answering a question, or continuing attention to the utterance. A speaker can assess his listener's responses almost instantaneously: approbation, such as nodding or smiling; puzzlement, such as furrowing of brows or scratching of the head; boredom, such as coughing, yawning, or stretching. The skillful speaker is alert for such responses, called **feedback,** so that he can make proper adjustments in his utterance.

Since the writer does not meet his reader face to face, he is deprived of immediate feedback altogether. A playwright must see his work produced before he can fully assess it. After an essayist, novelist, or poet has published his work, further revision is usually out of the question. The professional writer therefore revises and polishes his manuscript to attain the ease, clarity, and precision that the reader has a right to expect.

Still another difference between speech and writing has to do with features present in speech but not in writing. These are **stress,** loudness of voice; **musical pitch,** the vibrations of the vocal chords; and **juncture,** the manner of transition from one sound to another or of terminating an utterance. In English, a few covering patterns of stress, pitch, and juncture, called **intonation,** provide a framework for the speaker to distinguish meanings of utterances, much as he distinguishes meanings of words by replacing one phoneme with another, like /k/ in *cold* with /g/ in *gold*. In the written sentence

Whom is he fighting, Jack?

it is impossible (except as it may be set in dialogue or otherwise made clear in context) to tell whether someone is addressing Jack or fighting him. In speech, with its more detailed system of signals, a lower pitch on *Jack* than elsewhere in the pattern means that someone is speaking to Jack: a higher pitch on *Jack* than in the rest of the pattern means that someone is fighting him. The sentence is ambiguous in writing, but not in speech.

Intonation is represented in writing by punctuation, but only partially and imperfectly so. A falling pitch contour on *Jack*, represented by a period, marks the first of the following pair of sentences as a statement; a rising pitch contour on *Jack*, represented by a question mark, makes the second pattern a question:

He's fighting Jack.
He's fighting Jack?

Both of the following sentences are questions, but the first usually has a falling pitch contour at the end, and the second, a rising contour. Each contour is represented by a question mark:

What is he fighting?
Is he fighting?

However imperfect the correspondence between intonation and punctuation, a knowledge of their points of convergence can be helpful in punctuation. A fuller treatment of the subject will be found in Chapters 17–20.

A final contrast between speech and writing concerns the extra-linguistic features that accompany the spoken language but not writing. These are nuances of voice, gesture, movement, and appearance. A speaker can communicate enthusiasm, levity, solemnity, or irony through modulation of his voice. The utterance "For Brutus was an honorable man" may be either genuinely praiseworthy or ironically cutting, depending on how it is said. A speaker, moreover, can employ gestures and movement to convey emotions. He can frown, point, or raise his arms, shake or nod his head. Through appearance he can communicate status. A military uniform, for example, discloses nationality, branch of service, and commissioned or enlisted status. A lettered sweater proclaims athletic achievement. All these extralinguistic features must be rendered in writing through sequences of words on paper. The writer then must find ways to compensate for these features present in the spoken language but absent in writing.

EXERCISES

1. An American and an Englishman can order "breakfast" in one another's country and be understood, yet a typical English and American breakfast differ markedly. What constitutes a typical breakfast in your part of the U.S.? How closely does your concept of a breakfast correspond to that generally associated with it in the United States? What comprises a typical English breakfast? A Continental breakfast? Could misunderstandings occur between an American tourist and a French hotel proprietor whose room rates include breakfast?

2. Comment on the following:
   1. Meanings are socially determined.
   2. We control language only to the extent that we have experienced meaning. (What about the statement sometimes made by a person that he knows something but cannot express it?)
   3. The best way to expand one's vocabulary is to memorize a word a day.
   4. Thousands of languages are spoken in the world, but there is no language that has not been mastered by anyone even of low intelligence.

    5.   A rooster crows because he is a rooster, but a man speaks because he is a man.

3.   Select a subject with which you are familiar, such as photography, music, or a sport. Then list some of the technical jargon that you commonly use in talking about this subject. Explain the most important terms.

4.   List the characteristics of a speaker's "oral" style in a lecture, a forum discussion, a news conference, or a sermon. What features contribute to the total communication?

5.   What is meant by "feedback"? Is it present in a telephone conversation? In a classroom lecture? In an actor's performance? Observe feedback signals in a lecture or discussion and write a report on your findings.

6.   Start a folder or notebook for transcribing interesting grammatical and stylistic features, unusual or striking uses of punctuation, diction, etc., that you encounter in your reading.

I] From Sentence to Discourse

2) *Basic Pattern* N V—*Simple Expansions*

WRITING AND GRAMMAR

Some students become inarticulate when they begin to write. Though otherwise competent, they worry about how to compose a sentence and become virtually paralyzed by the sight of a blank page. Others worry about what to say, and still others about where to begin. We will deal with all of these concerns, beginning with an aspect of the subject about which students really know more than they think, but about which they become most easily discouraged: how to structure their thoughts in grammatically acceptable ways.

A word of reassurance then is in order. We certainly know how to handle our native language, and after twelve years of formal schooling, most of us speak in socially accepted ways, preferring "They were in these streets" to "They was in them streets," or "He and I won't polish the car" to "Him and me ain't polishing the car." And all of us know grammar, if by grammar we mean the rules by which we form sentences in our minds and articulate them through our speech organs. As the Introduction has pointed out, we use English from early childhood and learn its patterns subconsciously. We readily distinguish grammatical from ungrammatical arrangements of words:

His sister invited him to Palm Beach.
His Palm Beach to invited sister him.

13

We accept the first pattern but reject the second, because its word order does not follow the rules by which we form English sentences. We grasp "He is there" as a statement and "Is he there" as a question because the word order is different. But different arrangements of words can signal similar meanings:

He gave Ginger some advice.
He gave some advice to Ginger.

And certain arrangements of words can be meaningful, even if the content is nonsense:

The skyscraper became a streetcar.
Whoever gave Ginger some advice has been melted down for cooking fat.

Except in fairytales, skyscrapers never change into streetcars, and people are unlikely to be melted down for cooking fat. But grammar and philosophical speculation are not the same.

In time we command a wider range of grammatical patterns. We need think only of the variety of our reading, from the daily sports page to textbooks, plays, stories, and novels. Some of us may wonder why we do not write as fluently as we speak or read. This is not surprising. We speak and read more than we write; our aural and oral grasp of language patterns has been consolidated through years of practice.

Our discussion of sentences begins with patterns that may seem elementary. But many seemingly complicated patterns are indeed elementary, once their parts are exposed for inspection. These parts are like the individual parts of a watch—impressive and delicate. Putting them together is a formidable task, and the watchmaker who does this has mastered his craft. Just as he adds a second hand, a timer, a calendar to the watch to serve the purpose for which it is intended, so the writer builds his sentence to make it more meaningful. Like the watchmaker, he must cultivate his craft.

NOUNS AND VERBS

The first sentence pattern to be discussed consists of a **noun** (**N**) and a **verb** (**V**):

N	V
Hope	remains.
Time	flies.
Students	complained.
Boys	sang.
Books	satisfy.
Musicians	practiced.

Nouns like *musicians, books, time* and verbs like *practice, satisfy, remains* belong to word classes whose members are numberless. They make up the core of the English vocabulary. Of the new words constantly added to the language—like *debrief, countdown, one-upmanship*—the majority are nouns and verbs. These, as well as adjectives and adverbs, which will be taken up later, comprise the major word classes of English.

Just as an American citizen may belong to different social, political, or religious groups without impairing his status as a citizen, so members of the major word classes may belong to different subclasses, or subsets, without affecting their status as nouns or verbs. An individual may perform as an engineer during the day, as a naval reservist one or two evenings a week, and as a member of a sailing club on weekends. Or he may simply hold a job in a corporation, but share no membership in other groups. Similarly, a noun may perform as a member of one subclass, like *boy, table, student,* called **common nouns;** *Jack, Greenwich Village, Venus,* called **proper nouns.** A common noun names the members of a class of things; a proper noun, the distinctive, specific member of a class. A noun may also perform as a member of both subclasses, like *hope* or *Hope,* where the first, a common noun, designates a state of mind, and the second, a proper noun, refers to a hospital training ship. The contrast is indicated in writing by capitalization of the proper noun, but subsets of major word classes can also be recognized in other ways. In the sentence pattern introduced in the preceding paragraph, all verbs perform as members of a subset called **intransitive verbs** (V_i). No verb is followed by a direct object or some other complement. But verbs like *sing, satisfy, practice* can also be members of other subsets. In "The boys sang two encores," "Books satisfy most tastes," and "The musicians practiced their accompaniment," *sang, satisfy,* and *practice* are **transitive verbs** (V_t). Each verb is followed by a direct object.

Membership in the major word classes is also flexible, and a word may sometimes perform as a noun and sometimes as a verb. In "The jet stands ready," we grasp *jet* as a noun; in "The passengers jet leisurely," we grasp *jet* as a verb. In the first sentence *jet* occurs in a noun position and in the second sentence it occurs in a verb position. Other nouns and verbs can be freely substituted in each position, respectively:

The *jet* stands ready.   The passengers *jet* leisurely.
    plane   speed
    transport   sail
    boat   fly
    car   rest

Position alone, however, is not the only signal for separating nouns from verbs. Nor is it the most reliable one. Most English nouns are distinguished by their ability to form the singular and plural number:

The passenger speeds leisurely.
The passengers speed leisurely.

In a detailed grammar of English the singular and plural number of a noun would be indicated as follows:

$N_{sing.}$	V	Hope remains.
$N_{pl.}$	V	Hopes remain.

In this book, however, such explicit treatment is unnecessary.

If the ability to form singular and plural number distinguishes nouns, the ability to form present and past tense sets verbs apart from other word classes:

N   V
Hope remains.
Hope remained.

We will indicate tense by the symbol **T**, which allows us to designate either the present or past:

N T V $\rightarrow$ N **present** V
N T V $\rightarrow$ N **past**   V

The arrow means that the formula at the left is to be rewritten more explicitly at the right:

N T V → N   **present V**
            Hope remains.
            Boys sing.
N T V → N   **past V**
            Hope remained.
            Boys sang.

For the present tense, of course, only the third person singular requires the suffix -*s*; for the past, the suffix is -*ed* for regular verbs. *Be*
has three forms for the present (*am, is, are*) and two for the past (*was,
were*). Verbs like *sing, put, write* have special forms for the past.[1]

Besides position and inflectional suffixes, nouns and verbs may be
distinguished by derivational forms, prefixes and suffixes that usually
affect the class membership of the word to which they are added:

NOUN-FORMING SUFFIXES

-or: act **+** -or   → actor (*also* resistor, resonator)
-ness: big **+** -ness → bigness (*also* wantonness, suppleness)
-ity: minor **+** -ity → minority (*also* triviality, modernity)

VERB-FORMING PREFIXES

be-:   be- **+** cloud → becloud (*also* befriend, bewitch)
em-:   em- **+** bitter → embitter (*also* embody, embowel)

VERB-FORMING SUFFIXES

-ize: formal **+** -ize → formalize (*also* generalize, liberalize)
-en: soft **+** -en   → soften (*also* weaken, brighten)

Finally, nouns and verbs can be identified by function words like *a,
the, can, might,* which will be taken up later in this chapter.

In a sentence, word classes are usually signaled by more than one
grammatical marker. Indeed, without enough markers, a word
cannot be assigned to its class:

Transport jets across the Atlantic.

It is impossible to tell whether a transport jets across the Atlantic or
whether someone is told to transport jets across the Atlantic:

[1] See p. 301.

The transport jets across the Atlantic.
Transport the jets across the Atlantic.

Introduction of the noun marker *the* resolves the ambiguity.

A special relationship exists between the grammatical forms of *transport* and *jet* in sentences like "The transport jets across the Atlantic" and "The transports jet across the Atlantic." In the first sentence, the singular noun *transport* is followed by the singular, or -*s*, form of the verb *jets*. In the second sentence, the plural noun *transports* is followed by the simple form of the verb *jet* (without the -*s*). A noun related or *tied* to a verb this way is called the **subject,** and the verb that follows, the **predicate.** Both subject and predicate may be expanded into extremely complex structures, but the basic pattern of a sentence, its kernel, will always consist of one of a few simple structures like the one described here.

PRONOUNS

Nouns may be replaced by words from a small set called **pronouns** (N_p):

N	V_i	N_p	V_i
Musicians	practice.	*They*	practice.
Hope	remained.	*None*	remained.
Boys	sing.	*Most*	sing.
Books	satisfy.	*These*	satisfy.
Time	flies.	*It*	flies.
Students	complained.	*Who*	complained?

Pronouns are best classified as a subgroup of nouns, since they occur in noun positions and perform noun functions. Pronouns include:[2]

(1)		(2)		(3)
I	(me)	my	mine	which
we	(us)	our	ours	what
he	(him)	his		this
she	(her)	her	hers	these
they	(them)	their	theirs	that
who	(whom)	whose		those
you		your	yours	both
it		its		all

[2] W. Nelson Francis, *The Structure of American English* (New York: Ronald Press, 1958), pp. 244–249.

(4)	(5)	(6)
some	anybody	each
more	anyone	another
most	everybody	nobody
many	everyone	either
any	someone	neither
few	no one	one
several	anything	other
much	everything	two . . . ninety-nine
none		

Choice of an appropriate pronoun sometimes is a problem with the first six paired pronouns in column (1), because standard English frowns on "Them complained" or "He caught Jane and I at the last moment."[3] Certain pronouns in columns (5) and (6) may present problems in punctuation. *Everyone, another, either,* and *neither,* for example, can take the possessive:

> everyone's belongings
> either's luck

One, other, and *two . . . ninety-nine* may be preceded by words like *the, all, any* (to be discussed in the next section); they may also take the plural; and *one* and *other,* the possessive:

> any six
> some twos
>
> one
> the ones
> one's livelihood
>
> any other person's income   any other's income
> all other persons' incomes   all others' incomes

Pronouns play an important part in discourse as sequence markers. (See pp. 125–126.)

DETERMINERS

Besides the major word classes, there are several smaller sets of words that have important grammatical functions. Their membership is fixed, and words added to the vocabulary are likely to be nouns,

---

[3] For discussion of choice of pronouns, see pp. 302–303.

verbs, adjectives, or adverbs, rather than members of these smaller sets, or function groups.

The first set, or function group, consists of **noun determiners**, or simply **determiners (D)**, that signal a noun is to follow:

(D)[4]	N	V_i
The	musicians	practice.
No	hope	remained.
Our	boys	sing.
Those	books	satisfy.

Proper nouns like *Bertha, Queen Elizabeth* are not usually preceded by determiners, though sentences like "Our Bertha remained" or "The *Queen Elizabeth* is the largest ship" are grammatical. Nor can determiners be used with nouns indiscriminately. *The time flies* is grammatical, but **a time flies* and **a sugar* are not.[5]

Determiners include:

a/an	this/these	neither	much
the	that/those	some	several
my	his	each	enough
our	her	other	both
your	its	another	any
their	few	all	one
no	many	more	two . . . ninety-nine
every	either	most	

Determiners like *the, no, some* have little meaning by themselves. Combined with nouns as in *the musicians, no hope, some books,* they limit the meaning of the noun that follows.[6] The noun in such a construction is called the **head** and the word that expands the noun, its **attribute,** or **modifier.** The head is the essential part of the construction; the attribute, or modifier, is not. A fundamental principle of expansion can be observed here: As a modifier is combined with a

---

[4] Parentheses indicate that the enclosed item or items in a formula are optional. Both "the musicians practice" and "musicians practice" are grammatical, and the use of the determiner depends solely on meaning. Certain restrictions on the use of determiners are mentioned in this chapter, but the determiner system of English is too complex to be treated fully in an introductory text.

[5] An asterisk (*) symbolizes a nongrammatical construction or a construction unacceptable in writing.

[6] Some determiners also combine with adjectives as in "The poor always suffer most" or "The famous care little about trivialities."

head, a more specific meaning emerges from the expanded construction.

Most of the determiners in the list also appear as pronouns. Their classification depends on position:

(D)	N	V_i		N_p	V_i
Most	boys	sing.		*Most*	sing.
Those	books	satisfy.		*Those*	satisfy.
Neither	candidate	spoke.		*Neither*	spoke.
His	dog	won.		*His*	won.
Some	hope	remained.		*Some*	remained.

The italicized words in the first column are determiners, signaling nouns; those in the second column are pronouns in a noun position.

Some determiners in the list never appear as pronouns. We can say "Every boy sings," but not "*Every sings*"; "a candidate spoke," but not "*a spoke*." A few determiners have closely related forms that are pronouns:

(D)	N	V_i		N_p	V_i
No	hope	remained.		*None*	remained.
Your	candidate	spoke.		*Yours*	spoke.
Their	dog	won.		*Theirs*	won.

The italicized words in the first column are classified as determiners; those in the second column, as pronouns.

A determiner, as has been stated, limits the meaning of the noun with which it combines. A pronoun usually refers to a noun cited previously in a sentence, though it may also anticipate a noun, called its **antecedent.** Without an antecedent for *most, those, neither, his,* or *some,* the contextual meaning of sentences in column two would be unclear. We would not know that *most* referred to *boys, those* to *books, neither* to *candidate,* etc. Without a clear antecedent, moreover, a pronoun may be ambiguous:

John Barrie criticized his partner after he had left the office.

One cannot tell whether John Barrie or his partner had left the office, because *he* can refer to either.[7] Rephrasing of the sentence resolves the ambiguity:

After leaving the office, John Barrie criticized his partner.
John Barrie criticized his partner, who had left the office.

[7] See also reference of pronouns, pp. 289–290.

AUXILIARIES; AFFIX TRANSFORMATION ($\mathbf{T_{af}}$)

A verb may be introduced by a function word called an **auxiliary**. One or more auxiliaries may combine with a verb to form a verb phrase:

He may study.
He may   have studied.
He   has   been studying.
He might have   been studying.

The order of auxiliaries is fixed. In the examples, *have* follows *may* and *might*, members of a subset called **modals** (**M**); and *been* follows *has* and *have*.

The elaborate, yet systematic, machinery of the English auxiliary system can be represented by a simple formula:

T (M) (have -en) (be -ing) V

The parentheses mean that each of the enclosed elements is optional, and any or none of them may be used in a verb phrase. Only two elements, those outside the parentheses, the **T** (tense) and the **V** (verb), are obligatory. Modals (**M**), (**have -en**), with **-en** meaning past participle, and (**be -ing**), with **-ing** meaning present participle, may be selected singly or in combination, provided their order is maintained.

A few examples will show how verb phrases containing auxiliaries are formed. The first group of auxiliaries we will discuss are modals, which in addition to *may* and *might*, include the present tense forms *can, will, shall*, and *must*, and the past tense forms *could, would*, and *should*. A present tense modal is required if the present is designated for **T**:

N T M V → N$_p$ **present M   V**
                   He **present can study** →
                   He can study.

A past tense modal is used if the past is assigned to **T**:

N T M V → N$_p$ **past M   V**
                   He **past can study** →
                   He could study.

We can see that in verb phrases containing modals, the modal, not the verb, bears the tense form. We do not say "*He could studied*" or "*He could went." Indeed, whatever the first auxiliary in a verb phrase, the same rule applies: the auxiliary, not the verb, bears the tense. "He has studied," for example, is formed as follows:

N T have -en V → N$_p$ present have -en V
                 He   present have -en study
                 He has studied.

The tense applies to the first auxiliary in the verb phrase, in this instance, *have*. Similarly, the **-en** applies to the next form, the verb. A rule, rearranging forms like **T, -en,** and **-ing** so that each will apply to the proper word in the string can be stated as follows:

Af + v → v + Af

The rule, where **Af** (**affix,** that is, either a prefix or suffix) stands for **T, -en,** and **-ing,** and **v** for **M, have, be,** or **V,** says that a **T, -en,** or **-ing** immediately followed by a **v,** that is, by **M, have, be,** or **V,** must be switched around with that **v.** The rule, our first example of a transformation, puts the affix in its proper place, after the form to which it applies.

We will take up transformations more fully in the next few chapters, showing how complex grammatical structures can be derived from a few underlying strings by the application of specific rules, in much the same way that a variety of auxiliary structures can be derived from one underlying string by rules applied to this string. Thus the affix rule, symbolized hereafter by (**T$_{af}$**), will indicate the transformation **Af + v → v + Af** under the conditions specified.

With (**T$_{af}$**), we can now rewrite the preceding examples more explicitly:

	N$_p$ present M V →
	He **present may study** →
(**T$_{af}$**)	**Af + v** →
	He **may present study** →
	v + Af
	He may study.

	N$_p$ **past M V** →
	He **past may study** →
(**T$_{af}$**)	**Af + v** →
	He **may past study** →
	v + Af
	He might study.

```
            Nₚ present have -en  V       →
            He present have -en  V       →
            He present have -en  study →
(T_af)          Af  +   v    Af + v      →

            He have present study -en →
                v + Af       v + Af
```

He has studied.

A complete grammar of English would, in addition, contain rules for rewriting **may + past** as *might*; **study + -en** as *studied*; **have + present** in **context**ₛᵢₙg. as *has*.

The auxiliary formula provides for several combinations of auxiliaries, some of which are illustrated in the following examples. The first sequence contains a modal and *have*:

```
            N  T      M    have -en  V     →
            Nₚ present M    have -en  V     →
            He present may have -en   study →
(T_af)          Af  +  v   v    Af + v      →

            He may present have study -en →
                v + Af        v   v + Af  →
```

He may have studied.

Since no **Af** precedes *have*, the affix rule does not apply to *have*, as indeed we would not expect it to.

Here is an example containing a **be -ing**:

```
            N  T        be -ing V      →
            Nₚ present be -ing V        →
            He present be -ing study →
(T_af)          Af  +  v   Af + v      →

            He be  present study -ing →
                v + Af        v + Af
```

He is studying.

The next example contains a modal and **be -ing**:

```
            N  T  M    be -ing V      →
            Nₚ past M    be -ing V      →
            He past may be -ing study →
(T_af)          Af + v    v   Af + v    →
```

He **may past be study -ing** →
   v + Af   v v + Af

He might be studying.

All elements of the auxiliary formula are used in the following:

    N T   M   **have -en** **be -ing** V   →
    N_p **past M** **have -en** **be -ing** V   →
    He **past may have -en**   **be -ing** **study** →
(T_{af}) Af + v   v   Af + v Af + v

    He **may past have be -en study -ing**   →
    v + Af v   v + Af v + Af

He might have been studying.

The complexity of the English verb system is by no means exhausted by a display of its auxiliary structure, as the following instances show:

  used to study
  begins studying
  is supposed to keep on studying
  ought to try to begin studying
  hasn't dared to stop studying

But a detailed description of these constructions would be in order only in a full grammar of the English verb.

SUMMARY

One basic pattern, consisting of a simple subject and predicate and tied by agreement in number, has been presented:

     N V_i → Prices decline.
(D) N V_i → The price declines.
     N_p V_i → They decline.

We have discussed two major word classes: nouns (including noun substitutes or pronouns) and verbs; and two sets of function words (determiners and auxiliaries). Determiners combine with nouns, and auxiliaries with verbs: *Some prices might decline.*

We have taken up three subgroups of auxiliaries: modals (**M**), **have -en** and **be -ing.** Several explicit combinations are possible, depending on which optional items (in parentheses) are selected from the formula:

T	(M)	(have -en)	(be -ing)	V
present	will			decline
past	would			decline
present		has		declined
past		had		declined
present	will	have		declined
past	would	have		declined
present			is	declining
past			was	declining
present	will		be	declining
past	would		be	declining
present		has	been	declining
past		had	been	declining
present	will	have	been	declining
past	would	have	been	declining

The affix transformation, (T_{af}), where **Af** may be a **T, -en, -ing**; and **v** may be an **M, have, be,** or **V**, inverts elements of a string as follows: **Af + v → v + Af.** No sentence can be generated until this rule has been applied. For example:

N   T   (M) V
prices **past can** decline →
       Af + v

prices **can   past** decline →
       v + Af

Prices could decline.

EXERCISES

1. If we know grammar both in the sense of using the right word at the right time and of recognizing and producing large numbers of sentences without conscious effort, what is the purpose of studying grammatical structures in a course in writing?

2. Can grammar be defined as a form of behavior? Explain.

3. How many tenses can you identify in English? How do we express future time? What inferences can you draw about the relationship of tense to time?

4. Identify the grammatical signals in Lewis Carroll's "Jabberwocky" from *Alice in Wonderland*:

> 'Twas brillig, and the slithy toves
> > Did gyre and gimble in the wabe:
> All mimsy were the borogroves,
> > And the mome raths outgrabe.

SUGGESTION:
Distinguish inflectional and derivational forms, function words, and signals of word order. Could any of the markers conceivably be ambiguous? For intellectual amusement, substitute common words for the nonsense words in the four-line stanza.

5. Members of the major word classes are extremely fluid, and often used in new ways or formed by analogy with other current words. For example, nouns like *host* and *guest* are commonly used as verbs in the context of television. A word like *prestigeful* is formed by analogy with *health—healthful*. Consult newspapers and magazines (1) for five instances of common words used in new grammatical contexts and (2) for five words formed by analogy.

NOTE:
Be sure you indicate the source as well as the full context of each of your examples.

6. How many grammatical markers signal each noun and verb in the following? Which items are ambiguous? Why?

    1. She disliked him.
    2. His friends disliked him.
    3. His closest friends criticized his temper.
    4. Official protests.
    5. Sports briefs.

The following are newspaper headlines:

    6. "Big 3 Air Plan to Avoid Risk of War"—*Pacific Stars and Stripes*, August 8, 1963, p. 5.
    7. "Chest Pains Back; Ike Comfortable"—*Detroit News*, November 11, 1965, p. 1 A.
    8. "U.S. Acts to Curb Road Deaths"—*Detroit News*, December 12, 1965, p. 5 H.

9. "Earmuff Weather for Pontiac Today"—*Pontiac Press*, December 6, 1965, p. 1.
10. "Russian Moon Shot on Course"—*Pontiac Press*, December 6, 1965, p. 1 B.

7. Are the types of ambiguity in the following items the same or different?

1. "Candidate Bares Running Mate."
2. Highway sign before a village: "No Truck Passing in Village."

8. Write sentences based on the following, using a determiner and members from two subgroups of auxiliaries.

EXAMPLE:

(D)	N	T	M	(have -en)	(be- ing)	V
	prisoners	past	can	have -en		escape
(T$_{af}$) Some	prisoners	can	past	have		escape -en
Some	prisoners	could	have	escaped.		

1. dignitaries arrive
2. attempts fail
3. plans develop
4. students participate
5. official protests

9. Replace the subject in each of the expanded sentences in Exercise 8 with two different pronouns.

EXAMPLE: Some prisoners could have escaped.
Some   could have escaped.
Most   could have escaped.

10. Write sentences based on the following formulas.

1. N T V$_i$
2. D N T V$_i$
3. N$_p$ T V$_i$
4. D N T M V$_i$
5. D N T have -en V$_i$
6. D N T M have -en V$_i$
7. D N T be -ing V$_i$
8. D N T M be -ing V$_i$
9. D N T have -en be -ing V$_i$
10. D N T M have -en be -ing V$_i$

3) Basic Patterns and Transformations

PATTERN (D) N $\begin{Bmatrix} V_1 \\ be \end{Bmatrix}$ Aj: ADJECTIVES

Adjectives (**Aj**) like *easy, careful, expensive, interesting* can be identified most readily in the pattern N$\begin{Bmatrix} V_1 \\ be \end{Bmatrix}$ Aj. This pattern consists of a noun tied to a verb like *become, seem, sound, taste, remain,* called a **linking verb** (**V₁**), or to forms of *be*, followed by an adjective.[1] The formula allows for the selection of a linking verb or a form of *be :*

(D)	N	V₁	Aj
This	story	sounds	scandalous.
Some	rules	seemed	strict.
His	party	became	boisterous.
The	sauce	tasted	good.
	Attitudes	remained	firm.

(D)	N	be	Aj
This	story	is	scandalous.
Some	rules	are	strict.
His	party	was	boisterous.
The	sauce	was	good.
	Attitudes	were	firm.

[1] *Be* is treated separately from other linking verbs because of its unique behavior in questions and similar constructions. See Chapter 9.

The adjective in each instance can be front-shifted:[2]

(D) N	V_1	Aj	(D) Aj	N
This story	sounds	scandalous. →	this scandalous	story
Attitudes remained firm.		→	firm	attitudes

(D) N	be	Aj	(D) Aj	N
His party	was	boisterous. →	his boisterous	party
Attitudes were firm.		→	firm	attitudes

Adjective Transformation (T_{aj})

The type of operation illustrated in the preceding section, the second example of a transformation, may involve the transposition of an element in a sentence, such as a word or phrase, from one position to another. It may involve the addition of a word, phrase, or sentence, or the deletion of part of a sentence. A transformation is a process or statement of a process showing the structural relationship of two constructions with explicit rules specifying how one construction may be derived from the other. The transformation shown above, symbolized by (T_{aj}) and called an **adjective transformation,** generates a noun phrase from a sentence.

The adjective transformation (T_{aj}) differs from the affix transformation (T_{af}), introduced in the last chapter, in that we may apply (T_{aj}) to a given construction or not, as we choose, our decision depending on stylistic requirements or other factors. We can say that (T_{aj}) is optional. The affix transformation, on the other hand, is obligatory; it is necessary for forming a verb phrase. All the transformations save one (T_{do}, p. 107) to be taken up in this and following chapters are optional ones.

Transformations can make the beginning writer aware of stylistic choices. In a given context either "Attitudes were firm" or "firm attitudes" can be selected, whichever fits better. Or at a more complex level:

---

[2] Words like *afraid* and *mere* do not work this way and would have to be treated as special instances. We can say, "The children were afraid," but not, "*the afraid children"; "a mere child," but not "*the child seemed mere." The native speaker learns these exceptions easily and sometimes uses them to gain an unusual or humorous effect by stretching the language a bit: "Herb Small, the actor, resented being so mere."

Dr. Johnson has taught two advanced mathematics courses and served as a consultant to an engineering firm.

OR: In addition to serving as a consultant to an engineering firm, Dr. Johnson has taught two advanced mathematics courses.

Besides developing stylistic awareness, transformations can explain certain types of ambiguity. For instance:

The Spanish students seemed lively.

One cannot tell if the students are Spanish or if they are studying Spanish. The reason is that the noun phrase "the Spanish students" can be derived from the pattern N $\begin{Bmatrix} V_1 \\ be \end{Bmatrix}$ Aj, "The students were Spanish," or "The students seemed Spanish," or from the pattern N V N, "The students studied Spanish" (which is taken up in the next chapter). The ambiguity illustrated here tends to be restricted to writing. Speech markers signal the right meaning through contrastive stress. Heavy stress on *Spanish* marks the phrase as a compound noun; heavy stress on *students* marks it as an adjective-noun combination. The first means the students who study Spanish, and the second the students who are Spanish.

PATTERN N be Av: ADVERBS

An adverb (**Av**) like *out, then, readily, outside, across* may be used to expand the basic pattern N V_i.[3] For example:

N	V_i	(Av)
Hope	remained	here.
Bertha	complained	bitterly.
He	walked	out.
The musicians	rehearsed	later.
They	stood	proudly.
Few boys	worked	hard.

If a form of *be* is tied to the subject, an adverb is required to complete the sentence:

[3] For problems involving adverbs in writing, see pp. 304–305.

N		be	Av
The students		are	inside.
They		were	downstairs.
He		was	out.
She		is	up.
The engineer		is	below.

Deletion Transformation (T_{del})

Forms of *be* in **N be Av** may be deleted, though not directly, by a transformation (T_{del}), where **del** stands for deletion:[4]

(D) N		be	Av		(D) N		Av
The students		are	inside.	→	the students		inside
One engineer		was	below.	→	one engineer		below
The time		is	now.	→	the time		now
All	passengers	are	aboard.	→	all	passengers	aboard
	Insects	are	everywhere. →			insects	everywhere

The positioning of an adverb sometimes affects the meaning of a sentence:

The boys sang downstairs.
The boys downstairs sang.

The first sentence tells where the boys sang. The second sentence tells where those who sang were and implies that there may have been other boys elsewhere. The first sentence has the construction **N V_i** (boys sang), but the second, which is more complex grammatically, derives from two sentences (see Chapter 6).

Adverbs may appear consecutively:

(D) N	V_i	(Av)	(Av)	(Av)
The musicians	rehearsed	here		later.
Bertha	complained		bitterly	then.
I	walked	there		frequently.
Our boys	sing		loudly	sometimes.
Our boys	sing	here	loudly	sometimes.

---

[4] An intermediate operation (converting the predicate into a relative clause) has been omitted:

The students are below. → the students who are below → the students below.

N	be	Av	Av
She	is	never	up.
They	were	down	already.
He	was	out	then.
The engineer	is	here	below.

In contrast to other major word classes, adverbs are readily movable. Their flexibility makes it possible to shift emphasis:

They stood	proudly.
They	proudly stood.
Proudly they	stood.
The musicians	rehearsed here later.
	later rehearsed here.
Later the musicians	rehearsed here.
Bertha	complained bitterly.
	bitterly complained.
Bitterly Bertha	complained.
Our boys	sing here sometimes.
	sometimes sing here.
Sometimes our boys	sing loudly here.
Here our boys	sing loudly sometimes.

The position following a verb can be filled by both adverbs and adjectives. It is therefore necessary to distinguish the two word classes. This is simple if the adverb is marked by the suffix *-ly* attached to certain adjectives like *bitter*, *sharp*, *true*:

The flower grew perfect.
The flower grew perfectly.

The first sentence means that the flower was perfect when it finished growing; the second, that it was perfect in its process of growing. The first sentence has the formula N V_i Aj; the second, N V_i Av.

Not all words with a *-ly* suffix are adverbs, however:

His voice seemed manly.
Our instructor looked friendly.
Their conduct was cowardly.

Manly, *friendly*, and *cowardly* are adjectives derived from nouns by the addition of *-ly* to *man, friend*, and *coward*. Each sentence, more-over, can undergo the adjective transformation N $\begin{Bmatrix} V \\ be \end{Bmatrix}$ Aj → Aj N.

We can say "his manly voice," "our friendly instructor," and "their cowardly conduct."

Sometimes it is impossible to tell whether a word is an adjective or an adverb:

The actor looked right.

If *right* is an adjective, the sentence means that the actor looked proper. If *right* is an adverb, the sentence means that the actor looked to the right. (See also pp. 304–305.)

QUALIFIERS (Q)

Adjectives and adverbs may be signaled by a small set called **qualifiers (Q)**:

	(Q)	Aj
The story sounds	*rather*	scandalous.
His party became	*pretty*	boisterous.
Some rules seem	*very*	strict.
The sauce tasted	*quite*	good.
Attitudes remained	*less*	firm.

	(Q)	(Av)
The musicians rehearsed	*much*	later.
Bertha complained	*most*	loudly.
Hope remained	*even*	then.
They walked	*too*	far.
He worked	*a bit*	harder.

Two qualifiers, *indeed* and *enough*, can follow adjectives and adverbs:

	Aj	(Q)
The story sounds	scandalous	*enough.*
The sauce tasted	good	*indeed.*

	(Av)	(Q)
Bertha complained	loudly	*enough.*
The musicians rehearsed	seldom	*indeed.*

One or more qualifiers may precede an adjective or adverb:

(Q)	(Q)	Aj		(Q)	(Q)	Av
rather	*less*	intense		*really*	*quite*	softly
somewhat	*more*	intelligent		*very*	*much*	later

Although qualifiers do not distinguish adjectives from adverbs, they nevertheless resolve certain types of ambiguity. For example:

He is an adult student.

The sentence can refer to a student who is an adult or to a student who, though he may be very young, is mature in his approach to learning. A qualifier before *adult* makes *adult* an adjective:

He is an *extremely* adult student.

Similarly, one cannot tell whether *entertaining* is a verb or an adjective in the following: .

Our guests were entertaining.

The sentence can mean that the guests put on a performance or that they were amusing. A qualifier makes *entertaining* an adjective:

Our guests were *very* entertaining.

Qualifiers, then, distinguish adjectives from nouns and verbs.

EXPLETIVES

Members of a small function group consisting of *it* and *there*, called **expletives,** serve as fillers at the beginning of a sentence. Here are some sentences beginning with the expletive *it*:

It rains.
It is raining.
It is rainy.
It is midnight.

The function word *it* should not be confused with the pronoun *it*. In the following sentence, *it* is an expletive:

It is the quite practical business of women to please.
    —CATHERINE DRINKER BOWEN, *The Atlantic*

In the next sentence, *it* is a pronoun whose antecedent is the noun *language:*

Language, like sleep, is not a substance but a process; in practice *it* is known to everyone, yet its theory all but defies formulation.
    —NELSON BROOKS, *Language and Language Learning*

There *Transformation* ($T_{(there)}$)

The expletive **there** is introduced by a transformation $T_{(there)}$, which reverses the N and a form of **be** in N **be** Av:

(D) N	be	Av		there be	(D) N		Av
A letter	is	inside.	→	There is	a letter	inside.
Few people	were	here.	→	There were few people here.

The expletive **there** should be kept distinct from the adverb *there*, which denotes place. In speech, the difference is marked by contrast in stress, but in writing no such contrast is apparent:

$$\text{Av} \qquad \text{there} \qquad\qquad \text{Av}$$

($T_{(there)}$)   Some papers are there. → There are some papers there.

In the following, the first instance of *there* is an adverb and the second an expletive:

> A journalist friend of mine, on assignment in Central America, once had occasion to hire a "stringer" (a local correspondent in a small town *there*). Since *there* was no newspaper in the town, the most likely candidate was one of the few English-speaking inhabitants who seemed to know his way around.—T. S. MATTHEWS, *The Atlantic*

Sentences beginning with the expletives **there** and **it** are sometimes wordy, and better alternatives are easily available:

> There are many who agree that . . .
> BETTER: Many agree that . . .
>
> It is my belief that . . .
> BETTER: I believe that . . .

SUMMARY

We have introduced two additional basic sentence patterns:

(D) N $\begin{Bmatrix} V_1 \\ be \end{Bmatrix}$ Aj   The speaker seemed dramatic.
                  The speaker was dramatic.
    N be   Av   Roger is outside.

Three new transformations:

(T_{aj}) (D)   N $\begin{Bmatrix} V_1 \\ be \end{Bmatrix}$ Aj   (D) Aj   N

       The speaker seemed dramatic. → the dramatic speaker
       The speaker was   dramatic. → the dramatic speaker

(T_{del}) (D)   N   be Av   (D) N   Av

       The sailors   are ashore. → the sailors ashore

(T_{there}) (D)   N   be Av   There be (D)   N   Av

       Some books   are here. → There are some books here.

Two sets of function words: qualifiers and expletives. Qualifiers precede adjectives and adverbs:

His statement was short.
His statement was *very* short.
Prices declined rapidly.
Prices declined *quite* rapidly.

Expletives introduce a sentence:

It was midnight.
There are some books there.

EXERCISES

1. Expand each of the following sentences with two appropriate adverbs either in consecutive or other positions.

    EXAMPLE: All prisoners could have escaped.

                     Av   Av
    All prisoners could have escaped instantaneously then.

              Av   Av
    All prisoners could easily have escaped later.

    1. Some hostility might have developed.
    2. Caution prevails.
    3. The crowd broke up.
    4. More lines were forming.
    5. My anxiety mounted.
    6. Her health had been deteriorating.
    7. The radiator was leaking.
    8. Our equipment had failed.

    9.   Six replacements landed.

  10.   Their determination will harden.

2.   Expand one of the adverbs in each sentence in Exercise 1 with an appropriate qualifier.

    EXAMPLE: All prisoners could have escaped instantaneously then.

$$Q$$

    All prisoners could have escaped almost instantaneously then.

3.   Apply (T_{del}), (T_{aj}), or (T_{there}), whichever is appropriate, to the following.

    EXAMPLE:

          (D) N   be   Av   → (D) N   Av

    (T_{del}) All prisoners were inside. → all   prisoners inside.

    1.   The dignitaries looked solemn.

    2.   No attempt seems hopeless.

    3.   Their use was commercial.

    4.   Students were everywhere.

    5.   The officials were Korean.

    6.   Some applicants were waiting outside.

    7.   The engine had sounded sluggish.

    8.   One item was crucial.

    9.   The negotiators appeared deadlocked.

  10.   Twenty pickets were marching around.

4.   Apply (T_{aj}) to the appropriate sentence in each pair below and incorporate the generated phrase in the other sentence.

    EXAMPLE: The prisoners could have escaped.

               The prisoners were unguarded. → the unguarded prisoners

               The unguarded prisoners could have escaped.

    1.   The replacements landed.
        The replacements were qualified.

    2.   This issue had been settled promptly.
        This issue was minor.

    3.   The dignitaries looked solemn.
        They advanced.

    4.   Some hostility might have developed.
        The hostility seemed isolated.

    5.   Our equipment is electrical.
        It failed.

5. Write sentences based on the following formulas:
    1. D N T V_i
    2. N_p T M V_i
    3. D N T M have -en V_i Av
    4. N T V_1 Aj
    5. D N T be Av
    6. D N T be Aj
    7. D N T be Q Aj
    8. N T be Q Aj N
    9. N_p T be D N Av
    10. D Aj N T M have -en be -ing V_i Q Av

4) Basic Patterns (Continued)

PATTERN N V_t N

One of the most common sentence patterns in English is N V_t N. In its basic form, N V_t N consists of a noun or pronoun tied to a member of the large subclass of verbs, called **transitive verbs** (V_t), and followed by a complement, usually a noun or pronoun, called the **direct object**:

(D)	N	V_t	(D)	N
	Voters	make		decisions.
His	constituents	ignored		him.
Most	scholars	avoided	a	controversy.
	They	like		it.
	I	admired	his	courage.
	They	accepted	the	trophy.

Roughly one third of the sentences in standard exposition belong to this pattern in its basic and expanded forms.

Passive Transformation (T_{pass})

A transformation can be applied to N V_t N making the direct object the subject of the derived sentence:

(D) N₁   V$_t$ (D) N₂
     Voters   make   decisions.   →
His constituents ignored   him.   →
Most scholars   avoided a   controversy. →

(D) N₂   **be -en** V   **by** (D) N₁
    Decisions   are   made   by   voters.
    He   was   ignored by his   constituents.
A   controversy was   avoided by most   scholars.

This transformation, called the **passive transformation** (T_{pass}), requires, in addition to the reversal of nouns, **be -en** and a prepositional phrase **by N**, in which the N is N₁ of the basic sentence. The **-en** in **be -en** applies to the following verb by means of (T_{af}).

The deletion transformation (T_{del}), introduced in the last chapter, drops the prepositional phrase from the generated sentence:[1]

N₂   **be -en** V   **by**   N₁
Decisions   are   made   by   voters.   →
He   was   ignored by his   constituents. →
A controversy   was   avoided by most scholars.   →

N₂   **be -en** V
Decisions   are   made.
He   was   ignored.
A controversy   was   avoided.

Deletion of the prepositional phrase eliminates reference to the performer or agent of the action and therefore marks an important change in meaning. "The controversy was avoided by most scholars" not only says that a majority of scholars abstained from a dispute, but clearly implies that a minority did not. "A controversy was avoided" deletes both stated and implied references to the agent and obviously has a different meaning.

The examples in the preceding paragraph and others in this book show that grammatical differences, that is, differences in structure, affect not only the meaning of a sentence but its style as well. Though grammar and style usually receive separate treatment in books on writing, they are more intricately and subtly linked than such arbitrary separation suggests. We shall therefore consciously point forward to the last part of this book and make whatever stylistic

[1] Prepositional phrases are taken up in the next chapter.

judgments seem warranted in the present section on grammatical structure, both to point to the often tenuous and elusive boundary between grammar and style and to assert their unity in finished discourse.

The use of the basic pattern or its passive transformation is a matter of choice. Clearly, the shifting of words affects both sentence rhythm and emphasis:

> The legislature passed the law.
> The law was passed by the legislature.
>
> The flood posed a threat.
> A threat was posed by the flood.

Sometimes the use of the passive results in stilted, as well as wordy writing, such as "The trophy was accepted by us" or "Their courage is admired by me," rather than the more vigorous "They accepted the trophy" or "I admire their courage."

A further reordering applying to only certain members of N V$_t$ N generates a compound noun:

> The writer writes fiction.   → fiction writer
> The management manages the company. → company management
> The chairman chairs the committee.   → committee chairman

In some sentences the verb can be shifted as well, with accompanying changes in its form:

> The apparatus supports prices. → price-support apparatus
> The program develops land.   → land-development program
> Actors starve for publicity.   → publicity-starved actors

Transformations that convert sentences into noun phrases will be taken up in Chapter 8.

The major word classes in pattern N V$_t$ N can be expanded in a variety of ways. Nouns may be introduced by determiners:

> Actors deserve applause.
> *Most* actors deserve some applause.

Verbs may be preceded by one or more auxiliaries:

> Most actors deserve some applause.
> Most actors *would* deserve some applause.

Verbs may be expanded by one or more adverbs:

Most actors would deserve some applause.
Most actors would *clearly* deserve some applause.

An adverb, in turn, may be preceded by a qualifier:

Most actors would *clearly* deserve some applause.
Most actors would *quite clearly* deserve some applause.

Adjectives, as has been shown, are introduced by $(\mathbf{T_{aj}})$:

Most actors would quite clearly deserve some applause.
Most actors are professional. → most professional actors
Most professional actors would quite clearly deserve some applause.

Also:

$\quad$ **(D)** $\quad$ Few scholars avoided the controversy.
$\quad$ **(T$_{aj}$)** $\quad$ Few *eminent* scholars avoided the controversy.
$\qquad\quad$ [*from* The scholars were eminent. → the eminent scholars]
$\quad$ **(T$_{aj}$)** $\quad$ Few eminent scholars avoided the *textual* controversy.
$\qquad\quad$ [*from* The controversy was textual. → the textual controversy]
$\quad$ **(Aux)** $\quad$ Few eminent scholars *would have* avoided the textual controversy.
$\quad$ **(Av)** $\quad$ Few eminent scholars would have *completely* avoided the textual controversy.

The meaning of a basic pattern is seldom as specific as that of an expanded one. Far from being merely ornamental, therefore, expansion is often necessary.

PATTERN N $\begin{Bmatrix} \mathbf{V_1} \\ \mathbf{be} \end{Bmatrix}$ N

The next pattern N $\begin{Bmatrix} \mathbf{V_1} \\ \mathbf{be} \end{Bmatrix}$ N contrasts with N V$_t$ N in having a linking verb (see p. 29) or a form of *be* instead of a transitive verb:

N	V₁	N		N	be	N
I	became	an apprentice.		The actors	are	students.
She	remained	his favorite.		The prince	is a	playboy.
Mitchell	appeared	a fool.		The interns	will be	teachers.

The noun following the linking verb or *be* is called a **predicate noun.**

Transposition Transformation (T_t)

The passive transformation cannot be applied to N $\begin{Bmatrix} V_1 \\ be \end{Bmatrix}$ N, for we do not say "*A fool was appeared by Mitchell" or "*People are been actors." But nouns in this pattern can be transposed by (T_t), where **t** stands for transposition, to achieve certain ironic, if not sarcastic, effects:

$N_1 \begin{Bmatrix} V_1 \\ be \end{Bmatrix}$	N_2		N_2	$N_1 \begin{Bmatrix} V_1 \\ be \end{Bmatrix}$
She remained	his favorite.	→	His favorite	she remained.
He was	a scholar.	→	A scholar	he was.

A compound noun can be generated by front-shifting the predicate noun of certain members of this pattern:

The actors are students.	→ student actors
The prince is a playboy.	→ playboy prince
The interns will be teachers.	→ teacher interns

PATTERN N V_{tg} N N

The next pattern, N V_{tg} N N, has in its basic form a noun or pronoun tied to a subclass of transitive verbs like *give* **g**(ive), *promise*, *offer* and followed by a complement of two nouns or pronouns. The first noun or pronoun is called the **indirect object,** and the second the **direct object:**

N	V_{tg}	N_2		N_3
They	gave	us		advice.
We	offered	them		encouragement.
The director	promised	him		this.
He	awarded	her	a	corsage.
The management	granted	Jackson	a	raise.
The company	offered	Smith	the	presidency.
The court	guaranteed	him		protection.

N_2 and N_3 may be interchanged by (T_t) with the preposition *to* preceding N_2:

N_1	V_{tg}	N_2	N_3	
They	gave	us	advice.	→
We	offered	them	encouragement.	→

N_1	V_{tg}	N_3	to N_2
They	gave	advice	to us.
We	offered	encouragement	to them.

(T_{pass}) can be applied, with either the indirect or direct object functioning as the subject of the derived sentence:

The court guaranteed him → He was guaranteed protection
  protection.   by the court.
                             Protection was guaranteed him
                             by the court.

The management granted → Jackson was granted a raise
  Jackson a raise.   by the management.
                             A raise was granted Jackson
                             by the management.

The director promised him → He was promised this by the
  this.   director.
                             This was promised him by the
                             director.

Some sentences of the type N V_{tg} N N can be inverted:

N_1	V_{tg}	N_2	N_3	
They	gave	us	advice.	→
The court	guaranteed	him	protection.	→

N_3	N_1	V_{tg}	N_2
Advice	they	gave	us.
Protection	the court	guaranteed	him.

Whenever the basic arrangement of a pattern is disturbed, attention is focused on the words out of regular sequence. Inversion therefore can be a dramatic device if used sparingly. Indeed, its force is its rare occurrence.[2]

PATTERN N V_{te} N N (and N V_{te} N Aj)

The last pattern taken up in this chapter, N V_{te} N N (or N V_{te} N Aj), consists in its basic form of a noun or pronoun tied to a subclass of transitive verbs like *elect* e(lect), *confirm*, *consider*, and followed by two complements. The first complement is called the **direct object**

[2] Rearrangement of sentence parts to focus attention in a certain way is also the strategy of constructing loose and periodic sentences. See pp. 342–345.

and the second complement, which may be either a noun or an adjective, the **object complement**:

N	V_{t_e}	N		N
The students	voted	Johnson	their	spokesman.
The court	confirmed	him		governor.
The judges	declared	him		winner.
She	considered	him	a	gentleman.
We	regard	Fred	a	scholar.
The class	made	*Othello*	its	choice.

N	V_{t_e}	N	Aj
The instructor	made	*Othello*	memorable.
We	consider	Fred	.exceptional.
The critic	thought	the play	disappointing.
She	regarded	her contribution	adequate.
They	made	it	meaningful.

The pattern N V_{t_e} N N looks deceptively like N V_{t_g} N N, but closer inspection reveals a difference:

N V_{t_e} N N   They elected Smith chairman.
N V_{t_g} N N   They offered Smith the chairmanship.

In the first sentence, the complements *Smith* and *chairman* refer to the same person. They are said to have the same referent. In the second sentence, the complements *Smith* and *chairmanship* have different referents. The patterns are distinguished by the subclasses of transitive verbs, which determine whether the complements have the same or different referents.[3]

The passive transformation can be applied to N V_{t_e} N N:

The court confirmed him governor. → He was confirmed governor
                                         by the court.
The students voted Johnson their   → Johnson was voted spokesman
   spokesman.   by the students.
The judges declared him winner.   → He was declared winner
                                         by the judges.

[3] Patterns like "They elected Smith chairman" and "The court confirmed him governor" differ from "We elected Smith this year" and "The court confirmed him Tuesday." The last two sentences are expansions of N V_t N with *this year* and *Tuesday* apparently derived from prepositional groups (*during this year, on Tuesday*) from which the preposition has been deleted.

EXPANSION OF N V_{t_g} N N; N V_{t_e} N N

Adjectives, adverbs, as well as function words, can be used to expand both N V_{t_g} N N and N V_{t_e} N N:

	N V_{t_g}	N		N
(Aux)	The firm *had* granted	Jackson	a	raise.
(T_{aj})	The firm had granted	Jackson	a *substantial*	raise.
	[*from* The raise was substantial.→		a substantial raise]	
(Av)	The firm had *never* granted Jackson		a substantial raise.	
(Q)	The firm had never granted Jackson a *very* substantial raise.			

	N V_{tg}	N by N
(T_{pass})	Jackson *was granted*	a raise by the firm.
(Aux)	Jackson *had been* granted	a raise by the firm.
(Av)	Jackson had *never* been granted	a raise by the firm.
(Q + Av)	Jackson had never been granted a raise by the firm *so quickly*.	

	N V_{t_e}	N	N
(D)	Eileen considers	him *an*	artist.
(T_{aj})	Eileen considers	him a *superior*	artist.
	[*from* An artist is superior.→ a superior artist]		
(Aux)	Eileen *must* consider	him a superior artist.	
(Av)	Eileen must *surely* consider him a superior artist.		

	N V_{t_e}	N	N by N
(T_{pass})	He *is considered*	an	artist by his peers.
(Aux)	He *would have been* considered	an	artist by his peers.
(Av)	He would *hardly* have been considered an		artist by his peers.
(Aj)	He would hardly have been considered a	*superior*	artist by his peers.
(Q)	He would hardly have been considered a *less* superior artist by his peers.		

SUMMARY

Four additional basic patterns have been introduced:

N V_t N — Students expect praise.

N $\begin{Bmatrix} V_1 \\ be \end{Bmatrix}$ N — Students become challenges.
Television is entertainment.

N V$_{tg}$ N N   The city presented him a plaque.

N V$_{te}$ N N   The nation considers them patriots.

All except N $\begin{Bmatrix} V_I \\ be \end{Bmatrix}$ N undergo the passive transformation (T$_{pass}$):

Students expect praise.   → Praise is expected by students.

The city awarded him a plaque.   → He was awarded a plaque by
                                                                    the city.

The nation considered them patriots. → They were considered patriots
                                                                    by the nation.

The phrase **by** N generated by the passive transformation may be dropped (T$_{del}$):

Praise is expected by students. → Praise is expected.

He was presented a plaque by
   the city.   → He was presented a plaque.

They were considered patriots
   by the nation.   → They were considered patriots.

Nouns in N $\begin{Bmatrix} V_I \\ be \end{Bmatrix}$ N can be transposed (T$_t$):

She seemed a blonde. → A blonde she seemed.

She was a blonde.   → A blonde she was.

Other sentence types may also be inverted:

Students expect praise, but low grades they abhor.

A student he is now; he may be someday a scholar.

Each of the four patterns may be expanded by adjectives (through T$_{aj}$), adverbs, and function words.

EXERCISES

1.   Identify the basic pattern in each of the following sentences:

EXAMPLE:

(D)   N   V

Most prisoners could have escaped accidentally.

Most prisoners escaped.

   1.   Each candidate passed his preliminary examination.
   2.   Social problems were much simpler then.

3. They certainly deserve some encouragement.
4. The presidency has been reportedly offered to the dean by the board of trustees.
5. A navigational error was responsible for the crash.
6. The sunbathers were exposed.
7. The mayor was unexpectedly overruled by his council.
8. The Prime Minister granted newly independent Malaysia immediate recognition.
9. No decision was made by the executive committee.
10. The dean might be replaced.

2. Expand each of the following sentences meaningfully in three steps, each time adding one of the following: an adjective [by (T_{aj})], determiner, auxiliary, or qualifier.

EXAMPLE:

Most prisoners escaped.
(T_{aj}) Most prisoners seemed defiant. → most *defiant* prisoners
Most defiant prisoners escaped.
(Aux) Most defiant prisoners *have* escaped.
(Q) Most defiant prisoners have *indeed* escaped.

1. Experts rated the plan a failure.
2. Their candidate seemed a winner.
3. The student council prescribed the fees.
4. The committee offered Hibbard the chairmanship.
5. Students are winners.

3. Apply (T_{pass}), wherever it is appropriate, to the expanded sentences in Exercise 2.

4. Write sentences based on the following formulas:

NOTE: Determiners (D) have been omitted from the formulas, but they may be freely added.

1. N T V_t N
2. N T M V_{tg} N N
3. N T M V_{te} N_p N
4. N T V_l N
5. N T have -en be -ing V_{tg} N_p N
6. N T have -en be Aj N
7. N T V_i Av Av
8. N T V_i Q Av
9. N T M be -ing V_t N Av
10. N_p T have -en V_{tg} N_p N_p

5) *Prepositional Phrases*

A preposition (**P**) is a function word like *of, in, to, for, at, on, from, with, by,* that usually combines with a noun or pronoun, called its **object**, and forms a construction known as a **prepositional phrase** (**P-phr**):

$$
\text{for}
\begin{cases}
\text{teachers} \\
\text{Mrs. Smith} \\
\text{her} \\
\text{him} \\
\text{them} \\
\text{us}
\end{cases}
\begin{array}{l}
\text{at} \\
\text{by} \\
\text{within} \\
\text{in front of} \\
\text{around} \\
\text{from behind}
\end{array}
\text{the house}
$$

Prepositions are important in showing relationships. Indeed, they play a role far out of proportion to their number. Professor Charles C. Fries lists nine prepositions—those mentioned in the first sentence—used in about 92 percent of the instances in which prepositions must be used. For the nine, the *Oxford English Dictionary* gives 329 meanings.[1] In a study of 208 expository sentences, for example, 426 prepositional phrases were counted, not including those in subordinate clauses, or an average of two per sentence. Some sentences of those counted had six and seven.

[1] Charles C. Fries, *American English Grammar* (New York: Appleton-Century-Crofts, 1940), pp. 112–113.

50

KINDS OF PREPOSITIONS

The most familiar are the simple prepositions, such as the nine listed above or the following, most of which can also perform as adverbs:

about	amid	concerning	out
above	among	down	over
across	around	like	regarding
after	as	near	
against	before	off	
along	behind	opposite	

Simple prepositions sometimes combine in pairs like *up and down, in and out, over and under* ("up and down the boulevard," "in and out the room," "over and under the bridge").

A compound preposition consists of two simple prepositions (written as one or two words):

across from	down from	over in
ahead of	down through	over on
along with	down to	over to
apart from	down upon	right about
as for	due to	right along
at about	except for	right between
away at	inside of	right from
away from	into	together with
back from	in with	upon
back in	off into	up against
back of	off to	up at
back through	on through	up by
back to	out against	up to
back toward	out for	within
back with	out of	without
because of	out through	
down by	over by	

A phrasal preposition consists of a preposition followed by a noun and another preposition, usually *to, of,* or *with:*

by way of	in line with	in touch with
in addition to	in need of	in trouble with

in advance of	in payment of	in tune with
in answer to	in place of	in view of
in care of	in regard to	on account of
in case of	in reply to	on behalf of
in charge of	in return for	on hand for
in connection with	in search of	on time for
in contrast to	in sight of	on top of
in danger of	in spite of	upon receipt of
in despair of	in store for	upon orders of
in doubt of	in support of	within range of
in excess of	in terms of	within reach of
in favor of	in time for	within sight of
in front of	in time to	

Combining Prepositional Phrases

Prepositional phrases combine with each of the four major word classes.

With nouns:

N	P-phr
Nations	of Europe
most	of it
year	before the war
crisis	at home
wages	together with fringe benefits
government	in relation to business
letters	in support of an application
shadows	in front of the curtain

With verbs:

V	P-phr
remain	for a year
served	as a consultant
inclined	to a belief
worked	within limits
housed	in barracks
refused	in spite of need
finished	in time for lunch
sleeps	within sight of his professor

With adjectives:

Aj	P-phr
capable	of valor
qualified	for an examination
close	to the president
optimistic	from the start
insistent	in support of his theory
ripe	in time for the holidays
rebellious	on account of her brother
equivocal	in spite of danger

With adverbs:

Av	P-phr
now	for a moment
immediately	by wire
slowly	around the curve
somewhere	among the natives
unquestionably	without taste
necessarily	up to midnight
quickly	off into space
hardly	within range of a solution

Prepositional phrases combining with nouns may have any of the four major word classes as object:

interest *in music*	(**N**)
a sense *of the significant*	(**Aj**)
popular rights *before then*	(**Av**)
hope *of serving* well	(**V**)

Sometimes another prepositional phrase functions as the object:

news from inside the bamboo curtain

The object of the preposition *from* is the prepositional phrase *inside the bamboo curtain.*

Prepositional phrases often combine with more than one word class in a sentence:

The visitors remained.
The visitors *from Colombia* remained.
The visitors *from Colombia* remained *for a week.*

His satire is implicit.
His satire *on politics* is implicit.
His satire *on politics* is implicit *in the dialogue*.

The collection was a success.
The collection *of ancient tales* was a success.
The collection of *ancient tales* was a success immediately *upon publication*.

In the first set, the prepositional phrases "from Colombia" and "for a week" combine with a noun ("visitors") and a verb ("remained") respectively; in the second set, two prepositional phrases expand a noun ("satire") and an adjective ("implicit") each; in the last set, they modify a noun ("collection") and an adverb ("immediately"). The object of a preposition may of course be expanded by other word classes as well as by another prepositional phrase:

in the department
in the chemistry department
in the largest chemistry department

the management
the management of the company
the management of the company without a board of directors

But too many consecutive prepositional phrases clutter up a sentence: "They left their home on Gunson Street in their new MG at ten in the morning for the lake region in the northern part of the State of Michigan." So does the use of two or more prepositions when only one is sufficient to convey the meaning:

The jalopy is being sold *for between* $75 and $95.
BETTER: The jalopy is being sold for $75 to $95.

He was born *at around* Easter.
BETTER: He was born *at* (or *around*) Easter.

He was told to keep children *out of from between* parked cars.
BETTER: He was told to keep children *from* parked cars.

INFINITIVES AND SEPARABLE VERBS

To followed by a simple verb or *be* forms a construction commonly called an **infinitive**:
to work
to write
to be

The question sometimes arises whether to place a word between *to* and the verb, that is, whether to split the infinitive. A so-called split infinitive is perfectly acceptable in standard written English if another construction would be ambiguous, awkward, or less emphatic:

> He wished *utterly to forget* his friends. [Ambiguous, for *utterly* can apply to either *wished* or *forget*.]
> He wished *to forget utterly* his friends. [Awkward.]
> He wished *to forget* his friends *utterly*. [Weak, sounding as though a thought had been tagged on.]
> NECESSARY SPLIT: He wished to utterly forget his friends.
>
> We were instructed *quickly to pull* the lever. [Ambiguous, since *quickly* can apply to either *instructed* or *to pull*.]
> We were instructed *to pull* the lever *quickly*. [Ambiguous, since *quickly* can apply to the whole sentence or to the infinitive phrase.]
> NECESSARY SPLIT: We were instructed to quickly pull the lever.

The examples show that an infinitive may be split to achieve clarity, smoothness, or force.

The selection of the right preposition sometimes poses a problem. "He took a course *with* Professor Smith," "He took a course *under* Professor Smith," or "He took a course *from* Professor Smith," are acceptable, but "He took a course *by* Professor Smith" is heard in only some parts of the United States. The ability of prepositions to form combinations with verbs, moreover, often forces choices among prepositional idioms like *agree to, agree with, agree on, agree in*; *compare with, compare to*; *differ from, differ with*, each of which has a distinct meaning and use, and therefore must be learned as an individual item.

> The warring countries *agreed to* a cease-fire.
> They *agreed on* details for implementing the terms of the cease-fire.
> They *agreed in* principle to negotiate their differences.
> They *agreed with* the mediator to avoid the use of force.
>
> The committee members *differed with* each other on how to raise funds for the hospital.
> The proposal to assess a 1 percent tax on all property owners *differed from* all other recommendations.
>
> My income was *compared with* his.
> His imagination was *compared to* a dried-up stream.

Students frequently inquire whether or not it is correct to place a preposition at the end of a sentence. In certain constructions this practice is not only desirable but necessary to avoid clumsy phrasing. For example:

> Almost instantly, I realized that this was the advice he had been waiting for.—ROBERT M. COATES, *The New Yorker*

> It was difficult to find anything to talk about.
> —ELIZABETH TAYLOR, *The New Yorker*

In the first sentence the preposition occurs in a relative clause in which the relative has been omitted. In such a construction the preposition quite properly follows its object. In the second sentence the same principle obtains, even though here the preposition follows an infinitive phrase.[2] Both "advice for which he had been waiting" and "advice which he had been waiting for" are acceptable, but "anything about which to talk" would be cumbersome. Here are other examples:

> Heroic daring and the imponderables of high civilization were the inheritance they [the Athenians] were born to.—EDITH HAMILTON, *The Greek Way*

> He [Socrates] was always the seeker, asking, not teaching; but his questions upset men's confidence in themselves and in all the comfortable conventions they lived by.—EDITH HAMILTON, *ibid.*

If the relative pronoun is not omitted, the preposition may or may not be shifted:[3]

> These are the principles by which he lives.

Both "by which he lives" and "which he lives by" are grammatical, but the first is more formal.

Sometimes what appears to be a preposition at the end of a sentence is an adverb that is part of the verb phrase, aptly called a **separable verb**.[4] The grammar of English allows:

> The engineer turned on the motor.
> *Or* The engineer turned the motor on.

---

[2] An infinitive with or without a complement or modifier.

[3] Relative pronouns are taken up in the next chapter.

[4] See W. Nelson Francis, *The Structure of American English* (New York: Ronald Press, 1958), p. 265.

The officer shot down the criminal.
Or The officer shot the criminal down.

Separable verbs with the object inside the verb phrase are common:

A little before noon, he saw a Japanese woman handing something out.
—JOHN HERSEY, *Hiroshima*

Her friends then left her to think that piece of news over.
—JOHN HERSEY, *ibid.*

A sentence containing a separable verb can be formally distinguished from one containing an intransitive verb followed by a prepositional phrase. Besides inserting a direct object into the verb phrase, we can apply (T_{pass}), as well as (T_{del}), to sentences containing separable verbs:

The motor was turned on (by the engineer).
The criminal was shot down (by the officer).

The following sentences, however, pattern differently:

The engineer turned on the road.
The officer shot down the alley.

Neither sentence, an example of **N V_i P-phr**, can undergo (T_{pass}). *On* and *down* are prepositions, not adverbs, in these sentences.

PREPOSITIONAL PHRASES IN SENTENCES

Prepositional phrases occur in basic patterns, especially in **N be Av** or **N V (Av)** where they replace the adverb:

(D) N   be   P-phr
The students were in the classroom.
The officials   are   with the legation.
The readings are   for comprehension.

(D) N   V   (P-phr)
The people   arrived   from the country.
The preposition appears   at the end.
The climax   occurred in Act II.

Prepositional phrases modifying nouns may be derived from different constructions. For example:

(D)	N	be	P-phr	
The	students	were	in the classroom.	→
The	officials	are	with the legation.	→
The	readings	are	for comprehension.	→
A	sign	is	by the road.	→
Their	student	is	from Norway.	→
The	woman	is	like Venus.	→
The	news	is	about the decision.	→

(D)	N	P-phr[5]
the	students	in the classroom
the	officials	with the legation
the	readings	for comprehension
a	sign	by the road
their	student	from Norway
a	woman	like Venus
the	news	about the decision

Or:

(D) N		V_t	(D) N	
The academy		reviewed	its awards.	→
The union		refused	a settlement.	→
Our class		chose	Poe.	→

(D) N's	N	of (D) N	
the academy's	review	of its	awards
the union's	refusal	of a	settlement
our class's	choice	of	Poe

Or: N V_t, where V_t is a form of **have**:

(D) N_1	have	(D) N_2		(D) N_2	of (D) N_1
The bank	has	a	manager. →	the manager	of the bank
The lady	has		charm. →	the charm	of the lady
The country	has	an	army. →	the army	of the country
The artist	has		pride. →	the pride	of the artist

Or:

(D) N_1	with	(D) N_2
→ the bank	with	the manager
→ the lady	with	charm
→ the country	with an	army
→ the artist	with	pride

[5] An intermediate step converting the predicate into a relative clause has been omitted: The students were in the room. → the students who were in the room → the students in the room.

Transformations like the preceding that convert sentences into noun phrases will be taken up in Chapter 8.

Considerable freedom is usually possible in transforming constructions that contain prepositional phrases:

N	P-phr		N	N
officials	with the legation	→	legation	officials
people	from the country	→	country	people
cards	for identification	→	identification	cards
preposition	at the end	→	end	preposition

Also:

N	P-phr		N	N
management	of the company	→	company	management
Constitution	of the United States	→	United States	Constitution *or*
			U.S.	Constitution
program	for urban renewal	→	urban renewal	program
requirement	for citizenship	→	citizenship	requirement

Time favors constructions like those in the right-hand column:

N	P-phr		P-phr	N
showmanship	on screen	→	on-screen	showmanship
facts	behind the scenes	→	behind-the-scenes	facts
architects	from out of town	→	out-of-town	architects

Here are other examples:

P-phr		Av
with rapidity	→	rapidly
with frequency	→	frequently

P-phr (P Aj N)		Av	V -en
with superb execution	→	superbly	executed
through skillful preparation	→	skillfully	prepared

P-phr (P Aj N)		Av	Aj
of high interest	→	highly	interesting
with remarkable resilience	→	remarkably	resilient

(D) N		P-phr	(D)	Aj	N
a	man	of pride	→ a	proud	man
a	contribution	of substance	→ a	substantial	contribution

V	P-phr		V	Av
walked	with grace	→	walked	gracefully
spoke	with pretentiousness	→	spoke	pretentiously

But "a cup of tea" is not "a teacup"; "a basket of bread," "a bread basket"; or "a house of light," "a lighthouse."

SUMMARY

A prepositional phrase consists of a preposition and its object. The preposition may be simple, compound, or phrasal, and the object either a noun or a pronoun. In a prepositional phrase expanding a noun, the object may be one of the four major word classes or another prepositional phrase:

SIMPLE PREPOSITION: *with* kindness
COMPOUND PREPOSITION: *out of* kindness
PHRASAL PREPOSITION: *in need of* kindness

                N
on account of Mary

                N$_p$
on account of her

    V -ing
for translating

                Aj
no rest for the weary

                Av
no rest for now

            P-phr
a song from out of the past

Prepositional phrases combine with each of the four major word classes:

N
disagreement during the summit conference

Aj
adequate within reason

Av
truly in harmony

V
imposed on all students

The object in a prepositional phrase may of course be expanded by another prepositional phrase:

imposed on all students with automobiles

where the prepositional phrase *with automobiles* is an expansion of *all students*.

The function word *to* combines with verbs to form infinitives; adverbs combine with verbs to form verb phrases (*or* compound verbs):

INFINITIVE: to turn

COMPOUND VERB: turn to
                 turn out
                 turn over

Nouns or pronouns can occur within a separable verb:

            turn on the light
            turn the light on
            turn it on
CONTRAST: turn on the corner

Prepositional phrases or constructions that contain prepositional phrases can often be transformed into other constructions:

N   P-phr   N   N
editor for the magazine → magazine editor

(D) N   P-phr   (D) Aj   N
an author of renown → a   renowned author

V   P-phr   V   Av
sang with brilliance → sang brilliantly

EXERCISES

1. In the following sets convert each sentence but one into a construction containing a prepositional phrase. Then incorporate the derived construction(s) in the remaining sentence.

    EXAMPLE: Japan has made great progress.
           The progress has been in seismo- → progress in seismo-
             logical engineering.   logical engineering
           Japan has made great progress in seismological engineering.

1. The author received his galley proofs.
    The galley proofs were from his publisher.

2. There is a very extensive market.
    The market is for exports.

3. Some curriculums are geared to economic needs.
    The community has needs.

4. He had few ideals.
    A physician has ideals.

5. The companies have capital resources.
    The government invited them.

6. The administration approved a slash.
    The slash was in the budget.

7. The audience clearly showed a preference.
    The preference was for plays.
    The plays had a message.

8. The President has friends.
    They formed an association.
    The association is for disseminating the truth.
    The truth is about programs.
    The administration has legislative programs.

9. The commission postponed the world junior-lightweight title fight.
    The postponement disappointed most fans.

10. The strikers defied the troops.
    Their defiance prolonged the costly dispute.
    The dispute was on the waterfront.

2. Convert each of the following constructions with its prepositional phrase into some other construction.

EXAMPLE: chairman of the board → board chairman

1. ended with abruptness
2. a study of character
3. with emotional involvement
4. history of culture
5. leadership of the party
6. discharged with honor
7. with startling similarity

8. through effective development
9. women of Naples
10. works with compulsion
11. research on nutrition
12. growth of the German economy
13. free from wrinkles
14. with proper punctuation
15. without adequate information
16. dispute on the waterfront
17. contender of top rank
18. spoke with aptness
19. operates with discretion
20. innovations in the department

3. In each of the following sentences convert phrases consisting of, or containing, one or more prepositional phrases into other constructions.

EXAMPLE:
    Sugar has always been available → Sugar has always been available
       for consumption by industries.   for industrial consumption.

1. The class in Russian prepared for its examination in vocabulary.
2. The Ambassador of France spoke with fervor on the common heritage of our two countries.
3. With bitterness the officials connected with the project denounced the slash in the budget by the government.
4. The Folk Arts Group performed six dances of ancient India and four numbers of modern American jazz.
5. The dances were characterized by a brilliant interpretation and followed by an ovation of five minutes.
6. He was determined to marry a woman of wealth, if not one of beauty.
7. Reports of the majority of newspapers agreed that the governor addressed the recalcitrant legislators with urgency, yet in a spirit of moderation.
8. They left their home on Gunson Street in their new MG at ten in the morning for the lake region in the northern part of the State of Michigan.
9. Despite an abundance of manpower, Laos has few workers with technical skills.
10. The resolution by the president to open membership in the club to nationals of foreign countries was received by the executive committee with approval.

4. Write sentences based on the following formulas. Use simple, compound, and phrasal prepositions to introduce prepositional phrases.

NOTE: Determiners (**D**) may be added wherever appropriate, and past or present tense (**T**) freely selected.

1. N P-phr V_i Av
2. N V_i P-phr Av Av
3. N V_i Av P-phr
4. N V_l Aj P-phr
5. N P-phr be Aj P-phr
6. N P-phr V_{t_e} N N P-phr
7. N V_l Aj P-phr (where P-phr is P N P Aj N)
8. N V_{t_g} N N P-phr (where P-phr is P D Aj)
9. N V_t N P-phr (where P-phr is P Av)
10. N V_t N P-phr (where P-phr is P V -ing Av)

6) Relative and Subordinate Clauses

RELATIVE CLAUSES

Relative Transformation (T_{rel})

A sentence may be expanded by an incorporating transformation that includes one of two sentences in the other. For example:

The judges reached a decision.
They had deliberated past midnight. } →
The judges who had deliberated past midnight reached a decision.

The drama club had built the set.
The set was acclaimed by all reviewers. } →
The drama club had built the set, which was acclaimed by all reviewers.

The speaker stared at the audience.
His emotions overwhelmed him. } →
The speaker, whose emotions overwhelmed him, stared at the audience.

The sentences involved in the transformation are the one from which the expansion derives, the **insert sentence** (**I**), and the one in which the expansion is used, the **matrix sentence** (**M**). "They had deliberated past midnight," "The set was acclaimed by all reviewers," and "His emotions overwhelmed him" are insert sentences; "The judges reached a decision," "The drama club had built the set," and "The speaker stared at the audience" are matrix sentences. In the insert sentence, a noun, pronoun, or determiner is replaced by a function word, called a **relative pronoun,** or **relative (R)**, which transforms the sentence into a **relative clause (R-cl)**. The generated clause is then included in the matrix sentence.

The transformation, symbolized by (T_{rel}), where **rel** stands for relative, differs from preceding ones insofar as it acts on two sentences rather than one:

> The judges reached a decision.
>
> (T_{rel}) *They* had deliberated past midnight. → *who* had deliberated past midnight
>
> The judges who had deliberated past midnight reached their decision.

> The drama club had built the set.
>
> (T_{rel}) *The set* was acclaimed by all reviewers. → *which* was acclaimed by all reviewers
>
> The drama club had built the set, which was acclaimed by all reviewers.

> The speaker stared at the audience.
>
> (T_{rel}) *His* eyes betrayed him. → *whose* eyes betrayed him
>
> The speaker, whose eyes betrayed him, stared at the audience.

The set of relatives is small:

who	whichever
which	whosever
that	whomever
whose	what
whom	whatever
whoever	

Of these, *who* and *whom* replace nouns denoting persons; *which,* animals and things; *that* and *whose*, persons, animals, or things. However, some writers shun *that* in referring to persons:

the girl (*who, that*) cried
the liner (*which, that*) sank
the family (*who, that*) lives across the street
the speaker *whose* emotions overwhelmed him
the family *whose* dog bit the postman
the tree *whose* leaves are scarlet
the committee (*that, which*) all members elected
the members (*whom, that*) the committee replaced

A relative has two simultaneous functions: it introduces a relative clause and it replaces a noun, pronoun, or determiner in the insert sentence:

> The committee will serve another year.
>
> (**T**$_{rel}$) *It* was appointed last fall. → *which* was appointed last fall
> The committee, which was appointed last fall, will serve another year.
>
> Bob Sled prefers selling electric toasters.
>
> (**T**$_{rel}$) *His* outdoor sport is skiing. → *whose* outdoor sport is skiing
> Bob Sled, whose outdoor sport is skiing, prefers selling electric toasters.

In each of the preceding sets, the subject of the matrix sentence is expanded. In the following, the direct object of the matrix sentence is expanded:

> The instructor selected the dictionary.
>
> (**T**$_{rel}$) *It* will be used in the course. → *that* will be used in the course
> The instructor selected the dictionary that will be used in the course.

In the next sentence, the object of the preposition is expanded:

> He has no interest in those poets.
>
> (**T**$_{rel}$) *They* demand too much from the reader. → *who* demand too much from the reader
> He has no interest in those poets who demand too much from the reader.

A relative replacing a noun, pronoun, or determiner in the direct object position is front-shifted:

> Eliot dated a Thai girl.
>
> (**T**$_{rel}$) He had met *her* at the dean's reception. → he had met *whom* at the dean's reception → *whom* he had met at the dean's reception
> Eliot dated a Thai girl whom he had met at the dean's reception.
>
> Eliot dated a Thai girl.
>
> (**T**$_{rel}$) He could not pronounce *her* name. → he could not pronounce *whose* name → *whose* name he could not pronounce
> Eliot dated a Thai girl whose name he could not pronounce.
>
> The gentleman was her agent.
>
> (**T**$_{rel}$) She invited *him*. → she invited *whom* → *whom* she invited
> The gentleman whom she invited was her agent.

Relatives are sometimes omitted in informal writing:

> The gentleman she invited was her agent.
> He was the kind of person she admired.
> The student showed little interest in the examination he missed.

Ambiguities sometimes occur when a prepositional phrase inter-venes between the relative clause and the expanded noun:

> the family across the street from the Joneses *whose* dog bit the postman
> the fireboat near the liner *that* sank

It is impossible to tell whether the dog belonged to the Joneses or to the family across from the Joneses, nor can one be certain whether it was the fireboat or the liner that sank. The relative in the first sentence can refer to either *the family* or *the Joneses*, and the relative in the second sentence to either *the fireboat* or *the liner*. One way of resolving the ambiguity is to recast each sentence:

> The family whose dog bit the postman lived across from the Joneses.
> The fireboat that sank near the liner had a six-foot gash in its side.

No ambiguity is present in the following, because the relatives have clearly defined antecedents, with *which* referring to *the street* and *who* to *the family*:

> the family across the street *which* is being repaired
> the family across the street *who* moved in yesterday

Nor is there any ambiguity in the next sentence, even though *which* can refer to either *the fireboat* or *the harbor*:

> the fireboat near the harbor which sank

Harbors, though they may settle a few inches annually, do not usually sink into the ocean.

SUBORDINATE CLAUSES

Subordinating Transformation (T_{sub})

Relative clauses expand nouns but not verbs and their comple-ments, that is, an adjective, noun, or nouns following a transitive verb, a form of *be* or other linking verb. A verb and its complement may be expanded by an incorporating transformation that includes one of two sentences in the other through a function word called a **subordinating conjunction** or **subordinator (S)**:

> The instructor left.
> His contract was not renewed. $\Big\} \rightarrow$
> The instructor left *because* his contract was not renewed.
>
> The judges reached a decision.
> They had deliberated past midnight. $\Big\} \rightarrow$
> The judges reached a decision *after* they had deliberated past midnight.

The transformation, symbolized by (T_{sub}), where **sub** stands for subordination, changes the insert sentence into a **subordinate clause (S-cl)**. As in (T_{rel}), the generated clause is then inserted in the matrix sentence. Structurally, however, (T_{sub}) functions differently from (T_{rel}): in (T_{rel}), the relative pronoun replaces a noun, pronoun, or determiner in the insert sentence; in (T_{sub}), the subordinator replaces nothing. It simply introduces the insert sentence, which remains fully intact. Both relative clauses and subordinate clauses are, of course, "subordinate" or "dependent" in the sense that they are included in, or are a part of, another sentence.

Subordinators include:

after	because	since	where
although	before	so that	whereas
as	how	that	wherever
as if	in order that	though	while
as (often, soon, far) as	if	unless	why
as though	provided that	until	when

Inspection of the list reveals some overlapping with relatives. Just as some words perform as nouns or verbs, so *that* may perform as a relative or subordinator:

> The council proposed a plan *that* all members could accept.
> The council accepted the condition *that* it would disband within a year.

In the first sentence *that* is a relative and in the second a subordinator.

Which one of two sentences to subordinate depends largely on context and grammatical requirements:

> The judges who reached a decision had deliberated past midnight.
> The judges who had deliberated past midnight reached a decision.
> The judges reached a decision after they had deliberated past midnight.
> The judges deliberated past midnight. They reached a decision.

The first sentence emphasizes the length of the judges' deliberations. The second and third sentences emphasize the end of the deliberations. The last set, consisting of two short consecutive sentences, gives equal emphasis to both actions.

The choice of punctuation significantly affects the meaning of a sentence that contains a relative clause:

> The judges who had deliberated past midnight reached a decision.
> The judges, who had deliberated past midnight, reached a decision.

The first sentence points out that only those judges who deliberated past midnight arrived at a decision. It implies that there were other judges who did not take part in the deliberations. The meaning of *judges* is limited or restricted; there is no internal punctuation to set the relative clause off from the rest of the sentence. A clause that limits, restricts, or defines the meaning of its antecedent is called a **restrictive clause.** The second sentence asserts that the judges reached a decision, then adds that they stayed past midnight. The relative clause, set off by commas, expands the whole sentence, not any single word. It is said to be **nonrestrictive.** Nonrestrictive clauses are set off by a comma or commas; restrictive clauses are not.[1] Thus:

> The questionnaire, which was prepared by a faculty committee, will evaluate instructors.
> The questionnaire which was prepared by a faculty committee will evaluate instructors.
> *Or:* The questionnaire that was prepared by a faculty committee will evaluate instructors.[2]

Similarly:

> Miss Winslow will decline the role unless the studio improves her contract.
> Miss Winslow will decline the role, unless the studio improves her contract.

[1] See pp. 230–233 for a discussion of features of intonation which are often useful in distinguishing restrictive and nonrestrictive clauses.

[2] Some writers prefer *that* in restrictive clauses and *which* in nonrestrictive clauses, but this practice is by no means universal. See, for example, the quotations by J. Lederer and E. Burdick, p. 73; C. Amory, p. 132; R. E. Spiller, p. 234. In each of these quotations, *which* presumably introduces a restrictive clause. For a liberal approach to this matter of usage, see Bergen Evans and Cornelia Evans, *A Dictionary of Contemporary American Usage* (New York: Random House, 1957), pp. 505–506 ("that; which"). For a conservative point of view, see Margaret Nicholson, *A Dictionary of American-English Usage*: Based on Fowler's *Modern English Usage* (New York: Oxford University Press, 1957), pp. 576–580 ("that" rel. pron.).

The first sentence says that under certain conditions Miss Winslow will not accept the part. The subordinate clause "unless the studio improves her contract" tells under what conditions Miss Winslow will decline the role. It is restrictive. The second sentence tells what Miss Winslow will do, then qualifies her decision. The subordinate clause expands the whole sentence, not just part of it. It is nonrestrictive.

AS SENTENCE ADJUNCTS

A dependent clause that expands a sentence is called a **sentence adjunct.**

Subordinate clauses performing as sentence adjuncts often appear at the beginning of a sentence:

Unless the studio improves her contract, Miss Winslow will decline the role.

When Wagner trumpeted unprepared major ninths at us in *Tannhäuser,* we stopped our ear.—G. B. SHAW, *Sixteen Self Sketches*

They also occur in the middle of a sentence:

Slang, as we should know, is one of the great sources of language.
—D. W. BROGAN, *The American Character*

The reason print did not destroy the Catholic Church, although it broke the Church's monopoly, is that in good time print was adapted to the uses of the Church.—GILBERT SELDES, *The Public Arts*

He ate breakfast and then, because the morning was already hot, undressed down to his underwear and went out on the porch to read the paper.—JOHN HERSEY, *Hiroshima*

At the end of a sentence the meaning determines whether a subordinate clause is a sentence adjunct or not. In the following, the first is a sentence adjunct, the second is not:

He had slept badly the night before, because there had been several air-raid warnings.—JOHN HERSEY, *Hiroshima*

The social and political role of American education cannot be understood if it is thought of as being primarily a means of formal instruction.
—D. W. BROGAN, *The American Character*

Relative clauses performing as sentence adjuncts are introduced by relatives like *whatever*, *whoever*, or by a relative preceded by the phrase *no matter:*

> Whatever he decides, he is unlikely to regret his choice.
> No matter what he decides, he is unlikely to regret his choice.

IN NOUN POSITIONS

In addition to performing as sentence adjuncts, relative and subordinate clauses may occupy noun positions:

> That they have the right to select their own candidates is beyond dispute.
>
> That the poets also were aloof is the greatest pity because radio was made for them.—GILBERT SELDES, *The Public Arts*
>
> What is most needed in these tense times is the will to compromise.
> —U THANT, *Saturday Review*
>
> What the first-generation American children learn to despise may include elements in their moral diet that are not replaced.
> —D. W. BROGAN, *The American Character*

The subject position of the first two sentences is filled by subordinate clauses, the subject position of the last two by relative clauses. In the following, the direct object position is occupied by a relative and a subordinate clause, respectively:

> In one way and another I have used in my writings whatever has happened to me in the course of my life.
> —SOMERSET MAUGHAM, *The Summing Up*
>
> I personally think that the grimmest place on earth is the Bahamas during the winter season.—GEOFFREY BOCCA, *Saturday Review*

A relative clause can also function as the object of a preposition:

> The rise, at the turn of the century, of what James called "the softer pedagogy" is responsible for a debasement of language beyond all bounds of forgiveness.—JACQUES BARZUN, *Teacher in America*

A sentence may contain more than one relative or subordinate clause. In the following, a subordinate clause ("though I have no academic qualifications") is nested within another ("that . . . I am in fact much more highly educated than most university scholars") functioning as the direct object:

> I cannot too often repeat that though I have no academic qualifications
> I am in fact much more highly educated than most university scholars.
> —G. B. SHAW, *Sixteen Self Sketches*

The next sentence contains a subordinate clause in the subject position
("Why our representatives abroad have not learned the languages
they need or studied basic sources of information such as Mao's
writings") with a relative clause nested inside of it ("they need");
and a relative clause ("which involves the entire American nation")
that expands the predicate noun *question:*

> Why our representatives abroad have not learned the languages they need
> or studied basic sources of information such as Mao's writings is a
> question which involves the entire American nation.
> —WILLIAM J. LEDERER and EUGENE BURDICK, *The Ugly American*

Other combinations, without any attempt to explain them, are displayed in the following:

> Since the ability to play bridge is one of the marks of Americanism in a
> suburb, it is reasonable that there should be a bridge club in schools.
> —D. W. BROGAN, *The American Character*

> Although I feel sorry for them, I can after a fashion understand those
> people who say they can't read fiction.
> —GRANVILLE HICKS, *Saturday Review*

> In Martinique, when the whistle blew for the tourists to get back on the
> ship, I had a quick, wild, and lovely moment when I decided I wouldn't
> get back on the ship.—JAMES THURBER, *My Life and Hard Times*

SUMMARY

A sentence may be included in another either by $(\mathbf{T_{rel}})$ or $(\mathbf{T_{sub}})$.
Included sentences generated by $(\mathbf{T_{rel}})$ are called relative clauses;
those generated by $(\mathbf{T_{sub}})$, subordinate clauses. Nouns are expanded
by relative clauses; verbs and their complements by subordinate
clauses; and sentences by both:

N V Av	The swimmers trained hard.
N R-cl be Aj P-phr	The swimmers who trained hard were certain of victory.
N V Av S-cl	The swimmers trained hard because they were certain of victory.

S-cl, N V Av	Although the swimmers were certain of victory, they trained hard.
R-cl, N be Aj P-phr	Whatever training the swimmers had, they were certain of victory.

Relative and subordinate clauses may occupy noun positions in a sentence:

R-cl V$_t$ N P-phr	Whatever training the swimmers had will help them to victory.
S-cl be N P-phr	That the swimmers hoped for a victory was no surprise to us.
N V$_t$ S-cl	The swimmers believed that they would win a victory.

EXERCISES

1. Apply ($\mathbf{T_{rel}}$) to one sentence in each pair below and expand an appropriate element in the matrix sentence with the generated relative clause.

    EXAMPLE: Galvez confessed to the Mercury holdup.
    > He also named his accomplices. → who also named his accomplices
    >
    > Galvez, who also named his accomplices, confessed to the Mercury holdup.

    1. Our governor is an excellent golfer.
        He also cooks.

    2. Six hundred sociologists to the conference on juvenile delinquency began to converge on Fort Lauderdale.
        The host city had made the best offer for housing and feeding the delegates.

    3. The mayor presented a two-year scholarship to Melda Pippin.
        She is the youngest pineapple queen ever chosen.

    4. The young sailor was rushed back to the United States on "sick leave."
        He had become engaged to a native grandmother in Tahiti.

    5. New responsibilities descended upon Marguerite MacMillan.
        Her pedigreed dachshund had a litter of five puppies.

6. He urged lifting of the ban.
    It restricts suburban taxis from picking up fares in the city.

7. The county board refused to repair the city's flooded streets.
    The suburban voters expressed full confidence in the board.

8. The village ordinance required playing of the national anthem
    before the showing of each movie.
    The village council passed the ordinance by a vote of 6 to 5.

9. For the first time since the signing of the trade agreement with
    the U.S., the Philippines is expected to exceed her duty-free
    quota.
    Under this agreement coconut oil is subject to restrictions.

10. Her companion is doubtless unaware of her moodiness.
    He may be anyone.

2. Identify the insert (**I**) and matrix sentences (**M**) underlying each of the
    expanded patterns in Exercise 1. Then indicate (1) whether a subject or
    object in the matrix sentence has been expanded, and (2) whether a
    subject, object, or determiner in the insert sentence has been replaced
    by a relative. (For punctuation of restrictive and nonrestrictive elements,
    see p. 244.)

    EXAMPLE: (**M**)   Galvez confessed to the Mercury holdup.
    (**I**)   He also named his accomplices.
    Galvez, who also named his accomplices, confessed to
    the Mercury holdup.

    (1)   Subject in **M** expanded
    (2)   Subject in **I** replaced by *who*

3. Apply (T_{sub}) to one sentence in each pair below and expand the matrix
    sentence with the generated subordinate clause.

    EXAMPLE: An assignment is of little value.
    The reasons for it are explained. → unless the reasons for it
    are explained
    Unless the reasons for it are explained, an assignment is of
    little value.

    1. The dean of the college gave his full support to the team-teaching
        project.
        He had consulted with his department heads.

2. The diplomats agreed to yet another meeting, and they expressed cautious optimism.
   They again reported no progress.

3. Our letter cannot possibly have been lost.
   A first-class sticker was on the envelope and the address was plainly marked.

4. He urged his administrators to submit weekly progress reports.
   They could make better recommendations for dealing with violators of the law.

5. A student can elect seven courses each term.
   The quality of education becomes suspect.

6. Olson will run for public office.
   He expects to win.

7. The president refused all offers of aid.
   He received a guarantee of noninterference.

8. She was determined to visit the Greek islands this summer.
   She would have to mortgage her home.

9. Long lines began forming in front of the box office before dawn and the luckless fans refused to be discouraged.
   All tickets to the World Series had been sold out.

10. From the airport she rushed to her hotel, registered, took an elevator to her room, slipped into her cocktail dress, waited, and began to have doubts about the constancy of her husband.
    She had forgotten to set her watch back an hour.

4. Identify the inset (**I**) and matrix sentences (**M**) underlying each of the expanded patterns in Exercise 3. Then indicate whether each generated subordinate clause functions as a sentence adjunct or as a modifier of the verb and complement.

EXAMPLE: An assignment is of little value.
        The reasons for it are explained. → unless the reasons for it are explained
        Unless the reasons for it are explained, an assignment is of little value.

        The generated **S-cl** at the beginning of the sentence, set off by a comma, functions as a sentence adjunct.

5. Apply either (T_{rel}) or (T_{sub}), whichever is appropriate, to one of the sentences in each pair below and place the generated clause in a noun position of the other sentence.

EXAMPLE:

He admitted it.

(T_{sub}) He held up the Mercury drugstore. → that he held up the Mercury drugstore

He admitted that he held up the Mercury drugstore.

1. The traffic bureau will enforce new speed regulations in the suburbs.
   The police chief announced it.

2. She had called American junior officers "soldiers of fortune."
   She denied it.

3. The rainfall this season was the highest in twenty years.
   This is hardly a surprise to anyone.

4. Anyone is eligible.
   He may submit an application.

5. The department added eight or nine new instructors.
   No one really knows it.

6. The directive ordered the commissioner to explain it.
   He had given his staff the afternoon off.

7. This has always impressed him most about the United States.
   It is the helpfulness of its citizens.

8. He put his complete trust in it.
   Responsible advisers called it "total involvement."

9. Generate a subordinate clause and place it in the subject position of the matrix sentence:
   Rita Fowler learned something.
   This is enough of a miracle.

10. Generate a relative clause and place it in the subject position of the matrix sentence:
    Rita Fowler learned something.
    This is enough of a miracle.

6. Identify the noun position in each generated sentence of Exercise 5 that has been replaced by a relative or subordinate clause.

    EXAMPLE: He admitted that he held up the Mercury drugstore.

    > The direct object of the matrix sentence has been replaced by a S-cl.

7. In the following sets apply (T_{rel}) or (T_{sub}) to every sentence but one and incorporate the generated clause(s) in the matrix sentence.

    1. Southeast Asia is an ageless region.
        The sense of history is new.
        Neighbors are scarcely aware of their common experience and mutual interests.
        Each country is inflamed by an intense—almost anachronistic—spirit of nationalism.

    2. Southeast Asians smoulder over the memory of exploitation.
        They suffered exploitation as colonials.
        They feel this.

    3. Asians know this.
        They must diversify and expand their agricultural production and embark upon some kind of industrialization.

    4. They have an environment of poverty.
        They seek to replace it in the fastest and most thorough fashion possible.

    5. The following are consecutive sentences:

        a. Most of the contemporary leaders of Southeast Asia are men.
            They have had the benefit of a western education and have risen to prominence on the issues of anti-imperialism and nationalism.

        b. They have little sympathy for communism.
            They have not hesitated to cooperate with communists as a matter of expediency.

        c. They know this.
            The communists will turn against them.
            The time seems favorable.—Adapted from CLAUDE A. BUSS, *Southeast Asia and the World Today* (Princeton, 1958), ch. 1.

8. Write sentences based on the following formulas:

NOTE: Determiners (**D**) may be added wherever appropriate and the present or past tense (**T**) freely added.

1. N R-cl V$_t$ N
2. N V$_t$ N R-cl
3. N V$_t$ S-cl
4. N R-cl V$_t$ S-cl
5. N P-phr V$_i$ Av S-cl
6. S-cl, N V$_i$ Av
7. S-cl, N R-cl V$_t$ N
8. R-cl, N be Aj P-phr
9. N V$_t$ N P-phr R-cl
10. S-cl be N R-cl

7) *Conjunction*

COORDINATING CONJUNCTIONS

A productive process of expansion is compounding or **conjunction.** Most simply, conjunction refers to the joining of elements of grammatically equal rank. Function words used in this transformation are called **coordinating conjunctions** or simply **conjunctions** (**C**). They include:

and	for	than
or	yet	
nor	but	

Conjunction Transformation (T_{conj})

Elements joined by (T_{conj}), where **conj** stands for conjunction, include words, phrases, clauses, and sentences:

Donna is an alert student. ⎫
She is an articulate student. ⎭ →
Donna is an alert *and* articulate student.

Jerry Donohoe might capture a gold medal in track. ⎫
He could also capture a gold medal in swimming. ⎭ →
Jerry Donohoe might capture a gold medal in track *or* in swimming.

All Founders Society patrons were invited to attend a tea at the art museum.

The museum closes down for complete renovation.⎫
Its curator leaves on a buying mission to Europe. ⎭ →

All Founders Society patrons were invited to attend a tea at the art museum before it closed down for complete renovation *and* before its curator left on a buying mission to Europe.

The antique auction started at 11 A.M.⎫
Few buyers showed up. ⎭ →

The antique auction started at 11 A.M., *but* few buyers showed up.[1]

Adjectives are joined in the first set, prepositional phrases in the second, subordinate clauses in the third, and sentences in the fourth. In addition to (T_{conj}), the joined coordinate clauses in the third set are included in the matrix sentence by (T_{sub}) with appropriate adjustments in tense sequence.[2]

Words repeated in the same construction may be dropped in (T_{conj}):

Jack is majoring in history.⎫
Dick is majoring in speech.⎭ →
Jack is majoring in history and Dick in speech.

Jane will take a trip to England. ⎫
Betty will take a trip to England.⎭ →
Jane will take a trip to England and so will Betty.

In the first set, the duplicated verb phrase is deleted. In the second set, only the subject of the second sentence is retained, with *so* replacing the deleted items.

Elements joined by a conjunction are grammatically equal in rank, as the examples have shown. Nouns may be joined with nouns, verbs with verbs, prepositional phrases with prepositional phrases, relative clauses with relative clauses. When the compounded elements are unequal in rank, an ungrammatical sentence that may seem awkward, and foolish besides, may result:

*He is highly competent and a graduate student.

These patterns underlie the sentence:

He is highly competent.
He is a graduate student.

---

[1] For punctuation of sentences joined by conjunction, see pp. 241–242.
[2] For (T_{sub}) see Chapter 6.

But (T_{conj}) cannot apply to an adjective phrase ("highly competent") and a compound noun ("graduate student"), though of course we can say:

He is a highly competent graduate student.

The following also violates the rules of conjunction:

*The final disaster occurs when Othello discovers Desdemona's purity and that he has been duped.

The compounded elements "of Desdemona's purity" and "that he has been duped" are not of equal rank, as their derivations show:

Desdemona has purity. → Desdemona's purity
Othello learns X.[3]
Othello learns of Desdemona's purity.

Someone has duped him. → He has been duped (by someone).
Othello learns X.
Othello learns that he has been duped.

*Othello learns of Desdemona's purity and that he has been duped.

A prepositional phrase and a subordinate clause cannot be properly joined. Revision is possible as follows:

Othello learns of Desdemona's purity.⎫
Othello learns of Iago's deception.   ⎬ →
Othello learns of Desdemona's purity and Iago's deception.

The final disaster occurs when Othello learns of Desdemona's purity and Iago's deception.

The elements on either side of the conjunction are prepositional phrases, with the second preposition omitted.

If properly compounded elements are of equal grammatical rank, they need not be internally equivalent. For example:

In a sense we know about juvenile delinquency only from its failures, the lads who are most disturbed and have the least general ability—except that one important ability of getting caught.
—PAUL GOODMAN, *Growing Up Absurd*

In recent years, academicians from the fields of sociology, cultural anthropology, social psychology, and even psychoanalysis have descended on

---

[3] X symbolizes (*or* represents) the slot filled by the insert sentence or phrase.

advertising with their assorted insights, bodies of theory, and nostrums, and have secured a truly remarkable amount of publicity for their efforts.—MARTIN MAYER, *Harper's Magazine*

In the first quotation, the compound relative clause has the underlying patterns **N be Aj** and **N V$_t$ N**; in the second quotation, the compound predicate consists of an expanded **V$_i$ (P-phr)** and **V$_t$ N**. Similarly, sentences to which (**T$_{conj}$**) has been applied need not have the same basic pattern:

> Scientific research has become the right arm of modern technology, and to some people modern technology is plainly evil.
> —DAVID E. LILIENTHAL, *This I Do Believe*
> [The patterns are **N V$_t$ N** and **N be Aj**.]

> Most of the students—there may have been twelve or fifteen, men and women—were well past thirty, and probably all of them taught French literature somewhere or other.—VINCENT SHEEAN, *Personal History*
> [The patterns are **N be P-phr** and **N V$_t$ N**.]

But (**T$_{conj}$**) is sometimes ineffectively applied by the beginner:

> Mrs. Bird was the lucky contest winner.⎫
> She received a phonograph.   ⎬ →
>   ⎭
> Mrs. Bird was the lucky contest winner and she received a phonograph.

Better stylistic alternatives are available:

> Mrs. Bird, who was the lucky contest winner, received a phonograph.
> [(**T$_{rel}$**) has been applied.]

> Mrs. Bird, the lucky contest winner, received a phonograph.
> [(**T$_{nom}$**) has been applied.][4]

> Mrs. Bird was the lucky contest winner. She received a phonograph.
> [Two short consecutive sentences perhaps imply that Mrs. Bird really expected to win a Mustang or a trip to Europe.]

When three or more members of a construction of grammatically equal rank are joined, the conjunction between each save the last two members may be omitted and replaced by a comma. Such a construction is called a **series**:[5]

---

[4] The transformation generating an appositive will be taken up in the next chapter.
[5] For punctuation of a series, see p. 242.

Man has always sacrificed truth to his vanity, comfort and advantage.
—SOMERSET MAUGHAM, *The Summing Up*

Contrast: For the complete life, the perfect pattern, includes old age as well as youth and maturity.—SOMERSET MAUGHAM, *ibid.*

Sometimes the conjunction between the last two members is also omitted:

Civilization, a much abused word, stands for a high matter quite apart from telephones and electric lights. It is a matter of imponderables, of delight in the things of the mind, of love and beauty, of honor, grace, courtesy, delicate feeling.—EDITH HAMILTON, *The Greek Way*

Members of a series may be single words or phrases, as in the preceding examples, or other constructions. In the following, the series consists of three subordinate clauses:

There is no point in trying to make the United States out to be a country without faults, where everything is fine between labor and management, where there are no civil rights difficulties, and where we have no unemployment problems.—ROBERT KENNEDY, *Saturday Review*

Independent clauses combine in a series in the next example:

[Mark Twain] grew up in the agrarian society of Missouri while it was still frontier country; he spent several years in the Far West during the pioneering period; and he settled finally in the industrial East, where he lived in close association with a number of big business magnates.—HENRY B. PARKES, *The American People: Their Civilization and Character*

The most effective series usually consists of three or four members, but stylistic or contextual demands invite departures from the norm:

We must come to the realization that *new* knowledge, some criticism and some dissent and some new ideas, will be required to level out cycles of our economy, to merge our markets with the world's, to get "farm surpluses" into empty stomachs, to replace men with machines and swords with plowshares without causing unemployment, and to create a more meaningful place in society for those whose life's work is done.
—ADLAI E. STEVENSON, *What I Think*

The poet . . . is not a mixture of a prophet, a seer, a priest and a medicine man. He may be any manner of man: as moral as Tennyson, as pagan as Keats; as classic as Housman, as romantic as Swinburne; as optimistic as Browning, as pessimistic as Hardy; as mystic as Blake, as practical as Pope; as subtle as de la Mare, as simple as Herrick.
—ELIZABETH DREW, *Discovering Poetry*

In the first quotation, the repetition of infinitive phrases underlines the need for action; in the second quotation, the repetition of polarities in a series of correlative constructions emphasizes that a poet may be any manner of man.

Certain elements are sometimes improperly interpreted as a series:

*Eloise is a wearisome, poor, acting play.

The writer could mean that *Eloise* is a poor-acting play or that it is a poor acting-play. Whatever his intent, *wearisome, poor,* and *acting* cannot be members of the same series, as their derivations show:

The play was wearisome. → the wearisome play
The play was poor.   → the poor play
The play acted poorly.   → the poor-acting play

One can write:

Eloise is a wearisome, poor acting-play.
Or: Eloise is a wearisome, poor-acting play.

Also:

a prosy, ornate, artificial play
a witty, contrived, entertaining play

The rule underlying compounding applies: only elements of grammatically equal rank can be members of a series. The same rule applies to larger constructions, though less stringently:

[The Japanese worker] is better educated and better trained than almost any other worker, and he works cheerfully, hard, and for long hours.
—PETER F. DRUCKER, *Harper's Magazine*

For my own satisfaction, for my amusement and to gratify what feels to me like an organic need, I have shaped my life in accordance with a certain design, with a beginning, a middle and an end, as from people I have met here and there I have constructed a play, a novel or a short story.—SOMERSET MAUGHAM, *The Summing Up*

Two adverbs and a prepositional phrase ("cheerfully, hard, and for long hours") perform as a series in the first sentence; two prepositional phrases and an infinitive phrase ("for my own satisfaction, for my amusement and to gratify what feels to me like an organic need") in the second. Some grammatical flexibility is therefore possible if it is stylistically motivated. When demands of grammatical form conflict with those of style, the writer has to decide which to satisfy.

CORRELATIVES

Certain conjunctions, called **correlatives**, operate in pairs:

both . . . and	not (only) . . . but (also)
either . . . or	not . . . as
neither . . . nor	whether . . . or

Like single conjunctions, correlatives join elements of grammatically equal rank:

> The revolutionary changes that have occurred since 1890 in the world of science—especially in physics but also in chemistry, biology, and the sciences of man—have been due *not* so much to new facts *as* to new ways of thinking about facts.—JOHN B. CARROLL, ed., *Language, Thought and Reality: Selected Writings of Benjamin Lee Whorf*

> The week is the week *not only* because it has seven days *but* because they are in a fixed order.—EDWARD T. HALL, *The Silent Language*

In the first sentence the correlatives join prepositional phrases; in the second, subordinate clauses.

SUMMARY

Elements of grammatically equal rank can be joined by conjunction ($\mathbf{T_{conj}}$):

serious *yet* witty
on the beach *and* along the coast
those who expect to attend the lecture *or* those who will remain at home
They left, *but* we continued to dance until dawn.

Three or more compounded elements constitute a series:

He is tall, gray-haired, and good-looking.

He denied having been in the vicinity of the theft; he denied possession of the stolen photographs; and he denied being a friend of Dona Diego, the movie starlet.

Conjunctions operating in pairs, called correlatives, are used to join constructions of grammatically equal rank:

both men *and* women
either those who expect to go *or* those who will stay at home

EXERCISES (T_{conj})

1.   Apply (T_{conj}) to whatever elements in the following sentences can be most appropriately combined. Make whatever minor adjustments in wording may be necessary.

EXAMPLE: He refused to claim victory.
             He did not intend to make a statement } →
                at this time.
             He refused to claim a victory, nor did he intend to make a statement at this time.

1.   Few statements about Asia-West relations can ever be wholly true. They cannot be wholly false either.

2.   Asians are held together by their common experience of Western dominance.
      They are united by their fierce desire to be completely free of it.

3.   Their awareness of the West may be outright hostility.
      It may be abject fondness.

4.   White executives command at least twice the salary given to a Filipino of equal ability.
      The same holds true for other white employees.

5.   A majority of Filipino movie stars are Caucasians.
      Many are Eurasians who have chosen Filipino screen names.

6.   In Manila foreigners are lionized.
      An American guest of honor is a status symbol.

7.   A white person is as outlandish in a remote Filipino village as a polar bear.
      He is as rare too.

8.   At the apogee of the Spanish regime, white foreigners never made up more than one percent of the entire population.
      The same holds true of the American occupation.

9.   The Japanese seem to know just what they want from the West.
      They also know what to discard.

10. Indonesians treat their Eurasians with lofty contempt.
      They view Americans with humorous condescension.

                           —Adapted from CARMEN GUERRERO NAPKIL,
                           "Do Asians Have an Inferiority Complex?"
                           The Asia Magazine (Manila), September 1,
                           1963, p. 3.

2. Apply (T_{conj}) to the following:

EXAMPLE: He refused to claim victory.
He refused to make a statement. $\Big\} \rightarrow$
He refused either to claim victory or to make a statement.

1. A college professor is expected to instruct.
   He is expected to publish scholarly books and articles.

2. Our government supports private education.
   It offers grants-in-aid to private institutions.
   It encourages higher salaries for teachers.

3. *Lifting Anchors* is a musical comedy that should have a long run.
   It is colorful and lively and brash.

4. Miss Sevilla is not primarily known as a writer.
   She is known as a hunter of big game.

5. She has gained eminence in hunting circles.
   She has earned distinction in public life.

6. She is her country's official hostess.
   She is shy.
   She is soft spoken.
   She is charming.

7. Hogan made four stopovers on his round-the-world flight:
   He spent two weeks sightseeing in Japan.
   He spent nine days shopping in Hongkong.
   Then he spent two weeks visiting relatives in Switzerland.
   He spent another two weeks resting up on the French Riviera.

8. Her performance was characterized by majestic grandeur.
   There was no absence of depth of interpretation either.

9. Many of the town's younger set were seen at the fashion preview.
   We spotted Peachy Perez, the Spanish Minister's niece, and Virgie Moreno, the South American beauty. Then there were Lucy Brown, the Senator's daughter, and Grace Shore, the well-known skater.

10. The worth of a sport is not victory. It is sportsmanship.

8) *Nominalization*

V- ing PHRASES

Nominalization Transformation (T_{nom})

The transformation of a sentence into a noun phrase is known as **nominalization.** (T_{nom}), where **nom** stands for nominalization, can be applied to a sentence in a variety of ways. For example:

N	V	(Comp)	N's	V -ing	(Comp)
They	sing.		→ their	singing	
John	left	the city.	→ John's	leaving	the city

The subject is changed into the possessive (note that **N's** has the same function as **D**) and *-ing* added to the simple form of the verb (*sing, leave*). The sentence may or may not have a complement (**Comp**), that is, an object, predicate noun, or adjective. Here are other examples:

They opposed the tax bill.   → their opposing the tax bill
You elected him spokesman. → your electing him spokesman
I offered Jane a lawyer.   → my offering Jane a lawyer
She became an instructor.   → her becoming an instructor
We look foolish.   → our looking foolish
Albert is a scholar.   → Albert's being a scholar

The generated phrase may fill a noun position in a matrix sentence:

We like it. → We like their singing.

I regretted it.	→ I regretted John's leaving the city.
He cannot understand it.	→ He cannot understand their opposing the tax bill.
It was a great mistake.	→ Her becoming an instructor was a great mistake.
This makes us happy.	→ Our looking foolish makes us happy.
It is hardly a surprise to anyone.	→ Albert's being a scholar is hardly a surprise to anyone.

In the first three sentences, the nominalized phrases fill object positions; and in the last three, subject positions.

Tense endings and auxiliaries except forms of *have* and *be* are dropped from the verb phrase:

They sing.
They sang.   } their singing
They can sing.

They have sung.
They had sung. } their having sung

V- ing phrases with *be,* deriving from the passive, are taken up later in this chapter.

The next transformation generates this noun phrase:

N	**V**	**(Comp)**	→	**N**	**V -ing**	**(Comp)**
They	sing.		→	them	singing	
He	planned	a trip.	→	him	planning	a trip
Elsie	took	her test.	→	Elsie	taking	her test

The common form of the noun or the objective form of the pronoun is employed in the generated phrases, in contrast to the possessive form of the noun and pronoun in the earlier examples. Thus:

They sing. → { their singing
            them singing

Elsie took her test. → { Elsie's taking her test
                        Elsie taking her test

The generated phrases may be inserted in a matrix sentence:

We heard their singing.
We heard them singing.

We approved of Elsie's taking the test.
We approved of Elsie taking the test.

In constructions such as the following, the possessive form of personal pronouns is preferred. The N form is increasingly used with nouns, but both N's and N are used with proper nouns:

> The dean wondered about the students returning to their dormitories.
> We had no knowledge of Mr. Flaherty's promising Mirabelle a part.
> We had no knowledge of the director promising Mirabelle a part.
> We had no knowledge of his promising Mirabelle a part.

With certain nouns, as well as pronouns, the N's form is avoided altogether:

> He spoke of all people getting a square deal.
> They objected to anyone entering the building.

Other transformations generating noun phrases include these:

N	V	→ V -ing	N
Bells	ring.	→ ringing	bells
The congressmen	flew.	→ flying	congressmen
Negotiations	collapsed.	→ collapsing	negotiations

Here the N, rather than the V -ing, is the phrase head, and the V -ing simply a modifier. In the next set, on the other hand, the V -ing is the phrase head, and the prepositional phrase a modifier:

N	V	→ V -ing	of N
Bells	ring.	→ ringing	of bells
The congressmen	shouted.	→ shouting	of congressmen
Negotiations	collapsed.	→ collapsing	of negotiations

Ambiguities occur when nominalized constructions deriving from different patterns overlap. For example:

> The killing of criminals must be stopped.

The sentence can mean either (1) that murders committed by criminals must be stopped, or (2) that violence resulting in the death of criminals must be brought under control. The phrase "killing of criminals" can derive from

N	V_i	→ V -ing of N
Criminals	kill.	→ killing of criminals

N	V_t	N	→ V -ing of N
Or: Someone	kills	criminals.	→ killing of criminals

In the first sentence, *kill* is an intransitive verb; in the second, a transitive verb.

Here is another example:

Our entertaining guests will make the party a success.

The subject of the sentence can derive from either

N   V$_t$ N   → N's V -ing   N
We entertain guests. → our entertaining guests

or

(D) N   V$_i$ → (D) V -ing   N
Our guests entertain. → our entertaining guests

Additional grammatical markers resolve the ambiguity:

Our entertaining *the* guests *is* bound to make the party a success.
Our entertaining guests *are* bound to make the party a success.

In the first sentence it is *we* who entertain; in the second sentence the *guests* entertain.

to V PHRASES

In the next set of nominalizations, the noun phrases contain instances of **to V** (infinitive) rather than **V -ing** (participle or gerund):

N	V	(Comp)	for N	to V	(Comp)
They	sing.		→ for them	to sing	
Their prices	declined.		→ for their prices	to decline	
Hope	remains.		→ for hope	to remain	
The legislature	debated	the bill.	→ for the legislature	to debate	the bill

As in earlier transformations, auxiliaries except forms of *have* and *be* are dropped:

They shout.
They shouted.   → for them to shout
They will shout.

They are shouting.
They might be shouting. → for them to be shouting

They have shouted.   → for them to have shouted

They have been shouting. → for them to have been shouting

Also:

The students have elected
   Johnson their spokesman. → for the students to have elected
                        Johnson their spokesman

All judges had declared
   him winner. → for all judges to have declared
                        him winner

Our neighbors are raising
   chickens. → for our neighbors to be raising
                        chickens

The director had been
   promising her a part. → for the director to have been
                        promising her a part

A (T_{nom}), closely related to the last one, omits *for* in the generated construction:

N	V	(Comp)	
They	sing.		→
The legislature	debated	the bill.	→
The students	have elected	Johnson the spokesman.	→

N	to V	(Comp)
them	to sing	
the legislature	to debate	the bill
the students	to have elected	Johnson their spokesman

An important difference between noun phrases with *for* and without *for* is that only those introduced by *for* can fill the subject position:

For them to sing is hardly a pleasure.
We like them to sing.

Passive constructions may be nominalized, as the following examples show:

She was ignored. → her being ignored
               → for her to be ignored

She has been ignored. → her having been ignored
               → for her to have been ignored

Jackson will be granted a promotion.	→ Jackson's being granted a promotion
	→ Jackson being granted a promotion
	→ for Jackson to be granted a promotion
	→ Jackson to be granted a promotion
The papers were processed by the board.	→ the papers being processed by the board
	→ for the papers to be processed .by the board
	→ the papers to be processed by the board

OTHER NOMINALIZED CONSTRUCTIONS

Not all nominalized phrases require **V -ing** or **to V**. Indeed, certain transformations taken up in earlier chapters are actually instances of nominalization, though they have not been specifically identified as such. Included are compound nouns and noun phrases (see Chapters 4 and 5) and relative and subordinate clauses performing the functions of nouns (see Chapter 6). Other nominalizing transformations will be taken up in the remainder of this chapter.

Certain sentences of the type **N have N** can be nominalized as follows:

N_1	have	N_2		$N's_1$	N_2
Jim	has	relatives.	→	Jim's	relatives
Marguerite	has four	dachshunds.	→	Marguerite's four	dachshunds
The soldier	has	courage.	→	the soldier's	courage
Our country	has	laws.	→	our country's	laws

The generated noun phrases can be placed in matrix sentences like the following:

They are constantly bothering him.	→ Jim's relatives are constantly bothering him.
They will be entered in the international dog show at St. Tropez.	→ Marguerite's four dachshunds will be entered in the international dog show at St. Tropez.

Related constructions, like N_2 **of** N_1 and N_1 $\begin{Bmatrix} \textbf{of} \\ \textbf{with} \end{Bmatrix}$ N_2, have already been taken up in Chapter 5.

(T_{nom}) can be applied to a sentence by dropping the inflection of its verb and making the generated phrase the direct object of a verb like *let, make, see,* or *hear* in the matrix sentence:

The musicians practiced. → She heard the musicians practice.

He presented her a corsage. → I saw him present her a corsage.

The story sounds scandalous. → The girls made the story sound scandalous.

A similar operation obtains in the following:

He attends the university. → His family insists (that) he attend the university.

The school maintains high standards. → We demand (that) the school maintain high standards.

Phrases generated by (T_{nom}) should be distinguished from subordinate clauses which they resemble:

Gwendolyn heard the musicians rehearse.
Gwendolyn heard that the musicians rehearsed.

The first sentence says that Gwendolyn listened to the musicians who were rehearsing; the second sentence says that she received a report about the musicians' rehearsal. Here is another example:

Miss Stalker insists that the students be present at the ceremony.
Miss Stalker insists that the students were present at the ceremony.

In the first sentence Miss Stalker clearly requires the students to attend the ceremony. In the second sentence, she affirms, presumably against certain opposition, that the students had indeed been present. A sentence may assert, as well as imply.

In addition to occupying noun positions, as in the above examples, nominalized phrases can perform as sentence adjuncts:

Our boys sang vigorously.⎫
They won the competition.⎭ → Singing vigorously, our boys won the competition.

Or: Our boys, singing vigorously, won the competition.

The astronaut was thrilled
by a fine blast-off.   →   Thrilled by a fine blast-off, the
He was in high spirits.   astronaut was in high spirits.

Or: The astronaut, thrilled by a fine
blast-off, was in high spirits.

MISPLACED MODIFIERS

An important restriction applies to nominalized phrases that function as sentence adjuncts. Both the insert and matrix sentence must share a common subject. Otherwise the derived sentence will not be sensible. For example:

He ate lunch in Paradise.
The car broke down in   →   Eating lunch in Paradise, the
Bad Axe.   car broke down in Bad Axe.

The derived sentence contains what is commonly called a **dangling,** or **misplaced, modifier,** a construction often more amusing than obscure, but in any case ungrammatical.[1]

Nominalized phrases performing as sentence adjuncts contrast with nominalized phrases in noun positions, as the following sets show:

Singing vigorously, our boys won the competition.
Singing vigorously won our boys the competition.

Seeing the Queen eating a hot dog, he changed his views of royalty.
Seeing the Queen eating a hot dog changed his views of royalty.

Not having passed a single bill, the legislators lost their appeal to the voters.
Not having passed a single bill lost the legislators their appeal to the voters.

The first sentence of each pair contains a sentence adjunct; the second sentence, a nominalized phrase functioning as subject.

APPOSITION

(T_{nom}) applied to N R be N generates an **appositive,** a phrase with adjacent nouns sharing the same referent:[2]

[1] See also pp. 294–296.

[2] These constructions are derived from N be N. Thus, "Miss Willard is a professor"; "Cali is Colombia's third largest city."

N	R	be	N
Miss Willard	who	is	a professor →
Cali	which	is	Colombia's third largest city →
The editor of the school paper	who	was	a sociology major →

N	N
Miss Willard,	a professor
Cali,	Colombia's third largest city
the editor of the school paper,	a sociology major

The appositive may be inserted in a matrix sentence:

Miss Willard, a professor
X has been at Meadowbrook
University for ten years. → Miss Willard, a professor, has been at Meadowbrook University for ten years.

Or: A professor, Miss Willard has been at Meadowbrook University for ten years.

Cali, Colombia's third largest city
An American advisory group on city planning visited X. → An American advisory group on city planning visited Cali, Colombia's third largest city.

the editor of the school paper, a sociology major
X wrote a controversial article on falling in love in college. → The editor of the school paper, a sociology major, wrote a controversial article on falling in love in college.

Or: A sociology major, the editor wrote a controversial article on falling in love in college.

Certain restrictions apply to appositives, as the following contrasts show:

N,	N	N	N
Edgar Marlow,	the doctor	Doctor	Edgar Marlow
Bill Swift,	tennis champion	tennis champion	Bill Swift

The constructions in the right-hand column below are evidently
derived from

N_1	be	N_2		N_2	N_1
Willard	is	a professor	→	Professor	Willard
Bill Swift	is	a tennis champion	→	tennis champion	Bill Swift
Cloud	is	senator	→	Senator	Cloud

No punctuation separates the adjacent nouns in **N N**, called a **restrictive appositive,** but a comma sets off **N, N,** a **nonrestrictive
appositive.**[3] The use of a restrictive or nonrestrictive appositive
usually depends on context. For example:

> our tennis champion Bill Swift [Presumably there are other tennis
> champions.]
> our tennis champion, Bill Swift [Presumably there is only one cham-
> pion.]
> *Or:* Bill Swift, our tennis champion

Similarly:

> the *United States*, the fastest liner
> the fastest liner, the *United States*
> *But:* the liner *United States*

Nominalized constructions have many uses. In the following
sentence, for example, five **V -ing** phrases function as subject:

> Having a battalion of American civil servants building native housing
> with their own hands, creating irrigation in deserts, rigging electrical
> equipment, driving cars, or as menials, bargaining for fish in the
> market place, would have a great psychological impact.
> —WILLIAM J. LEDERER, *A Nation of Sheep*

In the next example, the infinitive phrase "to study the problem of
wasted manpower of youth" complements the object, "the University
of Colorado":

> Congress has authorized the University of Colorado to study the problem
> of wasted manpower of youth, and a report will be ready soon.
> —WILLIAM J. LEDERER, *ibid.*

[3] For a discussion of restrictive and nonrestrictive modifiers, see pp. 70–71. For
their punctuation, see pp. 244–246.

Several nominalized constructions appear in this passage:

> Private colleges particularly are likely to find the years immediately
> ahead traumatic. Recognizing the nature and dimensions of the
> approaching storm, Sidney G. Tickton, program associate of the Fund
> for the Advancement of Education, has been calling on the colleges to
> "plan ahead" for financial stability and educational effectiveness.
> —JAMES CASS, *Saturday Review*

In the second sentence, the phrase "Recognizing the nature and
dimensions of the approaching storm" performs as a sentence adjunct;
the nonrestrictive appositive "program associate of the Fund for the
Advancement of Education" expands the subject of the sentence,
"Sidney G. Tickton"; the infinitive phrase "to 'plan ahead' for
financial stability and educational effectiveness" complements the
object, "colleges."[4]

SUMMARY

Nominalization (T_{nom}) converts a sentence into a noun phrase:

N V	N's V -ing
The dog barks. →	the dog's barking
He barks.	

	N V -ing
	the dog barking
	him barking

for	N V
for the dog	to bark
for	him to bark

	N to V
	the dog to bark
	him to bark

	V -ing N
	barking dog

	V -ing of N
	barking of the dog

---

[4] The phrase "are likely to find" is not an instance of nominalization. The verb
phrase is ultimately derived from "will find," but the rules for generating this
construction are not taken up in this book.

Ambiguity occurs when constructions like **V -ing** N or **V -ing of** N derive from more than one source.

N	V	**V -ing of N**	
Policemen fired.		→ firing of policemen	
N$_1$	V	N$_2$	**V -ing of N$_2$**	**(by N$_1$)**
They fired policemen.		→ firing of policemen (by them)	

Forms of *have* and *be* remain part of the nominalized construction, but tense endings are dropped.

They study.	→ their studying
They are (were) studied.	→ their being studied
They have (had) studied.	→ their having studied
They have (had) been studied.	→ their having been studied
They study.	→ for them to study
They are (were) studying.	→ for them to be studying
They have (had) studied.	→ for them to have studied
They have (had) been studying.	→ for them to have been studying

A nominalized phrase can be derived from various sentence types:

We admire Mary.	→ for us to admire Mary
Mary is admired.	→ Mary's being admired
Mary has charm.	→ Mary's charm
Mary is the winner.	→ Mary, the winner

The generated phrase can perform different functions in a sentence:

Subject
He speaks softly. → *Speaking softly* is his habit.
To speak softly is his habit.

Object
He learned   *to speak softly.*
She taught   *him to speak softly.*
She thanked *him for speaking softly.*

Sentence adjunct
Speaking softly, he carried a big stick.

A nominalized phrase can perform as object of a matrix sentence containing a verb like *hear, make, let, insist, demand*:

The principal explained it. → I heard the principal explain it.

They are staying for
three weeks.   → She insisted (that) they stay for
three weeks.

EXERCISES

1. Apply (T_{nom}) to each of the following sentences, making whatever changes in verb form accompany the transformation. ( ) means that the formula is optional, applying to only some members of a class. { } means that one of the enclosed formulas must be selected.

EXAMPLE A:

N V

Melvin wrote. → **N's V -ing** Melvin's writing

      → **N V -ing** Melvin writing

      → **V -ing** $\begin{Bmatrix} of \\ by \end{Bmatrix}$ **N** writing of Melvin

      → **for N to V** for Melvin to write

      → **N to V** Melvin to write

1. A student reported.
2. The show began.
3. Critics cheered.
4. He gave.
5. The infant might improve.

EXAMPLE B:

 N_1 V_t N_2

The agency enforces the law.

→ **N's V -ing (of) N** the agency's enforcing (of) the law

→ **N V -ing N**   the agency enforcing the law

→ **V -ing of N by N** enforcing of the law by the agency

→ **for N to V N** for the agency to enforce the law

→ **N to V N**   the agency to enforce the law

→ **(N's N** $\begin{Bmatrix} in \\ to \\ of \end{Bmatrix}$ **N)**[5] the agency's enforcement of the law

→ $\begin{pmatrix} N_2 \text{ V -en } N_1 \\ N_2 \text{ N } N_1 \\ N_2 \text{ V -ing } N_1 \end{pmatrix}$[6] law-enforcement agency

         law-enforcing agency

[5] See p. 58.
[6] See p. 42.

1. The Congressmen slashed the budget.
2. The campaign prevented accidents.
3. He avoided the controversy.
4. The basketball team wound up a victorious season.
5. I admired his courage.

EXAMPLE C:

N_1 have N_2

The country has resources.

→ N_1 **have -ing** N_2 the country having resources

→ **for** N_1 **to have** N_2 for the country to have resources

→ N_1 **to have** N_2 the country to have resources

→ **N's$_1$** N_2 the country's resources

→ N_2 **of** N_1 the resources of the country

→ N_1 $\left\{ \begin{matrix} \text{of} \\ \text{with} \end{matrix} \right\}$ N_2 the country with resources

1. The company has a good safety record.
2. Professor Singalong has a Siamese cat.
3. The assistant manager has two children.
4. A teenager has a stock of slang.
5. The novel has suspense.

EXAMPLE D:

N V_1 N

He became a success. → **N's V -ing N**   his becoming a success

→ **N V -ing N**   him becoming a success

→ **for N to V N**   for him to become a success

→ **N to V N**   him to become a success

1. I became an apprentice.
2. Marion seemed a bungler.
3. Mitchell appeared their favorite.
4. She remains my favorite.
5. You stayed a friend.

EXAMPLE E:

N_1 be N_2

Our actors are students. → **N be -ing N**   our actors being students

→ **for N to be N** for our actors to be students

→ **N to be N**   our actors to be students

→ **(N_2 N_1)**   student actors

1. Their prince is a playboy.
2. Our students are teen-agers.
3. Television is entertainment.
4. Three cabinet members are women.
5. He was a scholar.

EXAMPLE F:
N V$_t$ N   N
We offered them encouragement.

→ **N's V -ing N N**   our offering them encouragement
→ **N V -ing N N**   us offering them encouragement
→ **for N to V N N**   for us to offer them encouragement
→ **N to V N N**   us to offer them encouragement

1. He gave Ruby a corsage.
2. I secured him a lawyer.
3. The management granted Jackson a raise.
4. The court guaranteed him protection.
5. They offered the Bullpups a plaque.

EXAMPLE G:
     N   V$_{te}$ N   N
The board elected Williams chairman.

→ **N V -ing N N**   the board electing Williams chairman
→ **for N to V N N** for the board to elect Williams chairman
→ **N to V N N**   the board to elect Williams chairman

1. The court confirmed Porter governor.
2. The referee declared the Bullpups winners.
3. The class had made *Othello* its choice.
4. We must regard Fred a scholar.
5. He considers them patriots.

2. Select two nominalized constructions from each set in Exercise 1 and place them in a noun position of an original matrix sentence.

EXAMPLE:
The agency enforces the law. → the agency's enforcement of the law
Each speaker commended X.
Each speaker commended the agency's enforcement of the law.

The agency enforces the law. → for the agency to enforce the law
The chief said that it is too great a responsibility.
The chief said that for the agency to enforce the law is too great a responsibility.

3. Apply (T_{nom}) to each of the following sentences in at least two ways.

   EXAMPLE: The budget was slashed. → the budget being slashed
                                                        for the budget to be slashed

   1. The critics were booed.
   2. Ruby was given a corsage by her fiancé.
   3. The Bullpups had been honored.
   4. Porter will be confirmed.
   5. His stand is universally respected.

4. Select five nominalized phrases from Exercise 3 and insert each in a noun position of an original matrix sentence.

   EXAMPLE: The budget was slashed. → the budget to be slashed
                    Most Americans want X.
                    Most Americans want the budget to be slashed.

5. Generate appositive constructions from the following:

   EXAMPLE:
   Bertha Bray, who was Mumford High's
       most popular history teacher   → Bertha Bray, Mumford
                                            High's most popular
                                             history teacher

   1. The nominees, who were exclusively foreign students
   2. The Italian exchange student, who is Carmen Padua from Venice
   3. N. V. M. Richter is the presiding judge.
   4. The recent first prize winner in graphic art, who was A. Landmark
   5. Blake is Michigan's representative.

6. Insert each of the appositives generated in Exercise 5 in a matrix sentence of your choice. Then indicate whether the appositive construction is restrictive, nonrestrictive, or whether it could be either.

   EXAMPLE:
   Bertha Bray, Mumford High's most popular history teacher
   X was given a gold medal upon her retirement.
   Bertha Bray, Mumford High's most popular history teacher, was given a gold medal upon her retirement. [Nonrestrictive]

7. Apply (T_{nom}) to a sentence in each of the following pairs. Then use the nominalized construction as the object of the matrix sentence.

   EXAMPLE: He requested it.
                   The students must be on time.
                   He requested that the students be on time.

1. A complete panel of examiners should be present at the interviews.
   The board demands it.

2. The fire razed five commercial blocks and destroyed the city's
   business section.
   Only one witness saw it.

3. The rumor backfired.
   He had let it.

4. Our moral standards should be defended.
   He advocates it.

5. She accepted the compliment.
   I heard her.

9) Negation, Questions, and Affirmation

The formation of negative, interrogative, and affirmative sentences presents few, if any, problems for the writer, and their treatment in a book on expository writing may be open to debate. But the generation of these sentence types shows the underlying regularity of the language, so that their inclusion is justifiable.

NEGATION

Negative Transformation (T_{not})

The negative transformation (T_{not}) can be illustrated by the sentence pattern **N V** containing a modal:

(D) N   T   M   V
his roommate **present can study**
                      will
                      may

(T_{not}) introduces the function word *not*, a function group by itself, after the second member in the auxiliary string:

(D) N   T   M   not   V
his roommate **present may not**   **study**
his roommate **present can not** (cannot) **study**

Since tense forms are added to the end of a verb or auxiliary, we

106

apply (T_{af}), introduced in Chapter 2, to invert the **T** and the **M**. (T_{af}), we may recall, switches any **Af** (a **T**, **-en**, or **-ing**) with a **v** (**M**, **have**, **be**, or **V**):

$$Af + v \rightarrow v + Af$$

Thus:

> his roommate **present can not study** $\rightarrow$
>   **Af** + **v** $\rightarrow$
> his roommate **can present not study** $\rightarrow$
>   **v** + **Af** $\rightarrow$
> His roommate **can not** (cannot) **study.**

Similarly:

> his roommate **present will study** $\rightarrow$ His roommate will not study.
> his roommate **present must study** $\rightarrow$ His roommate must not study.

Also:

> His roommate **past may study.** $\rightarrow$ His roommate **might not study.**
>   **will** $\rightarrow$ **would not**
>   **can** $\rightarrow$ **could not**

No matter how many auxiliaries occur in the verb phrase, the rule remains the same: **not** is introduced after the second member in the auxiliary string, whether that auxiliary is a modal, a form of *have* or *be:*

>   (D) N   T   have -en   be -ing   V
>   his roommate **present have -en   be -ing study** $\rightarrow$
> (T_{not}) his roommate **present have not -en be -ing study** $\rightarrow$
> (T_{af}) his roommate **have present not be -en study -ing** $\rightarrow$
>   His roommate has not been studying.
>
>   (D) N   T   M   have -en   be -ing   V
>   his roommate **past can   have -en   be -ing study** $\rightarrow$
> (T_{not}) his roommate **past can not have -en be -ing study** $\rightarrow$
> (T_{af}) his roommate **can past not have be -en study -ing** $\rightarrow$
>   His roommate could not have been studying.

Do *Transformation* (T_{do})

If the sentence to which (T_{not}) is applied contains no auxiliaries, a different procedure obtains:

>   (D) N   T   V   (D) N   T   not V
>   his roommate **present study** $\rightarrow$ his roommate **present not study**

Since the tense in this string cannot be assumed by the function word *not*, we therefore add the transformational rule (T_{do}):

$$Af \rightarrow do + Af$$

The rule inserts *do* as the carrier of the tense. Thus:

	his roommate **present not study** →
(T_{do})	his roommate **do present not study** →
	His roommate does not study.

Here are other examples of (T_{not}) that require the *do* transformation:

	N_p	T	V_t	(D) N
	he	**past become**	an apprentice →
(T_{not})	he	**past not become**	an apprentice →
(T_{do})	he	**do past not become**	an apprentice →
	He did not become an apprentice.

	(D) N	T	V_t	N_p
	his constituents **past**	**ignore** him →
(T_{not})	his constituents **past not**	**ignore** him →
(T_{do})	his constituents **do past not ignore** him →
	His constituents did not ignore him.

In sentences containing forms of *be*, (T_{not}) is applied as though *be* were an auxiliary:

	N_p	T	be	(D) N
	he	**present be**	a	scholar →
(T_{not})	he	**present be not** a	scholar →
(T_{af})	he	**be present not** a	scholar →
	He is not a scholar.

	(D) N	T	be	Aj
	the party **past be**	boisterous →
(T_{not})	the party **past be not** boisterous →
(T_{af})	the party **be past not** boisterous →
	The party was not boisterous.

Patterns with *have* offer an interesting contrast, because (T_{not}) can apply in two ways:

	N_p	T	V_t(have)	(D) N
	we	**present**	**have**	an opportunity →
(T_{not})	we	**present not**	**have**	an opportunity →
(T_{do})	we	**do present not have**	an opportunity →
	We do not have an opportunity.

	N$_p$	T	V$_t$(have)	(D) N	
	we	present	have	an	opportunity →
(T$_{not}$)	we	present	have not	an	opportunity →
(T$_{af}$)	we	have	present not	an	opportunity →
	We haven't an opportunity.				

Here are other examples:

These men have courage.   → These men do not (don't) have courage.

These men have not (haven't) any courage.

Our state has a balanced budget. → Our state does not (doesn't) have a balanced budget.

Our state has not (hasn't) a balanced budget.

Negation may of course be expressed in other ways besides (T$_{not}$). "These men have courage," for example, can be negated by a determiner: "These men have no courage." Or another verb can be chosen: "These men lack courage." Similarly:

We have some decisions to make.
We have no decisions to make.
We are spared from making decisions.

QUESTIONS

Yes-or-No Question Transformation (T$_q$)

The rules that develop negation also apply in part to the formation of certain types of questions. Simple questions, symbolized by (T$_q$), only require the reversal of the subject and two members of the auxiliary string:

	(D) N	T	M	V
	his roommate	present	can	study →
(T$_q$)		present	can his roommate	study →
(T$_{af}$)		can present	his roommate	study →
	Can his roommate study?			

(T$_q$), like (T$_{not}$), applies after the second member of the auxiliary string, no matter how many auxiliaries there may be:

(D) N   T   have -en   be -ing V
his roommate **past have -en   be -ing study** →
(T$_q$)   **past have** his roommate **-en be -ing study**   →
(T$_{af}$)   **have past** his roommate **be -en study -ing**   →
Had his roommate been studying?

(D) N   T   M   have -en   be -ing V
his roommate **past can   have -en   be -ing study** →
(T$_q$)   **past can** his roommate **have -en be -ing study**   →
(T$_{af}$)   **can past** his roommate **have be -en study -ing**   →
Could his roommate have been studying?

If the sentence has no auxiliaries, **do** performs as the tense bearer:

(D) N   T   V
his roommate **present**   **study** →
(T$_q$)   **present**   his roommate **study** →
(T$_{do}$)   **do present** his roommate **study** →
Does his roommate study?

Similarly:

His roommate studied.   → Did his roommate study?
They accepted the trophy. → Did they accept the trophy?
He became an apprentice. → Did he become an apprentice?

Sentences containing a form of **be** follow the same rule as for (T$_{not}$):

N$_p$ T   be   (D) N
he **present**   **be**   a   scholar →
(T$_q$)   **present**   **be** he a   scholar →
(T$_{af}$)   **be present**   he a   scholar →
Is he a scholar?

Sentences with **have** form two distinct question patterns, with the second pattern common in British usage:

N$_p$ T   V$_t$(**have**) N
they **present**   **have**   courage →
(T$_q$)   **present**   they **have**   courage →
(T$_{do}$)   **do present** they **have**   courage →
Do they have courage?

N$_p$ T   V$_t$(**have**)   N
they **present**   **have**   courage →
(T$_q$)   **present**   **have**   they courage →
(T$_{af}$)   **have present**   they courage →
Have they courage?

(T_{not}) and (T_q) may of course be combined, as in the following:

	(D) N	T	M	V
	his roommate	**present**	**can**	**study** →
(T_q)		**present**	**can** his roommate	**study** →
(T_{not})		**present**	**can not** his roommate	**study** →
(T_{af})			**can present not** his roommate	**study** →

Can not (cannot, can't) his roommate study?

Interrogative Transformation (T_w)

Questions formed by (T_q) can be further developed by a transformation (T_w), where **w** stands for function words like *who, what, where, which,* called **interrogatives**. (T_w) follows (T_q) in two steps, (T_{w_1}) and (T_{w_2}). First, (T_q) is applied:

	(D) N	T	V	N
	his roommate	**past study**	chemistry →	
(T_q)	**past** his roommate	**study** chemistry →		

Since an interrogative appears at the beginning of a sentence, the word or word phrase which it replaces must first be positioned initially by (T_{w_1}). Thus, if *chemistry* is to be replaced by an interrogative, then it must first be transposed:

	past his roommate **study** chemistry →
(T_{w_1})	*chemistry* **past** his roommate **study**

The interrogative may now be introduced by (T_{w_2}):

(T_{w_2}) **what past** his roommate **study**

The carrier of the tense is added next:

(T_{do}) **what do past** his roommate **study** →
What did his roommate study?

If an interrogative replaces the subject, the subject and tense are switched first:

	T	(D) N	V_t	N
	past	his roommate	**study**	chemistry →
(T_{w_1})		his roommate	**past study**	chemistry →
(T_{w_2}) **who**	**past**		**study**	chemistry →
(T_{af}) **who**			**study past**	chemistry →

Who studied chemistry?

The reversal of the subject and tense restores the original string, so that the interrogative can be positioned initially.

Here are some other examples of (T_w):

	N_p	T	V_t N	
	he	past	see John	→
(T_q)	past	he	see John	→
(T_{w_1})	John	past he see		→
(T_{w_2})	whom	past he see		→
(T_{do})	whom	do past he see		→
	Whom did he see?[1]			

And:

	N_p	T	V_t (D) N	
	he	past	select the novel	→
(T_q)	past	he	select the novel	→
(T_{w_1})	the novel past he select			→
(T_{w_2})	which past he select			→
(T_{do})	which do past he select			→
	Which did he select?			

A related sentence type, with the function word simply added, is shown by the following:

He flew to Manila.   → When did he fly to Manila?
He took the course. → When did he take the course?
He left.   → When did he leave?

Tag-end Questions

A question type, sometimes called a **tag-end question,** is illustrated by the following:

He has been studying every evening, hasn't he?
He is not taking the course, is he?
He did not fly to Manila, did he?

If the first part has no auxiliary, a form of *do* is used as tense bearer in the second:

The company awarded Smith the honor, didn't it?
He flew to Manila, didn't he?

[1] In ordinary speech *whom* is often replaced by *who* in the subject position. In formal writing *whom* is preferred.

Indirect Questions

Still another question-type, called an **indirect question**, is similar to the formation of indirect statements, except that the matrix sentence has a verb like *ask, inquire,* or *wonder*. For example:

He had been studying every evening.
We asked X.   → We asked whether he had been studying every evening.

           CONTRAST: We inquired, "Have you been studying every evening?"

The company awarded Smith the honor.
He asked X.   → He asked why the company awarded Smith the honor.

           CONTRAST: He asked, "Why did the company award Smith the honor?"

Indirect questions are followed by a period, not a question mark.

AFFIRMATION

Affirmative Transformation (T_A)

The last transformation taken up in this chapter introduces affirmation or emphasis in the verb group (T_A). The symbol **A**, denoting affirmation, is introduced after the second member in the auxiliary string:

	(D) N	T	M	V
	his roommate	**present**	**can**	**study** →
(T_A)	his roommate	**present**	**can** A	**study** →
(T_{af})	his roommate	**can**	**present** A	**study** →

A is indicated by italics in writing, by heavy stress in speech. Thus:

His roommate *can* study.

Sentences without auxiliaries require the tense bearer *do:*

	(D) N	T	V
	his roommate	**present**	**study** →
(T_A)	his roommate	**present**	A **study** →
(T_{do})	his roommate	**do present**	A **study** →
	His roommate	*does*	study.

The following pairs reveal interesting contrasts:

His roommate *does* study.
His roommate does a good job.

His roommate *did* study.
Did his roommate study?

Of the two instances of *does*, the first derives from "His roommate studies" to which (T_A) has been applied; the second is simply the transitive verb *do* in the formula N V_t N. Of the two instances of *did*, the first derives from "His roommate studied" to which (T_A) has been applied; the second is the tense bearer in the sentence "His roommate studied" which has undergone (T_q).

SUMMARY

Transformations that generate interrogative, negative, and affirmative sentences have an underlying similarity as these simplified formulas show:

	N	M	V	
(T_{not})	Fred	will	remain.	→ Fred will not remain.
(T_q)				→ Will Fred remain?
(T_w)				→ Who will remain?
(T_A)				→ Fred *will* remain.

	N	V	
(T_{not})	Fred	remains.	→ Fred does not remain.
(T_q)			→ Does Fred remain?
$(T_w$			→ Who remains?
(T_A)			→ Fred *does* remain.

	N	be	(D)	N	
(T_{not})	Fred	is	a	student.	→ ⎰Fred is not a student.
(T_q)					⎱Is Fred a student?
(T_w)					→ ⎰Who is a student?
					⎱Who is Fred?
(T_A)					→ Fred *is* a student.

$$N_p \quad V_t \text{ (have)} \quad (D)N$$

(T_{not}) They have   a   car. → $\begin{cases} \text{They do not have a car.} \\ \text{They haven't a car.} \end{cases}$

(T_q) → $\begin{cases} \text{Do they have a car?} \\ \text{Have they a car? [British]} \end{cases}$

(T_w) → $\begin{cases} \text{Who has a car?} \\ \text{What do they have?} \end{cases}$

(T_A) → They *have* a car.

(T_{do}), **Af → do + Af,** adds the tense bearer **do** when the verb phrase contains no auxiliaries.

Other question types are illustrated by the following:

INDIRECT QUESTION: He asked if the class could attend the special lecture.

TAG-END QUESTION: He asked if the class could attend the special lecture, didn't he?

EXERCISES

1. Apply (T_{not}) to the following strings, developing each transformation step by step.

EXAMPLE:

       N   T   M   V
       Jack **past shall** go →
(T_{not}) Jack **past shall** not go →
(T_{af}) Jack **shall past** not go →
       Jack should not (shouldn't) go.

1.   N   T   M   V   (D) N
    Robert **present will** accept the offer

2.   N   T   have -en V   (D) N
    Robert **past have -en** accept the offer

3.   N   T   be -ing V   (D) N
    Robert **present be -ing** accept the offer

4.   N   T   V   (D) N
    Robert **past** accept the offer

5. N_p T   V   (D) N
    He **past** avoid the office

2. Transform the following strings into questions, according to specific directions.

EXAMPLE:

       N   T   M   V

       Jack **past shall** go →

(T_q)   **past shall** Jack go →

(T_{af}) **shall past** Jack go →

       Should Jack go?

1. N   T   M V   (D) N
    Robert **present will** accept the offer
    [Apply (T_q).]

2. N   T   be -ing V   (D) N
    Robert **present be -ing** accept the offer
    [Apply (T_q).]

3. N   T   M have -en V   (D) N
    Robert **past can have -en** accept the offer
    [Apply (T_q) and (T_{not}).]

4. N   T   V   (D) N
    Robert **past** accept the offer
    [Apply (T_q), then (T_w) to *Robert*.]

5. N   T   V   (D) N
    Robert **past** meet the manager
    [Apply (T_q), then (T_w) to *manager*.]

3. Apply (T_A) to the following strings.

EXAMPLE:

       N   T   M   V

       Jack **past shall**   go →

(T_A)   Jack **past shall** A go →

(T_{af}) Jack **shall past** A go →

       Jack *should* go.

1. N   T   M V   (D) N
    Robert **present will** accept the offer

2. N   T   be -ing V   (D) N
    Robert **present be -ing** accept the offer

3. N   T   V   (D) N
    Robert **past** accept the offer

4. N   T   V Av **P-phr**
   Robert **past do** well in his studies

5. **(D)** N   T   **be Aj**
   the offer **present be** definite

10) *Grammar and Revision*

The preceding chapters have dealt only with the most common sentence types, and the samples should not be mistaken for a complete grammar of English. Certain sentence patterns and transformations have been treated only cursorily or not at all. Among these, for example, are transformations that delete part of a construction (T_{del}):

Perhaps they will change their minds.　→ Perhaps they will.
　　　　　　　　　　　　　　　　　　　 Perhaps.

No doubt he has reconsidered his decision. → No doubt he has.
　　　　　　　　　　　　　　　　　　　 → No doubt.

Also:

They eat beans.　　　　　　　　　　　 → They eat.
Miss Hinkel married Lieutenant Reeve.　 → Miss Hinkel married.

Or sentences containing members of a subclass of transitive verbs, sometimes called **middle verbs,** that do not undergo the passive transformation:[1]

The wedding cost a large sum of money.
She resembled her mother.
Miss Hinkel married Lieutenant Reeve.

[1] See Robert B. Lees, *The Grammar of English Nominalizations* (Bloomington, Ind.: Research Center in Anthropology, Folklore, and Linguistics, 1963), p. 8.

Neither "*A large sum of money was cost by the wedding" nor "*Her mother is resembled by her" is grammatical. Nor can "Lieutenant Reeve was married by Miss Hinkel" be accepted as the passive transformation of the example above, unless the writer meant that Miss Hinkel performed the ceremony. But then *married* would be a transitive verb.

However limited the present description, the knowledge gained from a study of grammatical structures should make the beginning writer aware of his freedom in selecting and arranging words to fit his needs. He should realize that even the most sophisticated sentences are built on or derived from a few basic types. The derivational history of the following sentence, for example, cited elsewhere (see p. 73), shows what basic sentence types underlie its complex structure:

> I cannot too often repeat that though I have no academic qualifications I am in fact much more highly educated than most university scholars.
> —G. B. SHAW, *Sixteen Self Sketches*

(T_{not}) I can repeat it.
I can often repeat it.   → I cannot often repeat it.
I cannot too often repeat it.

I am educated.
I am highly educated.
I am more highly educated.
I am in fact much more highly educated.

(T_{nom}) Most scholars are at a university. → university scholars
Most scholars are educated.   →
Most university scholars are educated.

(T_{con}) I am in fact much more highly → I am in fact much more highly
educated.   educated than most university scholars (are educated).

(T_{del}) I am in fact much more highly → I am in fact much more highly
educated than most university educated than most university
scholars (are educated).   scholars.

(T_{sub}) I cannot too often repeat it.   → I cannot too often repeat that I am in fact much more highly educated than most university scholars.

(T_{aj}) (The) qualifications are academic. → academic qualifications
I have no qualifications.   →
I have no academic qualifications.

($\mathbf{T_{sub}}$)   I have no academic qualifications. → I cannot too often repeat that though I have no academic qualifications I am in fact much more highly educated than most university scholars.

The following example shows how a knowledge of grammatical processes can help in revising:

> 1. John Galsworthy described his father as practical, tenacious, and conservative. 2. His father was in the sketch "A Portrait." 3. The elder Galsworthy was an out-and-out individualist. 4. He despised fanaticism. 5. He considered money "the symbol of a well-spent, well-ordered life." 6. He had values. 7. They were those of the upper-middle-class Victorian.

Sentences 1 and 2 can be combined by nominalizing the second sentence and inserting the generated phrase in the first, or matrix, sentence:

1. John Galsworthy described his father as practical, tenacious, and conservative.
2. His father was in the sketch "A Portrait."

→ John Galsworthy described his father in the sketch "A Portrait" as practical, tenacious, and conservative.

The predicates of sentences 4 and 5 can be compounded:

4. He despised fanaticism.
5. He considered money "the symbol of a well-spent, well-ordered life."

→ He despised fanaticism and considered money "the symbol of a well-spent, well-ordered life."

Sentence 3 can be nominalized:

3. The elder Galsworthy was an out-and-out individualist.

→ the elder Galsworthy, an out-and-out individualist

The generated appositive can be inverted:

an out-and-out individualist, the elder Galsworthy

It can replace the subject of the sentence derived from sentences 4 and 5:

He despised fanaticism and considered money "the symbol of a well-spent, well-ordered life."	→ An out-and-out individualist, the elder Galsworthy despised fanaticism and considered money "the symbol of a well-spent, well-ordered life."

Sentence 6 may also be nominalized:

6. He had values   → his values

The generated phrase can replace the subject of sentence 7:

7. They were those of the upper-middle-class Victorian.   → His values were those of the upper-middle-class Victorian.

The completely revised version reads as follows:

John Galsworthy described his father in the sketch "A Portrait" as practical, tenacious, and conservative. An out-and-out individualist, the elder Galsworthy despised fanaticism and considered money "the symbol of a well-spent, well-ordered life." His values were those of the upper-middle-class Victorian.

The original seven sentences have been reduced to three. Unnecessary repetition of *he* has been eliminated, and sentence relationships have been improved.

The samples in this and preceding chapters show how we derive complex grammatical constructions from a relatively few basic sentence types. Our focus on grammatical processes, however, by no means implies that other demands of good writing can be ignored. Purpose, organization, context, and style each claim and deserve attention, as we will see later.

SUMMARY: INVENTORY OF BASIC PATTERNS, TERMINOLOGY, AND TRANSFORMATIONS

The following inventory lists the major word classes, function groups, basic sentence types, and transformations taken up in Chapters 2–9, with the numbers at the right indicating the first page reference to each item:

MAJOR WORD CLASSES

Noun (**N**)	14
pronoun (**N$_p$**)	18
common noun	15
proper noun	15
Verb (**V**)	14
intransitive (**V$_i$**)	15
linking (**V$_l$**)	29
be	29
transitive (**V$_t$**)	15
(g)ive (**V$_{t_g}$**)	44
(e)lect (**V$_{t_e}$**)	45
separable	56
have	58
middle	118
Adjective (**Aj**)	29
Adverb (**Av**)	31

FUNCTION GROUPS

Determiner (**D**)	20
Auxiliary	22
modal (**M**)	22
have -en	22
be -ing	22
Qualifier (**Q**)	34
Expletive	35
Preposition (**P**)	50
Relative (**R**)	66
Subordinator (**S**)	69
Conjunction (**C**)	80
Correlative	86
Not	106
Interrogative	111
Do	107

BASIC SENTENCE TYPES

N V	14
N $\begin{Bmatrix} V_l \\ be \end{Bmatrix}$ Aj	29
N be Av	31
N V$_t$ N	40
N $\begin{Bmatrix} V_l \\ be \end{Bmatrix}$ N	43
N V$_{t_g}$ N N	44
N V$_{t_e}$ N N	45

TRANSFORMATIONS

(**T$_{aj}$**)	adjective	30
(**T$_{del}$**)	deletion	32
(**T$_{there}$**)	there	36
(**T$_{pass}$**)	passive	41
(**T$_t$**)	transposition	44
(**T$_{rel}$**)	relative	65
(**T$_{sub}$**)	subordination	68
(**T$_{conj}$**)	conjunction	80
(**T$_{nom}$**)	nominalization	89
(**T$_{not}$**)	negative	106
(**T$_q$**)	yes-or-no question	109
(**T$_w$**)	interrogative	111
(**T$_a$**)	affirmation	113
(**T$_{af}$**)	affix	23
(**T$_{do}$**)	do	107

EXERCISES

1. Using techniques developed in earlier chapters, construct a more sophisticated sentence from each of the following groups.

> EXAMPLE: Kathy's latest extracurricular activity has been as a member of the varsity inner-tube racing team.
>
> She swims with the thing inflated or deflated. I don't even know.
>
> Kathy's latest extracurricular activity has been as a member of the varsity inner-tube racing team, but I don't even know whether she swims with the thing inflated or deflated.
>
> [The second sentence has been inserted in the third by (T_{sub}), and the generated sentence combined with the first by (T_{conj}).]

1. Our team was defeated in each game of the season.
   Our home games were practically filled to capacity.

2. The Lotus Club grants guest privileges.
   The guest privileges are for a period of 15 days.
   Such privileges may be extended for another 15 days.

3. Norbert could have won the race.
   Everyone knows it.
   He had disobeyed the training rules.
   He had smoked.

4. He arrived in New York.
   He immediately scheduled a round of parties.
   The parties were for diplomats.
   He had ostensibly come to town for a funeral.

5. The elections were undoubtedly honest.
   Much bloodshed accompanied them.
   The bloodshed occurred among followers of the candidates.

6. The study of language can be made interesting.
   It can be made profitable.
   It is taught as a facet of culture.
   We experience the world through this facet of culture.

7. Roberta Baker is highly motivated.
    She is very articulate.
    She is well organized.
    She is a young executive.

8. We could not purchase stamps at a post office.
    This post office was remote.
    It was in a village.
    The village was Indonesian.
    The postmaster had become ill.
    His subordinates had no key to his desk.

9. American students are extremely informal.
    They attend classes in their undershirts.
    A visitor once said this.
    The visitor was Iranian.
    The undershirts were T-shirts.
    He didn't know it.

10. The editor replied.
    The article was interesting.
    It was valuable as the basis of lessons in a text.
    It was not sufficiently restricted.

2. Revise one of your papers with the express purpose of improving its
    sentence structure.

11) *Sequence Markers*

In most writing, sentences are rarely found in isolation. Rather, they occur as units in an extended treatment of a subject, that is, as segments of discourse. To achieve continuity in discourse, the writer can use a variety of structural devices, including **sequence markers,** words or phrases that link sentences. A sequence marker may be a substitute word, that is, a word that replaces another word, word group, or sentence. Or it may be a function word whose unique characteristic is to link sentences. Sequence signals should be distinguished from subordinators, which include one sentence in another; and from conjunctions, which expand words, word groups, and sentences. Certain conjunctions, however, also serve as sequence markers, as we shall see. Sequence markers include pronouns, auxiliaries, determiners, a small number of adverbs, conjunctions, conjunctive adverbs, and prepositional phrases.

PRONOUNS

Pronouns are the least dispensable of the sequence markers, for they not only preclude unnecessary repetition of a noun, but they keep the noun or noun phrase that they replace clearly identified in the reader's mind. A pronoun substitutes for a noun of a particular gender: *he* for *man, Mr. Smith,* or *boy*; *she* for *woman, Mrs. Smith,*

125

or *girl*; *it* for *typewriter*, *paper*, *ink*; *he*, *she*, or *it* for *baby*, *dog*; *she* or *it* for *ship*, *cow*, etc. For example:

> The notion of a vested interest has an engaging flexibility in our social usage. In ordinary intercourse *it* is an improper advantage enjoyed by a political minority to which the speaker does not himself belong. When the speaker himself enjoys *it*, *it* ceases to be a vested interest and becomes a hard-won reward.—JOHN K. GALBRAITH, *The Affluent Society*

The pronoun *it*, used three times in the last two sentences not only substitutes for the noun phrase "the notion of a vested interest," but also obviates the necessity of repeating the phrase or part of it. Here is another example:

> The journalist has to work against the clock. *This* is the limitation and the opportunity of his task.—LOUIS LYONS, *The Atlantic*

This substitutes for the phrase "to work against the clock," its antecedent.[1]

AUXILIARIES

Auxiliaries may replace a full verb as, for example, *can't* and *won't* in the following excerpt from an address to the 1962 convention of the National Council of Teachers of English:

> . . . it seems possible that if all of the other departments of the high school and the university were to cooperate in the teaching of writing—in the casual but regular correction of writing mistakes and the effort to maintain standards—then writing might improve in some noticeable way. It will be objected that other departments *can't* and *won't*.
> —PAUL ROBERTS, *The English Journal*

In the next example, *don't* replaces the full verb and complement of the preceding clause:

> Overproduction is one of the publisher's nightmares—another is the number of readers who walk the streets and might buy all kinds of books if only they passed a good bookstore; but they *don't*.—"Letter to a Young Man About to Enter Publishing," *Harper's Magazine*

[1] See also reference of pronouns, pp. 289–290.

DETERMINERS

Determiners performing as sequence signals refer to a noun or a noun phrase:

> There is a channel down which your work pours. *That* channel must be kept clear, free-running.—CATHERINE DRINKER BOWEN, *The Atlantic*

> One of the rites of spring in West Germany last week was the dunking of young Germans in huge wooden tubs full of water. Like most *such* playful survivals of more leisurely times, this was the celebration of a medieval tradition more honored in modern Germany than anywhere else: the apprentice system.—*Time*, May 3, 1963

In the first example, *that* in "that channel" refers to "a channel down which your work pours." In the second example, *such* in "such playful survivals" refers to "the dunking of young Germans in huge wooden tubs full of water."

The usefulness of sequence markers can easily be demonstrated by replacing the italicized pronouns and determiners in the following excerpt with the words which they replace:

> Newport is a small Rhode Island center of excesses. To start with, *its* trees are enormous, outsized. *Its* magnificent estates along the Cliff Walk, most of which went up in the late nineteenth century in a competitive building splurge by wealthy New York families, are so large that in many cases they can be converted instantly into religious and educational institutions. The Newport Preservation Society has turned *some* into museums; *others*, in these days of certain limitations for most, have appealed to the style of the Texans: *some* are already installed in palatial residences, the word is out, and *more* are on their way.—GEORGE PLIMPTON, *Harper's Magazine*

Here is the same passage with the pronouns and determiners replaced by their antecedents:

> Newport is a small Rhode Island center of excesses. To start with, the trees *of Newport* are enormous, outsized. The magnificent estates *of Newport* along the Cliff Walk, most of which went up in the late nineteenth century in a competitive building splurge by wealthy New York families, are so large that in many cases they can be converted instantly into religious and educational institutions. The Newport Preservation Society has turned some *estates* into museums; other *estates*, in these days of certain limitations for most, have appealed to the style of the Texans: some *Texans* are already installed in palatial residences, the word is out, and more *Texans* are on their way.

CONJUNCTIONS

Conjunctions like *and*, *but*, *nor*, *for*, *yet* function as sequence markers at the beginning of a sentence:

> At St. John's there is no counseling, no psychic snooping unless the student's intellectual efficiency has gone awry. *And* when girls go away for the weekend, their dignity as adults is unviolated: they leave word of their destination in sealed envelopes not to be opened except in an emergency.—DAVID BOROFF, *Saturday Review*

> Repressive and persecuting passions are very common, as the present state of the world only too amply proves. *But* they are not an inevitable part of human nature.—BERTRAND RUSSELL, *Unpopular Essays*

Conjunctions functioning as sequence markers differ from other conjunctions only by punctuation. The difference therefore is purely a convention of the written language. Conjunctions that function as sequence markers link sentences separated by a period; others link clauses connected by a comma to form a compound sentence.

ADVERBS

A few adverbs like *then*, *there*, *thus* sometimes replace a word or word group in a preceding sentence:

> But I dare not keep on except in rare cases; for instance, near the end of a scene. Even *then* it is dangerous. Fatigue will betray me and I shall spoil my scene with sentimentality or bombast.
> —CATHERINE DRINKER BOWEN, *The Atlantic*

The italicized *then* replaces the prepositional phrase "near the end of a scene" in the preceding sentence.

Some adverbs function as sequence markers without replacing anything:

actually	else	then
afterward	later	there
also	similarly	too
before	still	

A comma or commas sometimes set these adverbs off from the rest of the sentence:

Ross often summoned Hobard Weekes when a comma had popped up to worry him, and he would ask Weekes, "What is the rule?" *Then* he would run into Weekes later in the hall and say, "There isn't any rule."
—JAMES THURBER, *The Years with Ross*

In some old-fashioned English grammars to this day English nouns are declined in accordance with the Greco-Latin pattern: Nominative—*the book*, Genitive—*of the book*, Dative—*to the book*, Accusative—*the book*. *Actually*, case endings and declensions have disappeared from English, there seeming to be little justification for the artificial application of ancient classical patterns to modern English speech.
—JOSEPH BRAM, *Language and Society*

In some co-educational institutions, social life is traditionally sane, sober, and sensible; in others it is hectic. *Similarly*, a man's college or a woman's college may be a haven of sensible living, or it may be the base for feverish social activities.—JOHN W. GARDNER, *Harper's Magazine*

But these adverbs do not exclusively function as sequence markers. *Still* in the following is simply an adverb expanding *true:*

A skeptic may doubt that writers can be made by teaching, especially in an age that has seen most good grammar recede into mystery, but it is *still* true that writing can be improved by practice and conditioned by good reading.—LOUIS LYON, *The Atlantic*

CONJUNCTIVE ADVERBS

A group of function words, called **conjunctive adverbs,** perform chiefly as sequence markers, though they may have adverbial functions as well. Conjunctive adverbs include:

accordingly	however
furthermore	indeed
consequently	nevertheless
moreover	therefore
otherwise	thereafter
hence	thus

A conjunctive adverb may occur at the beginning or anywhere within the sequence sentence:

German industry has been plowing back into plant expansion and modernization about 44 percent of its profits. *Moreover*, stiff corporate

and individual taxes have enriched the state but limited the capital at the disposal of firms and persons. "The Atlantic Report: Germany."
—*The Atlantic*, December 1957

For us a "long time" can be almost anything—ten or twenty years, two or three months, a few weeks, or even a couple of days. The South Asian, *however*, feels that it is perfectly realistic to think of a "long time" in terms of thousands of years or even an endless period.
—EDWARD HALL, *The Silent Language*

Members of this set sometimes perform as adverbs with little, if any, connective function:

However distinguished the soloist may have been, Ted remained unimpressed.
They were allowed to come thus far.

Conjunctive adverbs show sequential relationships much like simple conjunctions, though more formally and precisely. The meaning denoted by *and*, for example, can be expressed more explicitly by connectives like *also, moreover, furthermore*.[2] But excessive use of conjunctive adverbs makes writing rigid and labored.

PREPOSITIONAL PHRASES AS CONNECTIVES

Certain prepositional phrases can serve as connectives. Among them are:

after a while	in addition	in time
as a result	in each case	in turn
by contrast	in other words	on the other hand
for instance	in the end	
for the first time	in the first place	
for example	in this way	

How they help to link sentences can be seen in the following:

The purpose of scientific language is control and prediction, that of esthetic language the intensification of direct experience. *In other words*, language must be understood in terms of the function it serves.
—JOSEPH BRAM, *Language and Society*

[2] A more detailed treatment of connectives is found in Harold Whitehall, *Structural Essentials of English* (New York: Harcourt, Brace & World, 1956), pp. 53–77.

For the essence of a sound style is that it cannot be reduced to rules—that it is a living and breathing thing, with something of the devilish in it— that it fits its proprietor tightly and yet ever so loosely, as his skin fits him. It is, *in fact*, quite as securely an integral part of him as that skin is.
—H. L. MENCKEN, *Prejudices: Fifth Series*

MISCELLANEOUS MARKERS AS CONNECTIVES

Other devices besides sequence markers contribute to discourse continuity. Set expressions like *no doubt, most important, to be sure, of course, after all*, have an unmistakable connective function:

> Whenever a text-book is written of real educational worth, you may be quite certain that some reviewer will say that it will be difficult to teach from it. *Of course* it will be difficult to teach from it. If it were easy, the book ought to be burned; for it cannot be educational.
> —ALFRED NORTH WHITEHEAD, *The Aims of Education*

> It is possible that *mortician* may owe its creation quite as much to the age-old and constant search for euphemisms for terms connected with death and burial as to the desire for professional status. There is, *after all*, a somewhat gruesome pun in the word *undertaker*, and though it has served the English from 1698 on, they do at times soften the effect by substituting *funeral furnisher.*—ALBERT MARCKWARDT, *American English*

Enumeration is often effective, as in the following passage, in which David Boroff describes phases of the academic program at St. John's College, Annapolis:

> The program is unique. Perhaps only St. John's—a port of last call for many of its students and faculty—could get away with it. *First*, there is a common course of study laid out for all four years for everybody—in effect, a four-year assignment given to a student when he matriculates. This creates a paradox which often baffles the outsider: St. John's is at once highly authoritarian and freewheeling, traditional, and bohemian. *Secondly*, the faculty—all called, with becoming modesty, tutors—teach almost everything. They may come with particular academic competencies, but they never rest on their Ph.D's. Everybody learns at St. John's.
> —DAVID BOROFF, *Saturday Review*

This chapter has been devoted to transitional devices that link sentences. We may think of transitions—whether pronouns, conjunctions, or prepositional phrases—as the bridgework of prose, for they are like bridges over rivers in that their function is to get us to the other side. But they are also like dental bridgework in that they should be as inconspicuous as possible. The beginning writer therefore must learn how to move his reader comfortably from sentence to sentence without invariably using too many of them.

EXERCISES

1. Identify all sequence markers in the following passages. Distinguish between those markers that merely link sentences and those that function as substitutes for words, phrases, or clauses.

   1. We would admire the courage and determination of John Quincy Adams if he served in the Senate today. We would respect his nonpartisan, nonsectional approach. But I am not so certain that we would like him as a person; and it is apparent that many of his colleagues, on both sides of the aisle, did not.
   —JOHN F. KENNEDY, *Profiles in Courage*

   2. Only a generation ago the newspapers boasted not only *bona fide* Society pages but also whole sections which were often almost entirely devoted to the goings on of Society. Now not only have these goings on, figuratively speaking, gone, but also we have no real Society pages, in the old sense, at all. Some newspapers, it is true, still do use the word, among them such a distinguished journal as *The New York Times*, but exactly what they mean by the term—particularly in the sense of who does and who does not come under its heading—would seem to be a difficult problem.
   —CLEVELAND AMORY, *Who Killed Society?*

   3. I passed all the other courses that I took at my University, but I could never pass botany. This was because all botany students had to spend several hours a week in a laboratory looking through a microscope at plant cells, and I could never see through a microscope.—JAMES THURBER, *My Life and Hard Times*

   4. Speech is so familiar a feature of daily life that we rarely pause to define it. It seems as natural to man as walking, and only less so than breathing. Yet it needs but a moment's reflection to convince us that this naturalness of speech is but an illusory feeling. The process of acquiring speech is, in sober fact, an utterly different sort of thing from the process of learning to walk.
   —EDWARD SAPIR, *Language*

5. A commonplace of life is that we do not get what we want all the time; i.e. our instincts, and the desires that derive from them, are constantly being frustrated. For instance, let us take the case of a child who wishes to drive—or even to be—an engine. Neither desire is likely to be satisfied in reality.
—RUPERT CRAWSHAY-WILLIAMS, *The Comforts of Unreason*

6. We can communicate scientific facts to each other without knowing or caring about each other's feelings; but before love, friendship, and community can be established among men so that we *want* to cooperate and become a society, there must be, as we have seen, a flow of sympathy between one man and another. This flow of sympathy is established, of course, by means of the affective uses of language. Most of the time, after all, we are not interested in keeping our feelings out of our discourse, but rather we are eager to express them as fully as we can.
—S. I. HAYAKAWA, *Language in Thought and Action*

7. It would be an error to assume that preliterate men show no awareness of specifically linguistic phenomena. Quite the contrary, most primitive groups are found in multicultural areas (such as New Guinea, West Africa, and the Amazon Basin) where they have become sensitive to their neighbors' "foreign" accents and to other differences in speech.—JOSEPH BRAM, *Language and Society*

8. Between the conclusion of *The Rambler* and the publication of the *Dictionary*, Johnson appears to have devoted himself chiefly to his work as lexicographer. He did, however, supply his friend, Mrs. Lennox, with a dedication to her *Shakespeare Illustrated* and published in *The Gentleman's Magazine* a brief biographical sketch of its founder, Edward Cave, who had just died, leaving an estate valued at more than eight thousand pounds. He also made one of a small group which contributed more or less regularly to an essay periodical called *The Adventurer*, with which his dear friend Dr. Bathurst also was associated.
—JOSEPH WOOD KRUTCH, *Samuel Johnson*

9. I seldom go out on limbs to crusade for individuals, much less a sport, my attitude towards public projects of this sort being with the "sink or swim" school. However, if ever an individual was pilloried by the shabby treatment he received from most of the press and the public, Jim Thorpe is that man.
—GRANTLAND RICE, *The Tumult and the Shouting*

10. We should study language, particularly our own language, just because it is a good thing to know. Of all the humane studies, it is the most humane, since it is the thing that is central and common and peculiar to mankind. If we find that study of it has practical value—improves our spelling, eliminates our comma faults—so much the better. But whether it does or not, it deserves a prominent place in the curriculum and particularly in what we might want still to call the composition class.

—PAUL ROBERTS, *The English Journal*

2. Choose an expository paragraph from a book or journal and make an analysis of the sequence markers in it.

3. Analyze one of your papers for the effective use of sequence markers and make whatever improvements seem indicated.

12) Discourse and the Paragraph

A paragraph is a convenience the writer provides for his reader. It is, roughly speaking, the counterpart of a pause or gesture by which the public speaker marks a change of direction or new development in his talk. Signals that the speaker communicates directly to his audience, the writer partially conveys through indentation of a line. In a sense, therefore, paragraphing is a kind of terminal punctuation, though, unlike terminal punctuation, it is optional rather than obligatory.

Good writing is possible without the periodic indentation of lines. But paragraphing is an admirable device that helps the reader follow the writer's organization. It is a visual aid as well, for no reader enjoys seeing sentences strung together without a break. Paragraphs that are too long seem formidable and unattractive, and often more inviting divisions can be made. Paragraphs that are too short seem choppy and usually reflect inadequate development of a topic.

If paragraphing is a device, we may inquire what principles underlie it. The question is difficult to answer, because the varied material that occurs between successive indentations eludes simple definition. An illustration will help to explain (the sentences are numbered for easy reference):

A CHALLENGE TO OUR ASSUMPTIONS

Harry A. Bullis

(1) Man's problem of survival today is not a case of "we or they." (2) Neither is the issue one of "win" or "not win." (3) It is, rather, to realize that every system, every ideology, is going through turbulent, revolutionary change; that *they* as well as *we* are changing. (4) Once this realization is made, the fanatical states of mind induced by the cold war, and inflamed by suspicious contempt, mistrust, and even outright hatred, can be safely abandoned. (5) For many of the things we feared about each other yesterday, and perhaps with justification, simply are not true today. (6) Take, for example, the nineteenth-century picture of capitalism which Communists continue to project. (7) This picture is of farmers and factory labor being exploited in order that capitalists might accumulate savings for investment in increased technological growth and production of more goods for more people. (8) But modern capitalism has changed. (9) Now the capitalist ideal is to make every man an owner. (10) The free world is not bent on burying Communism; rather it would work for a condition wherein every government rests on the consent of the governed. (11) Democracy in economic life is developing fast. (12) On the other hand, consider the picture of Communism that the free world continues to project. (13) Farmers and factory labor are exploited in order that Communist states might accumulate savings for investment in increased technological growth and the production of more goods for more people. (14) But modern Communism is also changing. (15) The principle of government by consent of the governed is edging into the minds of Communist peoples.

—*Saturday Review*, October 13, 1962

The excerpt, printed in this book as a single paragraph, actually appeared as four separate paragraphs on the editorial page of the October 13, 1962, issue of the *Saturday Review*. Half a dozen professors of English, asked whether or not they approved of the paragraphing as it appears in this book, offered a variety of comments, but none took exception to the arrangement of the material in one paragraph. (The indentations in the magazine article follow sentences 3, 5, and 11.) The division of discourse into paragraphs is often a matter of personal preference, and a writer or editor may have his own views on paragraphing. He may make a division on the basis of logic or for other compelling reasons. Some topics lend themselves to flexible arrangements; others demand a stricter organization. Whatever the nature of a paragraph, however, its structure involves certain fundamentals of composition.

UNITY

A good paragraph shares certain characteristics of a successful sentence. An effective sentence, as has been pointed out, is one whose words are properly related. It is not simply any string of words. "The committee elected Walker chairman" obviously differs in meaning from "The committee elected chairman Walker." And "Chairman Walker was elected by the committee" is a passive transformation of the second, not the first, sentence. Order and arrangement have a meaning of their own, which, together with the meanings of individual words, consititute the total meaning of a sentence.

In a similar way, paragraphs consist of more than just a string of sentences. A paragraph—or discourse—has meaning distinct from that of the individual sentences that constitute it. Its total meaning consists of its sentences and their arrangement, much as the meaning of a sentence differs from and is greater than the sum of the individual words that constitute it. In addition, the writer's assumptions that shape his treatment, the point of view toward his material and his reader, the overall strategy that informs his presentation and gives it significance—all these must be conveyed through words, sentences, and their arrangement.

How order and arrangement contribute to the total meaning of discourse is illustrated by the following portion of Admiral Hyman G. Rickover's testimony on U.S. education and training before a Congressional committee:

(1) Education, to me, means developing of the mind; it consists in transmission of the fundamentals of systematic knowledge and in development of the ability to utilize this knowledge for the solving of the myriad of problems which everyone encounters in his life.   (2) In a good school, students are constantly asked to apply what they have learned to new situations—this is what traditional examinations and tests are for.   (3) Thus, abstract knowledge is used in a practical way which prepares one for adult life when real problems must be solved rationally.   (4) The process of supplying both basic knowledge and ability to make practical use of this knowledge is properly termed "education."

(5) We must distinguish education from training, which is a process whereby youth acquire certain useful and socially approved habits; it is

"life adjustment," adjustment to the "peer" group, training in manners, good grooming and how to dress; it is miscellaneous know-how such as how to shop, budget, use the telephone, cook, drive a car; how to occupy one-self during one's leisure time as by flycasting or baton twirling; it is the acquiring of assorted vocational skills in such things as typewriting, wood-shop, machine shop, printshop.   (6) As in all human activities, the mind comes into play when one is trained in such skills and habits, but the mind does not develop through practicing manual skills or following habit. (7) Mastery of the English language has quite a different effect on one's intellectual capacities from that which comes through mastery of type-writing.   (8) Knowledge of history increases one's comprehension of world events, whereas homemaking or driver training—necessary and useful as they may be—do not.   (9) In most other countries training is largely left to home, to church and to learning through living or on the job—the schools concentrate on education.

(10) It is in education—that is in transmitting the fundamentals of knowledge, in developing the ability to think through sharpening the child's intellectual tools—that we fall down.   (11) Too much of our so-called education is mere training in various kinds of know-how.

—H. G. RICKOVER, *Education and Freedom*

Admiral Rickover propounds one central thesis: that American schools are concerned not so much with the teaching of fundamental knowl-edge as with the development of socially useful skills. To amplify this point, he first presents his concept of education and training, then examines the presence of each in our school system, and concludes by charging American schools with failing to educate students. However debatable some portions of the testimony may be, its presiding purpose gives it **unity,** an indispensable quality of effective discourse.

Each segment of the excerpt reflects the author's critical intent: (1) sentences 1–4, which define education; (2) sentences 5–6, which define training; (3) sentences 7–8, which illustrate the occurrence of each in our school system; (4) sentences 9–11, which assert the responsibilities of society toward education and training and the failure of U.S. schools to meet these responsibilities.

PROGRESSION

Another, more technical, way of looking at the structure of this self-contained excerpt is to let A stand for education and B for training. The author says that although some A is found in B, the presence of

A in B is not at all significant. A by no means equals B. American schools fall down on A. Too much of what they believe is A is really B. By patiently developing his theme, from the formulation of the concepts of education and training to the final assertion that U.S. schools are not discharging their obligations, the author achieves a second quality essential to successful discourse—**progression,** or **movement.**

COHERENCE

Analysis further shows that each sentence save the first is attached to the preceding one. Sentences 1–4, for example, assert that education has to do with intellectual development, with the transmission of "systematic" knowledge and the rational application of this knowledge to problems in actual life. Sentence 1 says that education involves the teaching of systematic knowledge and the utilization of this knowledge for solving problems. Sentence 2 says in a good school, tests and examinations serve as problem-solving exercises, and sentence 3 that examinations prepare students for later life as well, when real problems must be solved rationally. Sentence 4 restates the point that education supplies "basic knowledge" and "ability to make practical use of this knowledge." By properly relating successive sentences the author achieves **coherence,** another characteristic of successful discourse.

The Rickover excerpt shows that principles of organization apply to both spoken and written discourse and that paragraph divisions, which in this instance could have been made by an editor, are often optional. The first indentation coincides with the analysis of the discourse above, but the second indentation clearly marks a dramatic break, underlining the failure of U.S. schools to discharge their obligations. The indentation could have come after sentence 8 to correspond with the analysis, but a writer in control of his subject may indent for different reasons.

TOPIC SENTENCE

Successful discourse must have unity, coherence, and progression. Most expository paragraphs, moreover, contain what is called a **topic sentence,** usually consisting of a statement which requires definition, elaboration, or analysis, such as sentences 1 and 4 in the Rickover testimony or sentence 3 in the Bullis excerpt. Topic sentences occur anywhere in a paragraph, though perhaps most commonly at the beginning or end.

The presence of a topic sentence does not invariably guarantee a good paragraph, but ability to spot a topic sentence can be helpful in revising when the writer seeks to discover if his sentences are properly grouped together and given significance. Not every paragraph, however, has a stated topic sentence, which may, as often as not, be implied. Transitional paragraphs or those containing a long illustration may have no topic sentence at all, though a transitional paragraph may have as many as two, one relating to the preceding paragraph and the other to the paragraph that follows.

ILLUSTRATIONS OF ORGANIZATIONAL PRINCIPLES

The immediate usefulness of organizational principles becomes apparent in revising. The student should ask himself if his discourse has movement or progression, if each point is properly linked to the preceding and following points and to the overall design of the discourse, and if topic and supporting sentences are properly distributed. Inability to apply these basic principles of organization creates a variety of problems, the most common of which are (1) inadequately developed paragraphs, (2) incoherent paragraphs, and (3) unnecessarily detailed paragraphs.

Inadequate development of a topic often stems from the erroneous assumption that the reader will fill in the details himself. The result may be a series of unsupported generalizations:

```
     Henrik Ibsen's A Doll's House deals with woman's dependent
status in society, a subject still of concern today.  Another
theme running through the play is the tyranny of one individual
over another, specifically Torvald's domination of Nora.  Further
analysis reveals the theme of self-realization:  Nora's discovery
that she is the property of her husband, who has kept her ignor-
ant of the world outside.  When she becomes convinced that there
is no hope of change in the relationship with her husband, she
leaves him.  She is of course denounced for behaving "unnaturally."
```

The first sentence introduces the problem of woman's social status at the end of the nineteenth century, which, the writer says, still has significance today. He does not show how this problem finds expression both in the play and in contemporary life, but turns to the subject of domestic tyranny, which he immediately drops for the theme of self-discovery in the last three sentences. The paragraph, though it has movement, lacks unity and coherence, since sentence-to-sentence attachment and an overall design are missing.

A student might object to the analysis in the preceding paragraph by pointing out that each subject could well be treated later in the essay. Nonetheless the structure of the paragraph can be strengthened and the organization of the whole essay plainly displayed by indicating that three closely related, but distinct, themes emerge in Ibsen's *A Doll's House:* (1) woman's dependent status; (2) domestic tyranny; (3) self-discovery. The writer should never assume that his reader will understand easily what he writes unless he says clearly and precisely what he means.

Sometimes an inexperienced writer lets his subject elude him, and he develops his argument with irrelevant supporting points. The result may be a paragraph that lacks coherence:

```
    A dictionary cannot be regarded as the ultimate source of
correctness on questions of usage.  Basically, it is a reference
work similar to an encyclopedia, dwarf size.  We tend to use
more than one encyclopedia in our research for a term paper in
order to form a more adequate opinion; likewise, we should con-
sult more than one dictionary in order to ascertain the editors'
views on a particular usage.  Yet this is seldom done, because
we regard a dictionary as a sacred document.
```

The writer shifts gears in the second sentence, for instead of clarifying his opening statement, he lets himself be diverted by an unilluminating analogy, from which he draws the lame conclusion that since no single dictionary can provide a final answer to questions of usage, it is best to consult several. The conclusion sheds no light on the writer's thesis in the opening sentence that a dictionary cannot be considered an ultimate arbiter on questions of usage.

The beginner sometimes introduces excessive detail, especially in opening and closing paragraphs, as the following instance from a paper on Katherine Mansfield's story "Bliss" shows:

```
    A story is composed of many things.  First, of course, is the
plot.  This deals with the relating of facts that make up an event
or events around which the story revolves.  A mood transmitted by
the author to the reader is often found in a story.  This mood
can be one of happiness, sadness, hate, or love.  A theme around
which the story weaves itself is invariably present.  Characters
who react in certain ways to different situations are most often
seen.  Irony, saying one thing meaning the direct opposite, some-
times appears in a story.
    In Katherine Mansfield's "Bliss" many of these elements can
be found. . . .
```

The first paragraph consists of platitudes so transparent that they had best be eliminated in revision. The references to plot, mood, theme, character, and irony should be made only if they apply to the work under discussion. The writer must learn to strike a balance between excessive and insufficient detail, and to move forward at the right pace, neither giving an impression of superficiality nor boring his reader with clichés.

We should not overlook a point—often ignored because it seems so obvious—that discourse can be successful only if the writer fully controls his subject. Once this control has been achieved and tested, the subject frequently imposes its own pattern of development. Indeed, no amount of care given to principles of organization, to sentence structure, or to style can redeem an essay that lacks a basic grasp of the subject it purports to treat.

Attempts to impose orderliness on superficially conceived topics are, nevertheless, common among students. The result of one such attempt is the following, perhaps somewhat extreme, example (the name of the author is fictitious):

High School Was a Waste

by Samuel Purcell

I learned nothing in high school. I made good grades in English--C's usually, because I always could spell. But English is the most complicated language in the world, so complicated that no one can teach it to anyone else. My English teacher should have known this, but she kept on trying, the result of which was that I slept clear through all of her classes for four years. This is the first way high school was a waste.

Besides, my teachers were poorly prepared. They had all probably attended teachers colleges, and everyone knows that teachers colleges are third-rate. Except for my English teachers, no one spoke good English. The basketball coach always said "I seen" instead of "I saw." The trigonometry teacher knew nothing about vector spaces and linear transformations when I questioned him about some work I was doing on my own. And when I won the physics prize in the Science Fair I had to explain electron diffusion to the principal.

The teacher I had for government and world history for two years was a Canadian, who had no desire to become a United States citizen. When I asked him why he didn't teach in Canada, whether the living standard was too low for him, he got mad and expelled me from class. Canadians are backward and most of their country is wasteland. I believe in America for Americans. My Canadian teacher even said there would have been no Civil War if there had been no revolution against England, because England abolished slavery in 1813. He thought the United States would have been better off if we had remained in the British Commonwealth. I could not be expected to learn anything from an eccentric like that. This is the second way high school was a waste.

Every activity in my high school was based on athletics. We also had a language club, a press club, and a science club, but these didn't count. The really popular clubs were the booster club and the letterman club. We had one pep assembly every week, sometimes two. All the school dances were held after the games, except the Prom. The only important people in the school were the lettermen. I almost earned my letter in football, and I tried out for basketball. But I was too short to make the team. I got a letter in Band in my senior year, but I refused to wear it because it had a silver lyre on its crest. The only thing that saved me in high school was my car. I got my first car when I was sixteen, a Chevy.

Everything I learned in high school I learned by myself on my own time. The teachers were cantankerous and quarrelsome. You couldn't say anything without their wanting to argue.

The essay, by a basically knowledgeable student, has several major weaknesses: its sweeping generalizations and its lack of unity and coherence. The writer offers his generalizations, not so much to make a valid point as to impress both himself and his reader. A statement like "English is the most complicated language in the world" is hardly susceptible to analysis. Generalizations like "My teachers were poorly prepared" or "Every activity in my high school was based on athletics" show the writer's disposition to digress. The paragraph on Canada is a potpourri of personal impressions topped off by the biased observation, "I could not be expected to learn anything from an eccentric like that." The last paragraph lamely restates the writer's thesis and concludes with the unconvincing assertion that he could not talk to his teachers "without their wanting to argue."

An outline of the paper reveals its faulty logic:

Thesis: I learned nothing in my four years of high school.

I. Teachers are poorly trained at teachers colleges.
    A. A Canadian history teacher had an unfriendly attitude toward the U.S.
    B. Almost all the teachers spoke substandard English.
    C. The trigonometry teacher lacked up-to-date mathematical knowledge.
II. All activities in high school were related to athletics.
    A. There was much interest in the Booster and Letterman Clubs.
    B. Pep assemblies were important.
    C. Awards were given for participating in the band.

The thesis, first of all, is implausible, even though the student pointedly uses exaggeration as a device to achieve irony. He does not mean literally that he learned "nothing" in high school and that he slept through every single English class. Apparently he does, however, believe that (all) "Canadians are backward" and that (all) "teachers colleges are third-rate." He fails to distinguish between overstatement for effect and meaningless statement.

The logic of his presentation demolishes his thesis at once, even if we grant the spirit of the presentation. The alleged unfriendly attitude of his history teacher toward the U.S., for example, has nothing to do with the assertion that his teachers received poor training. The alleged substandard speech of his coach does not permit him to conclude that almost the entire staff speaks poor English. The second part of the essay with its emphasis on athletics bears little apparent relation to the thesis that the writer learned nothing in high school. There may of course be some relevance, but the writer does not perceive it. Prestige and acceptance in his school presumably exist for athletes but not for scholars. And though the exceptional student may have the drive to work without reinforcement, the average student may need it.

The outline has been hastily improvised by the student to give the essay an appearance of orderliness and to obscure its basic defects. The enumeration of ways in which high school was a waste fails to conceal the broad generalizations which are impossible of serious analysis. Indeed, the essay seems to proceed psychologically rather than logically as it should, and the reader learns more about the writer's personality than about the announced topic. This does not imply, of course, that the personality of the writer should be excluded from his work. On the contrary, countless great essays are held together only or primarily by it. But the personality that emerges—whether through style, point of view, logic of presentation, or choice of material—must be consistent. The Purcell essay lacks consistency, and for this reason, despite the humor of its exaggerated details, fails to impress.

In contrast to the preceding effort, the following essay is presented as a more successful attempt of student writing on a similar topic:

Instruction by Committee
by Gary Candelario

I attended high school in the pre-Sputnik period when life adjustment was the goal of the schools. Active hostilities in Korea had just ended, and government reports began to circulate which purported to show that the public school system was responsible for the poor showing of the American soldier in Korea. His low combat efficiency was blamed on a negative attitude, which, in turn, it was thought, was due to the failure of the schools to teach "democratic principles."

My high school therefore became a model of capitulation to local political pressure. Academic discipline was sacrificed to the theory of life adjustment both in and out of school. The curriculum was remodeled around such "democratic" concepts as personal hygiene, civic responsibility and participation, worthy home membership, vocational efficiency, and consumer education. Shakespeare, Shelley, and Shaw were shelved.

Instead of teaching, teachers assumed the role of guidance counselors. Every class became a hodgepodge of "democratic activity," and teaching was done by committees. There was a student-chairman for every conceivable subject, from sociology to communication skills. The school was deluged with mock United Nations, student legislatures, student patriotism assemblies-- anything which might help us to understand our society. The administration, faculty, and students were fully absorbed by a fantastic game of parliamentary "let's pretend."

One of the by-products of this period was our attitude toward English studies--particularly grammar. While the committee approach may work well in the social sciences, it brings with it built-in antagonism to English instruction. An English teacher cannot have a student-chairman in charge of the adverb. Nor should there be any style juries or sentence-construction committees. A composition cannot be examined profitably through a committee.

But some of my English teachers were apparently devoted to instruction by committee. We had to vote ourselves into committees to practice "telephone etiquette" and formal introductions-- somewhat difficult in blue jeans and a sweatshirt. Some of us were charged with selecting patriotic novels and still others with the reading of poetry, like Paul Revere's famous ride. Yet despite instruction by committee, the traditional grammatical programs were actively pursued: the double negative and "ain't" were the focus of a usage purge, and prepositions were to be avoided to end a sentence with. The textbooks said it was incorrect. I strongly suspect that some of our English teachers lost their sense of self- esteem and importance in this game of "let's pretend," for they

seemed embarrassed that grammar was so undemocratic. I also became
fed up, quit school, and joined the Marines.

One of the first things that impresses the reader of both essays is
that the Candelario paper makes less exaggerated claims, though it
also tends somewhat to oversimplify and overstate for effect, especially
when the writer asks us to believe that he left school primarily as a
protest against academic policy. Nor does the assertion that his high
school rebuilt its curriculum as a result of political pressure stand close
observation. Students of the history of education know that the trend
to life adjustment as an educational philosophy predated the Korean
War.

But the basic organizational qualities of unity, coherence, and progression the Candelario essay possesses in good measure, as the following outline shows:

Thesis: The educational philosophy of my high school promoted
academic mediocrity.

I. After the Korean War, the intellectual emphasis of our curriculum
was diluted, as a result of pressure, by the educational concept of life
adjustment.
A. Citizenship training was increasingly emphasized.
B. "Student committees" were set up in many subjects to insure
maximum student participation and practice in democratic
procedures.

II. Instruction by committee failed in English.
A. Oral English was taught by student committees in charge of
units on telephone conversations and formal introductions.
B. Choices by student committees were responsible for the selection
of mediocre literature.
C. Grammar with its authoritarian prescriptions could not be
taught by committees.

The two major points, (1) that the concept of life adjustment was
responsible for a watered-down curriculum, and (2) that learning by
committee failed dramatically in English, are amply supported, though
the writer could have defined the kind of political pressure on his
school and explained, however briefly, his notion of academic discipline, especially since academic discipline and life adjustment are not
necessarily incompatible. But the paper moves along briskly, the
writer's irony apparent as he contemplates his high school experience

from a distance and points his critical fingers in an unmistakable direction.

As a final illustration of unity, coherence, and progression, a critical, rather than an autobiographical, essay is presented as a sample of competent writing, submitted in response to a normal weekly assignment:

Oedipus as an Ideal Tragic Hero

by Nancy Kelley

The distinctive effect of tragedy, according to Aristotle, is its ability to evoke pity and fear. The tragic hero must possess qualities which excite these emotions. "Pity," says Aristotle, "is aroused by unmerited misfortune, fear by the misfortune of a man like ourselves."[1] The hero must be neither completely virtuous nor villainous. A completely virtuous man, in meeting with adversity, is more likely to evoke shock than pity. Conversely, the picture of a villain coming to his just deserts, while satisfying the moral sense, fails again of the higher tragic qualities. The ideal tragic hero must fall somewhere between these two extremes. Further, the cause of his tragic misfortune must stem, not from deliberate malice or vice, but from some flaw or frailty in his character.

Sophocles' tragic hero Oedipus is at once an idealized and a human figure, noble enough to inspire awe, yet human enough to arouse our sympathy.[2] He is basically virtuous as shown by his deep devotion to the people of Thebes, his sense of duty, and his determination to continue the search for truth in the face of impending danger. Yet despite his virtue, Oedipus is subject to the human passions and frailties of anger and misjudgment. He has misjudged the prophecy of Tiresias, the blind seer, and he suspects the loyalty of the Queen's brother, Creon. Although his rage at them is partially justifiable (since he feels he has been unjustly wronged), and his error understandable (since the knowledge necessary to save Thebes lies beyond his realm of penetration), these human qualities bring him close enough to reality to arouse fear at his misfortune.

A more difficult task, in applying Aristotle's criteria of the tragic hero to Oedipus, is the discovery of the tragic flaw. On the meager basis of human claims it is difficult to justify the magnitude of Oedipus' tragedy. His misfortune seems too great an atonement for mere anger, error, or pride. Indeed, the tragedy of Oedipus would seem to stem from his virtues rather than from his faults. For it is, after all, his dedication to a cause, his heroic search for truth, which brings him to destruction. The seeds of his misfortune, however, lie beyond control of the human mind; they are in the hands of Fate. In the final analysis, Oedipus' tragic flaw lies in the limitation of human reason. The intelligence with which Oedipus has saved the people of Thebes is human and cannot help him in the unequal struggle with destiny.

As King of Thebes, Oedipus wields power and commands respect. He is dedicated to his people and to the cause of truth. It is then from a position of lofty eminence that he falls, and this striking reversal of position makes his fall the more tragic. We see his tragic flaw, his imperfection as a human being, and in its culmination in his final destruction we experience a sense of tragic awe, of fear and pity.

---

[1]Aristotle, The Poetics, tr. S. H. Butcher (New York: Hill and Wang, 1961), p. 45.

[2]Sophocles, Oedipus Rex, tr. Dudley Fitts and Robert Fitzgerald, in Nine Great Plays, ed. Leonard F. Dean, rev. ed. (New York: Harcourt, Brace and World, Inc., 1956), pp. 60-112.

A critical paper such as this requires the student writer to move outward from his own experiences to those of others, experiences already fully articulated and ordered, whether by a reporter, critic, dramatist, or poet. One of the major problems then involves not so much the selection from, and articulation of, a stock of personal experiences, as the interpretation and evaluation of a written text or texts. Though techniques of research are not taken up until the next chapter, it is worth pointing out here that the principles of organization underlying a long investigative essay are substantially the same as those that inform the sample paper here.

The Kelley paper is admirably organized. It achieves unity by examining only certain qualities of a tragic hero and relating them to Sophocles' *Oedipus Rex.* Wisely, the writer attempts no definition of tragedy, nor does she make an effort to treat all elements of tragedy.

There are four clearly defined parts: (1) Aristotle's analysis of the characteristics of a tragic hero; (2) Oedipus as a tragic hero embodying these characteristics; (3) Oedipus' tragic flaw; (4) Oedipus' fall from eminence. The topic gets under way in the first sentence, which serves at once as an introduction and as an integral part of the essay. The writer's attitude toward her subject is most clearly set forth in the opening sentence of the third paragraph. Indeed the analysis of Oedipus' tragic flaw is perhaps the most admirable part of the paper, with its forthright distinction between fact and judgment. The last sentence recapitulates the topics dealt with in the essay.

In the present chapter, the paragraph has been described as a unit of discourse characterized by unity, coherence, and progression. It is a flexible unit, adaptable to the writer's different needs. As he learns to define his purpose, control his subject, and interest his reader, the student should use the paragraph as a convenient device to help in the organization of his paper, as well as a means to underline the overall strategy that informs that paper.

EXERCISES

1.   Explain the principles of organization underlying each of the following paragraphs or groups of paragraphs, with particular reference to the methods of attaining unity, coherence, and progression. Indicate whether or not each paragraph has a topic sentence and, if not, why not.

   1.   In our so-called civilized life print plays such an important part that educated people are apt to forget that *language is primarily speech*, i.e. chiefly conversation (dialogue), while the written (and

printed) word is only a kind of substitute—in many ways a most valuable, but in other respects a poor one—for the spoken and heard word. Many things that have vital importance in speech— stress, pitch, colour of the voice, thus especially those elements which give expression to emotions rather than to logical thinking— disappear in the comparatively rigid medium of writing, or are imperfectly rendered by such means as underlining (italicizing) and punctuation. What is called the life of language consists in oral intercourse with its continual give-and-take between speaker and hearer. It should also be always remembered that this linguistic intercourse takes place not in isolated words as we see them in dictionaries, but by means of connected communications, chiefly in the form of sentences, though not always such complete and well- arranged sentences as form the delight of logicians and rhetoricians. Such sentences are chiefly found in writing, but the enormous in- crease which has taken place during the last few centuries in educa- tion and reading has exercised a profound influence on grammar, even on that of everyday speech.—OTTO JESPERSEN, *Essentials of English Grammar* (London: George Allen & Unwin Ltd., 1933), p. 17.

2.　　We shall need compromises in the days ahead, to be sure. But these will be, or should be, compromises of issues, not of principles. We can compromise our political positions, but not ourselves. We can resolve the clash of interests without conceding our ideals. And even the necessity for the right kind of compromise does not eliminate the need for those idealists and reformers who keep our compromises moving ahead, who prevent all political situations from meeting the description supplied by Shaw: "smirched with compromise, rotted with opportunism, mildewed by expedience, stretched out of shape with wirepulling and putrefied with permea- tion." Compromise need not mean cowardice. Indeed it is frequently the compromisers and conciliators who are faced with the severest tests of political courage as they oppose the extremist views of their constituents. It was because Daniel Webster conscientiously favored compromise in 1850 that he earned a condemnation unsurpassed in the annals of political history.—JOHN F. KENNEDY, *Profiles in Courage* (New York: Harper & Row, 1955), pp. 19–20.

3.　　There are five components that make up a computer: input, control, arithmetic (or logic) unit, memory, and output. As machine intelligence expert, Dr. W. Ross Ashby, points out, we can get no more out of a brain—mechanical or human—than we put into it.

So we must have an input. The kind of input depends largely on the degree of sophistication of the machine we are considering.

With the abacus we set in the problem mechanically, with our fingers. Using a desk calculator we punch buttons: a more refined mechanical input. Punched cards or perforated tapes are much used input methods. As computers evolve rapidly, some of them can "read" for themselves and the input is visual. There are also computers that understand verbal commands.—D. S. HALACY, JR., *Computers: The Machines We Think With* (New York: Harper & Row, 1962), p. 51.

4.   To rejoice in life, to find the world beautiful and delightful to live in, was a mark of the Greek spirit which distinguished it from all that had gone before. It is a vital distinction. The joy of life is written upon everything the Greeks left behind and they who leave it out of account fail to reckon with something that is of first importance in understanding how the Greek achievement came to pass in the world of antiquity. It is not a fact that jumps to the eye for the reason that their literature is marked as strongly by sorrow. The Greeks knew to the full how bitter life is as well as how sweet. Joy and sorrow, exultation and tragedy, stand hand in hand in Greek literature, but there is no contradiction involved thereby. Those who do not know the one do not really know the other either. It is the depressed, the gray-minded people, who cannot rejoice just as they cannot agonize. The Greeks were not the victims of depression. Greek literature is not done in gray or with a low palette. It is all black and shining white or black and scarlet and gold. The Greeks were keenly aware, terribly aware, of life's uncertainty and the imminence of death. Over and over again they emphasize the brevity and the failure of all human endeavor, the swift passing of all that is beautiful and joyful. To Pindar, even as he glorifies the victor in the games, life is "a shadow's dream." But never, not in their darkest moments, do they lose their taste for life. It is always a wonder and a delight, the world a place of beauty, and they themselves rejoicing to be alive in it.—EDITH HAMILTON, *The Greek Way* (New York: W. W. Norton & Company, Inc., 1930, 1942), pp. 32–33.

5.   Whenever an American moves overseas, he suffers from a condition known as "culture shock." Culture shock is simply a removal or distortion of many of the familiar cues one encounters at home and the substitution for them of other cues which are strange. A good deal of what occurs in the organization and use of

space provides important leads as to the specific cues responsible for culture shock.

The Latin house is often built around a patio that is next to the sidewalk but hidden from outsiders behind a wall. It is not easy to describe the degree to which small architectural differences such as this affect outsiders. American Point Four technicians living in Latin America used to complain that they felt "left out" of things, that they were "shut off." Others kept wondering what was going on "behind those walls." In the United States, on the other hand, propinquity is the basis of a good many relationships. To us the neighbor is actually quite close. Being a neighbor endows one with certain rights and privileges, also responsibilities. You can borrow things, including food and drink, but you also have to take your neighbor to the hospital in an emergency. In this regard he has almost as much claim on you as a cousin. For these and other reasons the American tries to pick his neighborhood carefully, because he knows that he is going to be thrown into intimate contact with people. We do not understand why it is that when we live next to people abroad the sharing of adjacent space does not always conform to our own pattern. In France and England, for instance, the relations between neighbors are apt to be cooler than in the United States. Mere propinquity does not tie people together. In England neighbor children do not play as they do in our neighborhoods. When they do play, arrangements are sometimes made a month in advance as though they were coming from the other side of town!—EDWARD T. HALL, *The Silent Language* (New York: Fawcett Publications, Premier Book, 1961), p. 156.

2. Compare the relative length of paragraphs in books, learned and popular journals, and newspapers, and make an assessment of your findings.

3. Evaluate samples of your writing with respect to principles of organization. After making a detailed inventory of strengths and weaknesses, revise one of your papers on the basis of your criticism.

II] Research Techniques and Resources

II. Research Techniques and Methods

13) Research Techniques

INTRODUCTION

Research is fundamentally concerned with the discovery, organization and systematization of knowledge. It involves the careful selection, collation, and interpretation of evidence to help determine how a particular subject fits into the scheme of significant knowledge and how it advances knowledge. In the natural sciences such investigation, known as scientific research, has helped make man the partial conqueror of the physical universe by building on previous knowledge through scholarship and experimentation. In the humanities, scholarship has preserved the documents of earlier civilizations, assessed social, political, and intellectual movements, and interpreted the world's great works of art for us. Intelligent investigation, whether in the laboratory or in the library, is directly responsible for progress.

A student's first attempt at research is likely to be quite modest. Its principal aim may well be limited to the discovery of efficient ways of learning: the formulation of relationships or the exploration of a problem, whether of valence in atomic weight or the social contribution of John Steinbeck's novels.

Some students fear the research paper because certain misconceptions about it have been built up in their minds. The two most common of these are (1) that a research paper is factual and therefore dry; and (2) that the use of many sources must necessarily result in a hodgepodge of ideas. Both of these misconceptions are naïve. The first is mistaken because it assumes that whatever is factual is also dry. Poring over a telephone directory as a leisure activity indicates perhaps that the reader needs the help of a psychiatrist, but for a stranger attempting to locate friends in a city, the telephone directory is a useful, factual tool. A Sears catalog may not provide good bedtime reading, but in some foreign countries it has become the most sought-after item in U.S. Information Agency libraries, because it is a representative index to the American standard of life. Dryness and boredom are relative.

The second misconception that the use of many sources leads to a fragmentary paper is no less naïve. It is as though appreciation of a poem, symphony, or painting were impaired by analysis. On the contrary, mature appreciation is enhanced by study, for the poet, composer, or artist does not create by accident. Similarly, a hypothesis requires documented evidence. The assertion that General Eisenhower was more effective in public relations than in military strategy is an interesting speculation, but without supporting statements it is just that. Obviously such a generalization requires evidence that must be carefully examined for its reliability and bias.

CHOOSING AND NARROWING A TOPIC, SELECTING MATERIAL, AND FORMULATING A HYPOTHESIS

The four most common problems of the student researcher are (1) choosing a topic; (2) selecting and evaluating source material; (3) focusing and narrowing the topic; (4) formulating a hypothesis or a problem.

1. The selection of a topic demands thought and discrimination, because even a modest research project will make special demands on the student's time. The beginner therefore should try to ascertain as early as possible whether his topic is likely to submit to successful treatment.

Topics like the subsidization of college sports, the incidence of cancer and cigarette smoking, juvenile delinquency—which are likely to have been treated in high school—should be avoided. Biographical and historical accounts, which tend to be paraphrased, should also be left alone. A student interested in James Joyce, for example, might consider the relationship of the writer's early life to his autobiographical novel *A Portrait of the Artist as a Young Man* instead of making a purely biographical investigation.

A topic, moreover, must be viewed in the right perspective. A subject like "Why I Believe Fraternities Should be Eliminated from Colleges" is primarily argumentative, and if the student begins his research with the title thus fixed, he can do little except support his position. A serious defect of such an approach is that the student's mind has been made up in advance, no matter how compelling his arguments. The researcher, however, should pursue his subject with an open mind rather than argue a position, and present his judgments buttressed by objective evidence. Approached without bias, the fraternities topic seems unobjectionable, and comparative statistics on accidents, injuries, and fatalities in fraternity initiations compared with college football, for example, might be altogether enlightening. Indeed, the effort to make a considered judgment within this area—or on problems of censorship, South East Asia, or racial or religious discrimination—would seem instructive.

But an investigative paper need not be depersonalized. Students often ask whether they may include their opinions in a research report, assuming that there is a fundamental gap between knowledge gained from experience and knowledge gained from books. Some believe that knowledge derived from experience can be expressed with fervor and originality, but that knowledge derived from books must be translated into stilted prose. There is no reason why an investigative paper cannot have the same vitality expected from a revelation of personal experience. The knowledge from books which gives us access to the total of all recorded experiences—instead of limiting us to our own physical environment—can be just as vivid and compelling as direct personal experience.

2. After selecting his subject, the student should examine the availability of source material, for the authoritativeness of his final report will in large measure depend on the quality of his references. The resources of a college library are discussed in Chapter 16, but some observations on the quality and suitability of materials are appropriate here.

First of all, the student must dismiss the notion that whatever is published is inviolable and that print perforce confers dignity and authority on its author. The experienced researcher is alert to the purpose of a publication, its treatment of a subject, as much as he is to its content. The hallmark of an established publishing house is a greater imprint of confidence than the name of a fly-by-night publisher who may request a subvention from the author. University presses are likely to admit to publication only those works having the approval of experts, but not every publication by an established house or university press is noted by unerring excellence. The copyright date should be considered, for frequently reprinted and revised editions bear testimony to the merits of a book.

Besides the facts of publication, the researcher should consider the presiding aim of a book. If he requires a biography, he should decide whether to use an authorized, a definitive, or a fictionalized biography. A fictionalized biography of Michelangelo like Irving Stone's *The Agony and the Ecstasy* may have romantic appeal but may not be factually accurate, since the writer of fiction enjoys poetic license in rearranging facts to suit his purpose. An authorized biography like H. V. Marrot's *The Life and Letters of John Galsworthy* is usually accurate, but it is a commissioned work that must first be approved by the author or his family who commissioned it. Important facts therefore may sometimes be suppressed. A definitive biography like Richard Ellman's *James Joyce* relies on currently available scholarship and is likely to provide a respectable source of information, though not everyone may agree that Ellman is the only or the best. Indeed, it is advisable to find out whether there is more than one definitive treatment, whatever the subject.

The student should also develop a measure of sophistication about the qualifications of an author and of his purpose in writing a book or article. Albert Einstein was an obvious authority on nuclear physics, but perhaps not so astute a critic of politics. A biography of a presidential candidate published just before an election may well be politically inspired and biased. A popular article generally carries less authority than one in a professional journal.

A further sometimes useful distinction made by the researcher is between what are usually called primary and secondary sources. A primary source is an original document, like Lord Nelson's *Last Diary* or the first folio edition of *Hamlet*. Secondary sources are derivative in that they are based on primary sources. Examples would be a biography of Lord Nelson, like Oliver Warner's *Victory: the Life of Lord Nelson* (1958); or a critical study, like Harry Levin's *The Question of*

Hamlet (1959). Other secondary sources include most textbooks, histories (except eyewitness accounts), critical commentaries, and references. But depending on the subject, the distinction is not always so easy. The difference between *Hamlet*, a primary source, and a critical or textual study of *Hamlet*, a secondary source, is not the same as that between accounts of Nelson written by those who knew him and others written after both Nelson and all those who knew him were dead. With other subjects, moreover, there may be neither primary nor secondary, but only one or the other kind of source. In a study of Shakespearean criticism, for example, it would be difficult to decide what is a primary source and what a secondary source. *Primary* and *secondary* are technical terms and do not connote superiority or inferiority of one or the other type. They make possible a convenient division of sources. Finally, in search for material, the student should not hesitate to ask help from all those people he sees behind counters in the library. They are teachers too, and part of their job is to help him find the right sources.

3. Narrowing the topic to workable proportions prevents the treatment of a book-size subject in 1,500 or even 5,000 words. A history of American musical comedy cannot be presented in a short paper, nor can topics like "The Work of Tennessee Williams" or "The Characters in Arthur Miller's Plays." The classification of Miller's characters is of little interest unless it can be related to another, more significant, problem, such as the criticism of society implicit in Miller's treatment of middle- and lower-class characters. "The Work of Tennessee Williams" is a broad topic for an exhaustive study, but "The Disintegration of Williams' Heroines" or "Symbolism in *The Glass Menagerie*" is a more obtainable goal. Restriction of a subject is essential so that it can be explored in some depth and be informed by a significant purpose. The writer must be able to justify his work.

4. A hypothesis is a tentative, guiding idea which the investigator seeks to expound or demonstrate. Making a hypothesis enables him to focus better on his subject, maintain a consistent point of view, and dismiss peripheral matters. If he develops the hypothesis that the Security Council of the U.N. has a role in maintaining world peace, he can support his argument with an examination of the Security Council and its mode of operation, but if he says that the veto power possessed by each Council member is unfairly exploited by certain nations and fails to show how possession of this power affects world

peace, he has unwittingly confused two separate topics and neglected his hypothesis.

NOTE-TAKING AND NOTE CARDS

To the experienced researcher, note-taking is an essential step, because it is here that the structuring and interpreting of source material begins. In essence, note-taking requires ability to evaluate sources and to discriminate between what is likely to prove pertinent or not. It involves the ability to perceive purpose and point of view, the author's as well as the investigator's. It involves ability to recognize bias, fuzzy thinking, and faulty reasoning.

Even before starting his research, the student should have a fair idea where he is headed. Exploratory reading usually helps him clarify his aim and develop a hypothesis. Once the research has begun, however, he should develop the habit of reading, interpreting, and evaluating his sources simultaneously. He should learn to react to them—in writing—for memory is often untrustworthy. Quotations, paraphrases, and summaries may all appear on the same note card, provided they fall under one discrete heading. Opinions should be carefully separated [by brackets]. Most initial efforts, of course, will probably be more disheveled than those of the unerring and super-efficient researcher who has been at it for a decade or two, but the sooner the student adopts an efficient procedure—one that works—the more productive he will surely be. Here is a passage, followed by a possible note card based on an excerpt from Frederick L. Allen's *Only Yesterday* (New York: Harper & Row, 1957), a spirited account of America in the twenties:

At home, one of the most conspicuous results of prosperity was the conquest of the whole country by urban tastes and urban dress and the urban way of living. The rube disappeared. Girls in the villages of New Hampshire and Wyoming wore the same brief skirts and used the same lipsticks as their sisters in New York. The proletariat—or what the radicals of the Big Red Scare days had called the proletariat—gradually lost its class consciousness; the American Federation of Labor dwindled in membership and influence; the time had come when workingmen owned second-hand Buicks and applauded Jimmy Walker, not objecting in the least, it seemed, to his exquisite clothes, his valet, and his frequent visits to the millionaire-haunted sands of Palm Beach. It was no accident that men like

Mellon and Hoover and Morrow found their wealth an asset rather than a liability in public office, or that there was a widespread popular movement to make Henry Ford President in 1924. The possession of millions was a sign of success, and success was worshipped the country over.

—FREDERICK L. ALLEN, *Only Yesterday*, pp. 176–177.

Note Card

```
Post-war prosperity:  social patterns        Allen, Only Yesterday

176-  In the United States prosperity was accompanied by (1) the
177   spread of urban manners and fashions to the country, (2)
      the diminishing of class consciousness between rich and
      poor, and (3) the worship of wealth and its identification
      with success.

      (1)  short skirts and lipstick appeared in hinterland.
      (2)  A.F. of L. membership decreased; workers began to own
           cars.
      (3)  Henry Ford-for-President movement in 1924.  Mellon,
           Hoover, Morrow, wealthy men, held public office.

      [For the influence of advertising during this period, see
      Allen, pp. 176-177.]
```

The note card contains, first, a summary of the source material; second, illustrations of the three points contained in the summary; and third, a self-reminder by the writer—in brackets—to relate the information to Allen's treatment of advertising elsewhere in the book. The shortened bibliographical reference to the source is sufficient, because complete bibliographical information is almost always recorded on a separate bibliography card in the same way as a bibliographical entry at the end of a paper. (See pp. 178–179.)

QUOTING

Quoting means the verbatim transcription of material from another source. Since it is the easiest way of gathering information, the beginner is prone to fill his note cards with too many quotations, and to cite these quotations in his final paper. Often he thinks, incorrectly, that he can reduce the quotations to his own words later. This works well in theory but not in practice. For one thing, he postpones one of the essential steps of research, the interpretation and evaluation of his source material. Meanwhile, important details grow indistinct, the context of the quoted passage becomes blurred, and the original purpose of transcribing is forgotten. For this reason quotations should be kept to a minimum and reserved for unusually striking items which enhance, rather than weaken, the final paper. Some readers are as likely to skip quotations as not. A good rule of thumb, therefore, is to use as few of them as possible.

The writer must be careful to quote his material accurately and not omit key words or phrases. But he is perfectly free to exclude non-pertinent words or passages, provided the omission does not distort the quotation. For example:

> I believe—and I conceive the Constitution of the United States to rest . . . upon the fundamental proposition of the integrity of the individual; and that all government and all private institutions must be designed to promote and protect and defend the integrity and the dignity of the individual; that that is the essential meaning of the Constitution and the Bill of Rights. . . .—DAVID E. LILIENTHAL, *This I Do Believe*

The omission of two items, "as does religion" and "as it is essentially the meaning of religion" (shown by ellipses), does not affect the essence of the passage: that the Constitution is based on the concept of the inviolability of the individual. The omission of "and all private institutions," on the other hand, would be a serious misrepresentation of Mr. Lilienthal's statement.

PARAPHRASING

A paraphrase refers to the restatement of a passage with the meaning and intent of the original carefully preserved. It is more detailed than a summary. Here is a passage, followed by an unsatisfactory and a satisfactory paraphrase of a paragraph from Clyde Kluckhohn's *Mirror for Man:*

> Status in the United States is determined more by the number and price of automobiles, air-conditioning units, and the like owned by a family than by the number of their servants or the learning and aesthetic skills of family members. In fact, Americans usually are scared out of being artists. There is reverence only for the man who "does *things* in a big way." Most Americans do subscribe to the current Einstein legend, but *Time* has recently pointed out that many did not take this very

seriously until they were told that Einstein's "theories" had made the atomic bomb possible. It is significant that Edison is a household name, whereas only the professors have heard of Willard Gibbs.
—CLYDE KLUCKHOHN, *Mirror for Man*

Unsatisfactory paraphrase:

Status in the U.S. is determined by the price of automobiles, air-conditioning units, not by the number of servants or the knowledge and aesthetic skills of family members. Indeed, Americans usually are frightened out of being artistic. There is admiration only for the man who "does *things* in a big way." Most Americans subscribe to the current Einstein legend, but *Time* has recently shown that many did not take this very seriously until they were informed that Einstein's "theories" had been responsible for the atom bomb. It is significant that Edison is a household name, whereas only teachers have heard of Willard Gibbs.

The paraphrase is unsatisfactory because it follows the author's wording too closely, and because it changes the meaning of the passage. Some changes are merely grammatical: *atomic* to *atom* and *artists* to *artistic*. Words like *knowledge* and *teachers* are substituted for *learning*, and *professors*, as though synonyms could be interchanged indiscriminately. The omission of *more by . . . than* in the first sentence changes a tentative statement into a categorical one, and the phrase *had been responsible for the atom bomb* instead of *had made the atomic bomb possible* suggests that Einstein was morally accountable for the development of the bomb.

Here is an adequate paraphrase of the same paragraph:

Kluckhohn says that Americans define status more by material possessions like automobiles and air-conditioners than by number of servants or intellectual or aesthetic achievement. They admire the practical man rather than the artist or the intellectual. Although Einstein is popularly accepted, most people, according to an article in *Time* referred to by Kluckhohn, did not appreciate his importance until they learned that his theories had evolved the atomic bomb. All Americans have heard of Edison, but only a few are familiar with Willard Gibbs.

The paraphrase preserves the meaning of the original text, though the wording has been altered. The second and third sentences in the original have been condensed into one. The reference to *Time* has been kept to show the source of one of the author's illustrations.

SUMMARIZING

A summary is an abridgment, whether of a paragraph, article, or book, into a clear, concise statement, usually one-third or less the length of the original. A sentence or two generally suffice for a paragraph, and a paragraph is usually enough for an article. Here is a passage, followed by two summaries, from Jacques Barzun's *Teacher in America:*

> Above the beginner's level, the important fact is that writing cannot be taught exclusively in a course called English Composition. Writing can only be taught by the united efforts of the entire teaching staff. This holds good of any school, college, or university. Joint effort is needed, not merely to "enforce the rules"; it is needed to insure accuracy in every subject. How can an answer in physics or a translation from the French or an historical statement be called correct if the phrasing is loose or the key word wrong? Students argue that the reader of the paper knows perfectly well what is meant. Probably so, but a written exercise is designed to be read; it is not supposed to be a challenge to clairvoyance. My Italian-born tailor periodically sends me a postcard which runs: "Your clothes is ready and should come down for a fitting." I understand him, but the art I honor him for is cutting cloth, not precision of utterance. Now a student in college must be inspired to achieve in all subjects the utmost accuracy of perception combined with the utmost artistry of expression. The two merge and develop the sense of good workmanship, of preference for quality and truth, which is the chief mark of the genuinely educated man.
> —JACQUES BARZUN, *Teacher in America*

Summaries:

> The teaching of writing above the beginner's level cannot be restricted to a course in English composition, but must be shared by the whole faculty. The predominant aim of teaching writing should be understanding of, and accurate, felicitous, and correct expression in, every subject, for ability to use language responsibly and well characterizes the educated man.

> The ability to express oneself is important not only in education but in all phases of life. Syntactically correct composition is imperative for any subject, so that any person reading a composition is able to understand it fully. To be able to express himself in words is a true mark of an educated man.

Of the two summaries, both approximately fifty words, the first is clearly the better. It neatly sums up the three main points made in the original passage: (1) that the responsibility of teaching writing above the beginner's level rests on the entire faculty rather than on the instructor of English composition alone; (2) that the aim is to help a student achieve understanding of each subject and skill in expressing himself correctly and effectively; (3) that judicious command of language distinguishes an educated man.

The second summary, impaired by its lack of accuracy, overlooks at least one major point: that the obligation to teach writing should be shared by the entire teaching staff. It incorrectly attributes statements to Barzun who says nothing about the importance of writing well in "all phases of life." Nor does he say that "to be able to express himself in words is a true mark of an educated man." Presumably all of us can express ourselves in words, but not everyone can use language competently. Finally, the assertion that writing should be correct "so that any person reading a composition is able to understand it fully" is implied in the first sentence and hence unnecessary.

In a summary, then, the student should carefully distinguish main points from supporting evidence, so that misleading or incorrect statements will not be attributed to the source. He should also make certain that he does not distort the passage to be abridged.

A NOTE ON PLAGIARISM

Plagiarism (L. *plagiarius*, kidnapper) means the use of another writer's material without proper acknowledgment. Copying passages from printed sources without properly acknowledging them is as un-ethical as passing another student's paper off as one's own. There is a difference, to be sure, between plagiarism as a moral problem—as deliberate intent to deceive—and as an educational problem, the way some students are drawn into it a little at a time. The beginning writer may be careless in the use of quotation marks, or he may think that he has sufficiently paraphrased his material when he has changed only an occasional word or two. More importantly, he may present another writer's ideas as his own without realizing that he has plagiarized. Whether ideas are quoted or summarized, they must be acknowledged if they are someone else's. This is not only cour-teous but proper.

Sometimes it is difficult to decide whether an idea is unique or sufficiently well known to preclude documentation. General knowledge, such as the date of America's entry into World War II, the authorship of a play like *The Skin of Our Teeth* or *Streetcar Named Desire*, or a quote from Lincoln's Gettysburg Address, requires no citation, but George Jean Nathan's assessment of *Death of a Salesman*, for example, demands acknowledgment. Standard devices like footnotes are available for documenting information, but acknowledgments can also be incorporated in the text of a paper or listed at the end. Formal investigative papers require a critical apparatus consisting of footnotes and a bibliography. These will be taken up later.

OUTLINING

An outline reveals the structure of an article, chapter, or book. Its principal value is that it lets the writer verbalize his thoughts and see them in context. Putting thoughts on paper also stimulates the flow of ideas. Of course an outline is only as good as the writer's control of his material. An effective outline therefore depends on the student's mastery of his subject and his ability to discriminate between main and supporting points. Defects in outlining often indicate basic weaknesses in organization and call for careful analysis and rethinking.

Though the ideal time to outline is before composing the first draft, much can be said for the practice of outlining afterwards, especially for those students who have little luck with outlining in advance— and this undoubtedly includes the vast majority. The practice of refrigerating the first draft for a few days and then seeing whether it will submit to outline often proves to be a helpful, if somewhat shocking, experience. Certainly this is an expedient way of discovering gaps and other imperfections. However unconventional, such an approach to organization usually gets improved results for those who try it. It may also teach that economy of utterance and fullness of development are not mutually exclusive.

The three most common formal outlines are topic, sentence, and paragraph outlines. A topic outline consists of phrase heads and subheads related to each other and to the statement of purpose, which proclaims the thesis of the discourse. A sentence outline, consisting of complete statements, is necessarily more explicit than phrase heads in a topic outline. A paragraph outline abstracts each paragraph, thereby indicating more the sequence of paragraphs than the structure of the discourse as a whole.

Another type of outline is the preliminary outline, consisting of jottings by the writer as he evolves his design. The term *preliminary* is preferable to *working* outline, as it is sometimes called, because all types of outlines should in fact be working outlines. Their purpose is to help evolve a presentable scheme.

The following points should be remembered in outlining: (1) Parts logically related to each other should be presented under similar headings; that is, I and II should be equally important in relation to each other and to the topic as a whole. (2) A subdivision calls for at least two subheads, since logically nothing can be divided unless it yields two or more parts. A subdivision of point C, for example, requires subheads 1 and 2. (3) The grammatical structure of items under similar headings should be parallel; that is, if I and II are noun phrases, III should be a noun phrase. (4) Introductions and conclusions are omitted from outlines. The following sentence outline of Bertrand Russell's essay "The Functions of a Teacher"[1] illustrates these points:

I. The curtailment of the traditional rights of teachers to engage in the free pursuit of knowledge poses serious dangers.
   A. In totalitarian states the teaching of narrow nationalism has destroyed the concept of a common cultural heritage.
   B. In democratic societies there has been some tendency to appoint teachers on the basis of nationality rather than competence.

II. Serious consequences to education in democratic societies can be averted if the functions of the teacher are clearly understood.
   A. The teacher must be free to reject dogmatism.
   B. He must be free to pursue ideas dispassionately.
   C. He must be free to present the achievements of all mankind.
   D. He must want to develop young minds and to help students achieve a satisfying life.

III. At present teachers cannot discharge their functions adequately.
   A. They must train students for examinations rather than inspire them intellectually.
   B. They are expected to keep students ignorant of reality.
   C. They are dominated by bureaucrats and bigots.

[1] *Unpopular Essays* (New York: Simon & Schuster, 1950), pp. 112–123.

A formal outline gives the reader an overall view of a topic, as the example shows, but it is by no means essential to a presentation whose form and substance are skillfully wedded.

Note: For exercises, see the end of Chapter 15.

14) Documentation

In a report or investigative paper based on research in a library or elsewhere, acknowledgment of the sources consulted or used is made in the form of footnotes. Models of footnotes and a sample bibliography of books, periodicals, newspapers, and government publications are presented in this chapter.

FOOTNOTES

There are many different systems for handling footnotes. Certain forms of citations are preferred by some publishers as a matter of house style, and variations are found within specific fields.[1]

Footnotes are used for several purposes: primarily for the acknowledgment of borrowed material; for identifying for the reader the sources of quotations, statements of facts and opinions; for presenting

[1] The form of citations from books and periodicals used here and elsewhere in the present book follows the style recommended by the Modern Language Association (with one exception: the inclusion of the publisher's name, to conform to the Harper & Row style). The style recommended for government publications has been taken from the *Harper & Row Author's Manual* (New York: Harper & Row, 1966). The beginning student will find the material in this chapter adequate for his purposes, but if his needs exceed those discussed here, he should consult the *MLA Style Sheet* (rev. ed.), compiled by William R. Parker. A copy of the *MLA Style Sheet* may be obtained from Treasurer, MLA, 6 Washington Square North, New York, N.Y. 10003. The price is nominal.

material amplifying information in the text; and for cross references to other parts of the work.

The reference number is placed slightly above the line at the end of the quotation or after a statement borrowed from a source. Except for the dash, the number follows punctuation.

The footnotes, numbered consecutively in Arabic numbers through-out a short paper or a chapter, are placed at the bottom of the page containing the reference figure.

Books

Footnotes referring to books contain the following information given in this order:

1. Name(s) of author(s)
2. Title of article or chapter
3. Title of the work
4. Name(s) of editor(s)
5. Edition used, if not the first
6. Publishing information: place of publication (city), publisher, year of publication, volume number, page reference(s)

FOR A SINGLE BOOK BY A SINGLE AUTHOR

[1] Jacques Barzun, *Teacher in America* (Boston: Little, Brown, 1945), p. 48.

The following conventions should be noted:

1. The author's given name precedes his surname.
2. A comma separates the author's name from the title of the book.
3. The title of the book is italicized (underlined in typescript).
4. Parentheses are used to enclose the place and date of publication, and the name of the publisher. A colon follows the place of publication and a comma the name of the publisher. No punctuation is used before the open parenthesis.
5. A comma is used to separate the details of publication from the page number(s).
6. The abbreviation for *page* is *p.*; for *pages*, *pp.*
7. Unless the source cited has Roman numerals, Arabic numerals are used to designate page references.

FOR PARTIAL REFERENCE GIVEN IN TEXT

If a portion of the source is identified in the text, it is not repeated in the footnote:

In his *Teacher in America*, Jacques Barzun says, ". . ."[2]

Only the place, publisher, the date of publication, and the page reference are cited in the footnote:

[2] (Boston: Little, Brown, 1945), p. 48.

FOR REFERENCE TO A WORK OF MORE THAN ONE VOLUME

[3] Harley Granville-Barker, *Prefaces to Shakespeare* (Princeton: Princeton University Press, 1946), I, 108.

Note that (1) a capital Roman numeral is used to indicate the volume; (2) the abbreviation *p.* or *pp.* is omitted when a volume number is used.

FOR REFERENCE TO AN ARTICLE OR ESSAY IN A COLLECTION

[4] Sir John Fortescue, "George Whyte-Melville," in *The Eighteen-sixties*, ed. John Drinkwater (New York: The Macmillan Company, 1932), pp. 244–245.

Note that (1) the title of the essay is enclosed in quotation marks; (2) the editor's name follows the title of the book from which the essay is cited; (3) the abbreviation *ed.* is used, with no punctuation following.

If a collection has three or more editors, the name of one editor and the abbreviation *et al.* can be used, but only if the reference is to an article, not the collection. Note this example from the *MLA Style Sheet:*

[5] Baldwin Maxwell, "Middleton's *The Phoenix*," *Joseph Quincy Adams Memorial Studies*, ed. James G. McManaway et al. . . .

The abbreviation *et al.* may or may not be italicized.

FOR REFERENCE TO THE COLLECTED WORKS OF AN AUTHOR

[6] *The Poetical Works of Edmund Spenser*, ed. J. C. Smith and E. DeSelincourt (London: Oxford University Press, 1912), p. 56.

Note that (1) the author's name appears as part of the title; (2) the editors' names follow the title of the work, preceded by the abbreviation *ed.* ("edited by").

FOR REFERENCE TO A SIGNED OR UNSIGNED ARTICLE IN AN ENCYCLOPEDIA

A signed article:

[7] Lillyan Seymour, "Theatre," *Encyclopaedia Britannica* (1959), XXII, 28–44.

Note that the initials of an author's name appear at the end of an article, but the full name may be ascertained by consulting Volume I of the *Britannica*. The year of publication of the *Britannica* is synonymous with the edition. This practice is fairly recent, and older editions, such as the eleventh or fourteenth, should be clearly marked.

An unsigned article:

[8] "Proscenium," *Encyclopaedia Britannica* (1959), XVIII, 591.

With the exception of the author's name, the entry for an unsigned article is the same as that for a signed article.

FOR REFERENCE TO A SIGNED ARTICLE IN A SOURCE BOOK

[9] Harold Child, "Nineteenth-century Drama," *Cambridge History of English Literature*, ed. Sir A. W. Ward and A. R. Waller (Cambridge, Eng.: Cambridge University Press, 1932), XIII, 255–274.

The editors' names are included in the citation. Note also that it is desirable to identify the country—England—because there is a Cambridge, Massachusetts.

FOR LATER REFERENCES TO A CITED SOURCE

Footnotes referring to a previously cited source require only the author's name and page citation, provided the source is the only work by the author referred to:

[10] Barzun, p. 61.

If two or more works of an author are used, the citation must also include the title:

[11] Barzun, *Teacher in America*, p. 61.
[12] Barzun, *The House of Intellect*, p. 60.

A long title may be shortened in subsequent citations:

13 Edmund Spenser, *Complete Poetical Works*, ed. R. E. Neil Dodge (Boston: Houghton, 1908), pp. 112–116.

14 Spenser, *Works*, p. 56.

USE OF *ibid.*, *op. cit.*, *loc. cit.*

The use of the Latin abbreviations *ibid.* (*ibidem*, in the same place), *op. cit.* (*opere citato*, in the work cited), or *loc. cit.* (*loco citato*, in the place cited) is optional.

The abbreviation *ibid.* is used when the same source as in the immediately preceding note is cited. One could use *ibid.*, for example, for footnote 14 above.

14 *Ibid.*, p. 56.

The abbreviation is italicized and followed by a period. As the first word in the citation, it is capitalized.

The abbreviation *op. cit.* is used when a source is previously mentioned, but not in the immediately preceding footnote.

15 Elizabeth Longford, *Queen Victoria* (New York: Harper & Row, 1964), pp. 131–133.

16 . . .

17 Longford, *op. cit.*, p. 102.

Only the last name of the author is used. However, if there are two authors with the same last name, the first name or initials of both authors are retained.

The abbreviation *loc. cit.* is used to cite a particular passage referred to in an earlier note. The abbreviation appears with the author's name, but not with a page reference, since the page reference is the same as that of the passage cited.

FOR BOOKS OF THE BIBLE AND THE CLASSICS

After the first full citation in a footnote, abbreviated forms may be used *in the text* immediately following the quotation:

(Gen. i.1.)
(*Oth.* III.iii.105–106.)

Clearly it was the tragedy "of one that lov'd not wisely, but too well" (*Oth.* V.ii.344).

Note that (1) books of the Bible are not italicized; (2) periods—not commas—without spacing are used; (3) the period is included inside the parentheses if the quotation stands alone; the period is placed outside the close parenthesis if the quotation is incorporated in a sentence.

Periodicals and Newspapers

Footnotes referring to periodicals contain the following information:

1. Name(s) of author(s)
2. Title of article
3. Name of the periodical
4. Volume number
5. Year (month and date if applicable)
6. Page number(s)

[18] Richard M. Kain, "Galsworthy, the Last Victorian Liberal," *The Madison Quarterly*, IV (1944), 84–94.

Note that (1) the title of the article is enclosed in quotation marks; (2) the name of the journal is italicized; (3) a capital Roman numeral is used for the volume; (4) the year of the publication is enclosed in parentheses, followed by a comma; (5) *p.* or *pp.* is omitted because a volume number is used.

If the pagination of the journal is not cumulative, the day and month are cited in addition to the volume and year of publication:

[19] David Garnett, "Books in General," *New Statesmen*, IV (July 8, 1933), 46.

The style for newspapers is as follows:

[20] "A British Film Festival," *The Times*, June 17, 1931, p. 12.

Note that (1) the article—unsigned—is enclosed in quotation marks; (2) the name of the newspaper is underlined (the citation is to the London newspaper, not *The New York Times*); (3) the date is set off by commas, not enclosed in parentheses; (4) the page reference is preceded by *p.* because no volume number is used.

FOR GOVERNMENT DOCUMENTS AND PUBLICATIONS

The form for citations from government publications is the same as for a book.

[21] Hazel K. Stiebeling, "Food in Our Lives," in *Food: The Yearbook of Agriculture* (Washington, D.C.: U.S. Department of Agriculture, 1959), p. 5.

[22] *Juvenile Court Statistics*, No. 65 (Washington, D.C.: Children's Bureau, U.S. Department of Health, Education and Welfare, 1961), p. 11.

COMMON ABBREVIATIONS USED IN FOOTNOTES AND BIBLIOGRAPHIES

Abbreviations are used for titles of scholarly publications or dictionaries: PMLA (*Publications of the Modern Language Association*), CE (*College English*), OED (*Oxford English Dictionary*), DNB (*Dictionary of National Biography*). Other abbreviations frequently used in footnotes and bibliographies include the following:

anon.	anonymous
bk., bks.	book(s)
c. or ca. (*circa*)	about
cf. (*confer*)	compare
ch., chs., or chap., chaps.	chapter(s)
ed.	edited by, edition
e.g. (*exempli gratia*)	for example
f., ff.	following (f. indicates one following page; ff. more than one)
i.e. (*id est*)	that is
introd.	introduction
l., ll.	line(s)
n.	note (p. 91n. refers to a footnote in a source on p. 91)
n.d.	no date (of publication)
no., nos.	number(s)
n.p.	no place (of publication)
pref.	preface
pub. or publ.	published by
rev.	revised by
tr. or trans.	translated by, translation
vol., vols.	volume(s)

BIBLIOGRAPHY

An alphabetically arranged list of references used in a report is often included at the end of a documented paper. Although a bibliography is optional in a short paper, an alphabetical list of references is often useful to the critical reader, giving him an immediate idea of the range and quality of the investigator's sources.

A bibliography differs from a footnote as follows: (1) the author's given name follows his surname; (2) a period sets off the author's name from the title; (3) a period follows the title, or the name of the editor(s); (4) books, collections, or books in a series require no page references (only periodicals and newspapers do), but the total number of volumes in a series or collection is given. The following is a sample bibliography:

"A British Film Festival," *The Times*, June 17, 1931, p. 12.

Barzun, Jacques. *The House of Intellect*. New York: Harper & Row, 1959.

————. *Teacher in America*. Boston: Little, Brown, 1945.

Child, Harold. "Nineteenth-century Drama," *Cambridge History of English Literature*, ed. Sir A. W. Ward and A. R. Waller. 15 vols. Cambridge, Eng.: Cambridge University Press, 1932.

Fortescue, Sir John. "George Whyte-Melville," *The Eighteen-Sixties*, ed. John Drinkwater. New York: The Macmillan Company, 1932.

Garnett, David. "Books in General," *New Statesman*, VI (July 8, 1933), 46.

Granville-Barker, Harley. *Prefaces to Shakespeare*. 2 vols. Princeton: Princeton University Press, 1946.

Juvenile Court Statistics, No. 65. Washington, D.C.: Children's Bureau, U.S. Department of Health, Education and Welfare, 1961.

Kain, Richard M. "Galsworthy, the Last Victorian Liberal," *The Madison Quarterly*, IV (1944), 84–94.

"Proscenium," *Encyclopaedia Britannica* (1959), XVIII, 591.

Seymour, Lillyan. "Theatre," *Encyclopaedia Britannica* (1959), XXII, 28–44.

Spenser, Edmund. *The Poetical Works of Edmund Spenser*, ed. J. C. Smith and E. DeSelincourt. London: Oxford University Press, 1912.

The sample bibliography includes both primary and secondary sources, books as well as journals. The investigator may subdivide his list, but he should do so only if he has at least several items for each subheading. In an extensive appraisal of John Galsworthy, for example, he might find it useful to classify his references into (1) Galsworthy's writings, (2) biographical and critical studies of Galsworthy, and (3) historical and social background.

Note: For exercises, see the end of Chapter 15.

15) *Revision at Work*

Revision is rethinking to give a paper the appearance of effortless prose—effortless to the reader as though the writing had a life of its own. A sophisticated reader, of course, immediately recognizes such effort, for he knows that a well-written paper is not achieved by inspiration alone.

There are no strictly defined rules for revising. All generalizations about good writing apply, and these generalizations work for most purposes. Occasionally, a student may reach a point where he can evolve his own practices. He knows what will work for him. He may find that he can write most effectively in his first draft and that too many changes impede the flow and intensity of his prose. Or he may find that to write well, he has to write five or six drafts.

To professional writers revision is an integral part of composing. Somerset Maugham, commenting on the effortless quality of Colette's prose—and on his own—says this:

> I was exceedingly surprised to hear that she wrote everything over and over again. She told me that she would often spend a whole morning working upon a single page. But it does not matter how one gets the effect of ease. For my part, if I get it at all, it is only by strenuous effort. Nature seldom provides me with the word, the turn of phrase, that is appropriate without being far-fetched or commonplace.[1]

[1] Somerset Maugham, *The Summing Up* (Garden City, N.Y.: Doubleday, 1938), p. 43.

Although every American is familiar with the Declaration of Independence as it appears in the parchment copy, few know that it underwent a series of major changes before its acceptance by Congress. From the time Thomas Jefferson sent a draft to Benjamin Franklin until its presentation to Congress, twenty-six alterations were made in the document. Of these, twenty-three involved changes in wording and three the addition of new paragraphs.[2] Many of the revisions, such as those in the opening sentence, had far-reaching implications:[3]

When in the course of human events it becomes necessary for a *one* people to *dissolve the political bands which have connected them with another, and to* ~~advance from that subordination in~~ ~~which they have hitherto remained, & to~~ assume among the powers of the earth the *separate and equal* ~~equal & independent~~ station

to which the laws of nature & of nature's god entitle them,

a decent respect to the opinions of mankind requires that they should declare the causes which impel them to *the separation* ~~the~~ ~~change.~~

The writers of the Declaration, as Carl Becker points out, wished to assert that the colonists were a free people, exercising their rights "against a usurping king" not "against established political authority."[4] They were severing political bonds as equals, not advancing from a position of inferiority. The substitution of "separate and equal" for "equal and independent," and of "separation" for "change," moreover, shows that they were less concerned about forms of government than political separation from a ruler who had abused the "natural rights" of free men to "life, liberty and the pursuit of happiness."

Few writers achieve a finished prose style in their first draft. Initial efforts need to be rethought and refined. The first draft of this section, twice as long as the present version, contained an analogy that was at first appealing to its author. Revision was compared to a step in the

[2] Carl L. Becker, *The Declaration of Independence* (New York: Knopf, Vintage Books, 1958), p. 151.

[3] Becker, p. 160.

[4] Becker, p. 203.

construction of a wooden bookcase. The purchase of the wood, the cutting of the parts to shape, and the joining of the pieces were compared to the choice of a subject, research in the library, and organization of the material. Applying oil stain to bring out the grain and configurations of the wood was considered analogous to revising the manuscript so as to give it unity, coherence, and clarity. The final step—varnishing and polishing to bring out the softness of the wood and to make it seem as though the whole had been carved skillfully from a single piece—this step was held analogous to proofreading to eliminate minor imperfections and to making the writing seem easy and effortless to the reader, an attempt through the conscious application of art to conceal art.

This analogy is false. While the steps in building a bookcase and writing a paper may be comparable, the implication that they are alike in sequence is erroneous and therefore had to be abandoned. The purpose in building a bookcase is always the same, and if the builder knows his craft, he will always create a piece of furniture having essentially the same use, the same overall construction, and the same value to most people. As a composition evolves, however, the writer may find that his intention must be modified, that the facts he has uncovered demand a reappraisal of his work. He may have to change his outline, discard a long-cherished point of view, and in some instances abandon his topic and start afresh. Writing is a process that can be broken down and analyzed, as indeed it is in rhetoric texts and handbooks of composition. Yet the informed writer knows that after he has absorbed all the available wisdom on how to write, he must in the end rely on his own resources. In the process of composition he is necessarily alone, however useful the advice of teachers and handbooks. The analogy of writing to building a bookcase, while it is appealing because of its step-by-step procedure, is weakened when applied to the process of composition. That is why it was discarded from this section originally, though later restored to serve as an example of revision at work.

REVISING A RESEARCH PAPER

Another example of revision at work is the student research paper (pp. 184 ff.) with grammatical, stylistic, and interpretive problems. A commentary is found opposite each page of text.

The Style of W. Somerset Maugham

by Louise Landon

1   Maugham's style is the product of repeated failures--failures

2   to achieve a style that the novelist considered worthy of merit.

3   After long years of self-conscious imitation, he realized that his
,especially Dryden and Swift,
emulation of eighteenth-century models/restrained his own talents.
4   ~~search-for-a-style-was-keeping-him-from-saying-what-he-had-to-say.~~

H   his attempts
5   When he abandoned ~~this-effort,-he-could-write-more-freely-what-was~~

and evolved a style, uniquely his own, marked by
6   ~~in-his-heart,-and-it-was-natural-for-him-to-aim-for~~ lucidity, sim-

7   plicity, and euphony. ~~Thus-he-became-the-father-of-a-style-uniquely~~

8   ~~his-own-that-few-writers-have-been-able-to-equal-or-even-imitate-it.~~

9   ~~Maugham-is-neither-an-imitation-of-any-other-writers,-nor-a-combina-~~

10   ~~tion-of-successful-stylists.--Maugham-is-Maugham.~~

,
11   Lucidity ~~is~~ perhaps the ~~most~~ outstanding quality of Maugham's

style, derives its power from his precision and adequacy of detail.
12   ~~writing.--He-says-exactly-what-he-means,-leaving-nothing-to-the~~

He explicitly guides the reader's imagination up to the point where
13   ~~imagination-(except,-perhaps,-a-little-irony,-which-a-casual-reader~~

it ought to take over.
14   ~~could-miss).~~ In Of Human Bondage, Philip's various bondages are

COMMENTARY

LINE(S)

3–4   The reader is interested in knowing some of the writers whom Maugham imitated, because they reveal his literary tastes. Swift and Dryden are well known for their clear, incisive prose, their irony and wit. Maugham refers to these writers in *The Summing Up*.

4–5   That "his search for a style was keeping him from saying what he had to say" is not altogether true. The student evidently means that Maugham's imitation of other writers prevented him from giving spontaneous utterance to his own thoughts; that "his emulation of eighteenth-century models, especially Dryden and Swift, restrained his own talents."

5–7   "When he abandoned this effort, he could write more freely what was in his heart, and it was natural for him to aim for lucidity, simplicity, and euphony." The statement implies that Maugham's abandonment of models freed him to write whatever his heart dictated, and that his desire to write lucidly, simply, and euphoniously was quite natural. It is doubtful if any style can be attained "naturally." More likely, it involves long, laborious training. Maugham's imitation of models was part of this training.

7–10   These sentences seem to round out the opening paragraph by emphasizing Maugham's unique qualities as a stylist, but closer inspection shows that they contribute little to the subject. "Thus he became the father of a style" is reminiscent of clichés like "father of his country" or "father of the atomic submarine." Nor is there any evidence that Maugham developed a following among young writers. The hyperbole "few writers have been able to equal or even imitate it" [his style] would be difficult to prove. "Maugham is neither an imitation" is not quite correct; perhaps the student meant "imitator." "Maugham is *Maugham*" is gratuitous information. The last three sentences of the first paragraph are deleted in the revised version.

11   Qualifiers like "most," "very," "quite," often weaken rather than strengthen a sentence.

12–14   "He says exactly what he means, leaving nothing to the imagination (except, perhaps, a little irony, which a casual reader could miss)." The sentence does not express the writer's intent. Surely any artist is concerned with the imagination. If Maugham left "nothing to the imagination except perhaps a little irony, which a casual reader could

struggle to escape them

15   the undisguised backbone of the plot, ~~and~~ his ~~release-from-them~~

16   is always apparent to the reader. His ecstasy, for instance, upon

17   leaving school, is shadowed by passing doubts at getting his own

18   way; his sense of religious freedom is circumscribed by the sub-

19   conscious ties which remain; his admission of failure as an artist

20   is accompanied by a deep emotional release. These are but a few of

self-

21   the clearly defined milestones in Philip's progress toward ~~complete~~

fulfillment.

22 ~~release-from-bondage~~.

23   The second quality, simplicity, seems to come easily to Maugham,

gives us a glimpse of his struggle to

24   though in The Summing Up he ~~lets-us-glimpse-at-the-difficulty-he~~

achieve it.

25 ~~experienced-in-attaining-it,-and-tells-of-the-discipline-that-is~~

The simplicity of his style

26 ~~necessary-for-producing-effortless-prose.--He-gives-the-reader-an~~

lies in his choice of detail and

27 ~~appreciation-of-his-austerity-of-words,-which-is-easily-recognized~~

28 ~~in-his~~ characterization. The gold crosses worn by the Careys, for

suggest excessive religious formalism, which frustrates

29 instance, ~~are-an-immediate-sign-of-their-formality-in-religion~~,

Philip's desire to know God.

30 ~~which-also-suggests-a-reason-for-Philip's-failure-to-attain-a~~

31 ~~personal-relationship-with-God-during-the-years-he-spent-with-them~~.

LINE(S)

miss," he would hardly be worth reading. Perhaps the writer intended to convey the idea that Maugham "explicitly guides the reader's imagination up to the point where it ought to take over." The reference to irony in Maugham's style is too important really to be dismissed. Irony deserves some treatment in a discussion of Maugham's style.

Another objection is that the first sentence of this paragraph deals with lucidity, and the second with precision and explicitness which are not necessarily synonymous with lucidity, the sense of immediate understanding. Perhaps the student means that Maugham's lucidity derives its strength from his precision and adequancy of detail. The revision, in any event, is based on this assumption.

15–16　The phrase "release from them" implies that Philip, hero of the novel, is a passive character. This is partly true, but the writer underestimates Philip's struggle to achieve freedom from spiritual, intellectual, and emotional bondage. The revision asserts this more firmly.

21–22　"Self-fulfilment" in the revised version points to Philip's achievement in line with ideas conveyed by "milestones" and "progress."

23–26　The second part of the sentence attempts to say that Maugham struggled to achieve simplicity. Revision of the subordinate clause eliminates unnecessary words.

26–28　Insertion of "choice of detail" points forward to the next sentence.

28–31　"The gold crosses . . . them." The sentence requires clarification.

Maugham describes

32   ~~More-specifically~~, Mr. Carey's vanity ~~is-apparent-in~~ his "hair,

his   ;
33   worn long/ arranged over the scalp so as to conceal/baldness/"

Mrs. Carey's   nostalgia, her
34   ~~and-his-wife's~~ pathetic ~~triteness-is-paraphrased-in~~ "gray hair

35   . . . arranged in ringlets according to the fashion of her youth."

He artfully contrasts
36   ~~Perhaps-the-masterpiece-of-simplicity-in-characterization-is-his~~

...
37   ~~artful contrast~~ of Mildred's unwholesome "thin lips/ faint green

38   colour"and"bored look" to Sally's healthy attractiveness and bright

39   attitude.

fills
40   The third quality, euphony, ~~finds-its-way-into~~ almost every

T   include
41   page of the novel. ~~Among~~ ⟨t⟩he best examples ~~are~~ the descriptions

42   of the Parisian music-halls, ~~in-which-Maugham-speaks-of~~ "masses of

43   dingy red and tarnished gold . . . red-nosed comedians . . . fat

44   female singers . . . ~~aesthetic-delight-in-performing-dogs~~ . . .";

reminiscences of long cathedral services "through which he
45   Philip's ~~description-of-the-services-in-the-cathedral,-when-"every~~

had sat when every limb itched with the desire for movement"; and
46   ~~limb-itched-,-,-,-feet-like-ice-,-,-,-fingers-numb-and-heavy-,-,-,~~

his exhilaration atop a hill near the Rhine Valley when "unconsciously
47   ~~sickly-odour-of-pomatum,"--and-his-exhilaration-at-"tremendous~~

he thanked God that he no longer believed in Him."
48   ~~spaciousness-glowing-with-rich-gold-,-,-,-heart-beating-with-sheer~~

49   ~~joy-,-,-,-free-from-degrading-fears-,-,-,-free-from-prejudice-,-,-,~~

50   ~~could-breathe-more-freely-in-a-lighter-air,"--The-words-dance-along~~

LINE(S)

34–39   Revision eliminates such clumsy phrasing as "triteness is para-phrased" and "the masterpiece of simplicity in characterization is his artful contrast. . . ."

42   The deletion of "in which Maugham speaks of" changes the subordinate clause into an appositive and tightens the sentence.

44   The phrase "aesthetic delight in performing dogs" does not describe the music halls and violates sentence unity.

45–50   Major revision of the sentence is necessary because of the awkward merging of quotations.

51   ~~on-the-page,-leading-one-to-experience-Philip's-wild-delight-and~~

               The description of his uncle's death is poetic:
52   ~~lovely-freedom.---At-the-death-of-his-uncle,-the-words-are-poetry~~

53   ~~in-themselves:~~

54   The sun beat down hotly from a cloudless sky,
55   But the trees in the garden were pleasant and cool.
56   It was a lovely day.
57   A bluebottle buzzed against the window-pane . . .
58   The old man was dead.
59   The bluebottle buzzed, buzzed noisily against the
60   window-pane.

61   Maugham insists that lucidity, simplicity, and euphony need a

62   fourth ingredient to produce good writing: liveliness. At this,

                         rapidly and never tires the
63   too, he is a master. His story moves ~~quickly-from-one-scene-to~~

reader.
64   ~~another,-never-dwelling-in-one-place-long-enough-for-the-reader-to~~

65   ~~become-bored.~~ He uses enough suspense to maintain interest, enough

66   wit to insure sympathy for his characters, enough pathos to keep

67   the story human. It is as if each component were measured by a

68   gourmet's hand.

     Another quality, perhaps the least conspicuous of Maugham's
69   ~~Perhaps-the-most-inconspicuous-skill-in-Maugham's-inimitable~~

style,
70   ~~style,-and-the-one-which-sets-him-farthest-above-the-ordinary,-is~~

                       altogether   , is
71   one which he could not have developed ~~entirely~~ consciously, his

72   politeness to the reader. He says in <u>The Summing Up</u> that "good

LINE(S)

50–51   The sentence beginning "The words dance along the page" adds nothing to the discussion of euphony.

52–53   The phrase "at the death of his uncle," a dangling modifier, cannot logically modify the rest of the sentence.

54–60   The writer has improperly arranged the sentences as lines of poetry.

63–65   "His story moves quickly from one scene to another, never dwelling in one place long enough for the reader to become bored." The writer means that the story moves rapidly and never tires the reader.

69–70   "Perhaps the most inconspicuous skill in Maugham's inimitable style, and the one which sets him farthest above the ordinary. . . " is marked by fuzziness and exaggeration, eliminated in the revised version.

73 prose is an affair of good manners/' ~~but~such~~ . Good manners cannot be turned on

74 and off for the reader; they must be an inherent part of the

75 writer's own training. Maugham introduces each character to the

76 reader as he doubtless would personally. ~~Graciously~~, A gentleman, he says no

77 more than is necessary, so as not to strain the reader with too

78 many details in the first encounter. ~~It~is~satisfying~to~read~the~~

79 work of Maugham, because ~H~e writes <u>for</u> the reader, not <u>at</u> him.

80 That is why his work is satisfying.

LINE(S)

73   Repetition of "good manners" at the beginning of the sentence removes the ambiguous antecedent of "such."

78–79   "It is satisfying to read the work of Maugham . . ." is restated more forcefully at the end.

REVISED COPY OF "THE STYLE OF W. SOMERSET MAUGHAM,"
BY LOUISE LANDON

The Style of W. Somerset Maugham

by Louise Landon

Maugham's style is the product of repeated failures--failures
to achieve a style that the novelist considered worthy of merit.
After long years of self-conscious imitation, he realized that his
emulation of eighteenth-century models, especially Dryden and Swift,
restrained his own talents.[1] He abandoned his attempts and evolved
a style, uniquely his own, marked by lucidity, simplicity, and
euphony.[2]

Lucidity, perhaps the outstanding quality of Maugham's style,
derives its power from his precision and adequacy of detail. He
explicitly guides the reader's imagination up to the point where it
ought to take over. In Of Human Bondage, Philip's various bondages
are the undisguised backbone of the plot; his struggle to escape
them is always apparent to the reader. His ecstasy, for instance,
upon leaving school, is shadowed by passing doubts at getting his
own way; his sense of religious freedom is circumscribed by the
subconscious ties which remain; his admission of failure as an
artist is accompanied by a deep emotional release. These are but
a few of the clearly defined milestones in Philip's progress toward
self-fulfillment.

The second quality, simplicity, seems to come easily to Maugham,
though in The Summing Up he gives us a glimpse of his struggle to
achieve it.[3] The simplicity of his style lies in his choice of
detail and characterization. The gold crosses worn by the Careys,
for instance, suggest excessive religious formalism, which frustrates Philip's desire to know God. Maugham describes Mr. Carey's
vanity, his "hair, worn long, arranged over the scalp so as to

conceal his baldness"; Mrs. Carey's pathetic nostalgia, her "gray hair . . . arranged in ringlets according to the fashion of her youth."[4] He artfully contrasts Mildred's unwholesome "thin lips . . . faint green colour" and "bored look" to Sally's healthy attractiveness and bright attitude.[5]

The third quality, euphony, fills almost every page of the novel. The best examples include the description of the Paris music halls, "masses of dingy red and tarnished gold . . . red-nosed comedians . . . fat female singers"; Philip's reminiscences of long cathedral services "through which he had sat when every limb itched with the desire for movement"; and his exhilaration atop a hill near the Rhine valley when "unconsciously he thanked God that he no longer believed in Him."[6] The description of his uncle's death is poetic:

> The sun beat down hotly from a cloudless sky, but the trees in the garden were pleasant and cool. It was a lovely day. A bluebottle buzzed against the window-pane . . . the old man was dead. . . . The bluebottle buzzed, buzzed noisily against the window-pane.[7]

Maugham insists that lucidity, simplicity, and euphony need a fourth ingredient to produce good writing: liveliness.[8] At this, too, he is a master. His story moves rapidly and never tires the reader. He uses enough suspense to maintain interest, enough wit to insure sympathy for his characters, enough pathos to keep the story human. It is as if each component were measured by a gourmet's hand.

Another quality, perhaps the least conspicuous of Maugham's style, one which he could not have developed altogether consciously, is his politeness to the reader. He says in The Summing Up that "good prose is an affair of good manners."[9] Good manners cannot be turned on and off for the reader; they must be an inherent part of the writer's own training. Maugham introduces each character to the reader as he doubtless would personally. A gentleman, he says no more than is necessary, so as not to strain the reader with

too many details in the first encounter. He writes _for_ the reader,
not _at_ him. That is why his work is satisfying.

---

[1]W. Somerset Maugham, The Summing Up (Baltimore: Penguin
Books, 1946), p. 20.

[2]Ibid., p. 21.

[3]Ibid., pp. 23 ff.

[4]W. Somerset Maugham, Of Human Bondage (New York: Modern
Library, 1915), pp. 8, 13.

[5]Ibid., p. 330.

[6]Ibid., pp. 139, 140, 230.

[7]Ibid., p. 692.

[8]The Summing Up, p. 30.

[9]Ibid., p. 26.

Comments

The Landon paper by a second-term college freshman uses
Somerset Maugham's *The Summing Up*, an informal account of the
novelist's development as a writer, as a basic source for a short critical
study. The detailed discussion of style in *The Summing Up* defines
the student's purpose: to determine to what extent the qualities that
Maugham enumerates are present in one of his imaginative works.
Of Human Bondage, an autobiographical novel, serves this purpose
admirably.

Maugham's discussion of lucidity, simplicity, euphony, and liveliness, the ingredients of a style that he himself aimed for, easily
determines the structure of the paper. The problem of outlining,
therefore, resolves itself naturally. The student must gather examples
of each stylistic quality and incorporate them effectively into her
report. With some minor reservations she has done this competently,
though when the reader is told that Maugham "uses enough suspense
to maintain interest, enough wit to insure sympathy for his characters,
enough pathos to keep the story human," he is entitled to examples.

The final paragraph contains the student's appraisal of Maugham
as a stylist. Her reference to Maugham's politeness and to his regard
for the reader illustrates her ability to employ source material
skillfully.

Less successful than the organization and development of the topic is the student's command of sentence structure. The paper contains clumsy and awkwardly phrased constructions that lack precision and clarity. Among the more serious weaknesses is the writer's confusion of lucidity with simplicity in the second paragraph.

The revisions shorten the paper by approximately one-third, showing that the deleted phrases and sentences served merely as fillers. With these fillers eliminated and extra space at her disposal, the student writer could easily develop her theme further, perhaps adding a new dimension to her subject. But even with its abbreviated length —its blurred stretches of prose excised—the remaining sentences emerge markedly strengthened. Revision, it appears, is like a cross-examination in which the writer plays both the roles of prosecutor and defendant. Parts of the paper falter under scrutiny; others survive with minor alterations; still others stand up because of their vitality and spontaneity.

PROOFREADING

With revision successfully completed, only one other step remains— proofreading. Its purpose is simply to eliminate minor imperfections such as misspellings, mispunctuation, or tautologies. Minor blemishes, though they seldom impair the basic quality of a paper, nonetheless interrupt the flow of ideas. They are like a grease spot on a tie—just enough to spoil a good impression. Misspellings in particular have a way of causing raised eyebrows, though typographical errors elude even the most vigilant reader.

Finally, there are what may be called indispensable strategies in revision. Certainly, one of the best ways to give a composition its final inspection is to read it aloud. This has several advantages: the writer must slow down to the pace at which language is normally spoken, and doing so, he can spot errors more easily than he could through rapid, silent reading. By making a practice of actually hearing his composition, he can develop his responsiveness to the meaning and rhythm of prose. For this reason it also is worthwhile to listen to someone else read a draft aloud, for the writer can then hear his work as others hear it. Such practice helps close the distance between spoken and written utterance, showing that there are not two languages but one, with one form of it susceptible of greater precision and refinement.

Last, but not least, an excellent practice, as has already been pointed out elsewhere, is to shelve a paper for a few days in order to gain some distance from it. The closer we are, the less we are likely to see wrong —like the mother who has just been delivered of her first child: it is her very own and it is beautiful. So it is with a theme: only later do its shortcomings become apparent. Conversely, there is a point beyond which we are well advised to stop making revision, lest the spontaneity sometimes apparent in an earlier draft, be lost. Exactly where this point lies, everyone must determine for himself.

MANUSCRIPT FORM

In presenting his paper to the reader, the student should be governed by principles of common courtesy. He should make his manuscript pleasing in every way. A clean, well-ordered, legible paper is obviously better than a soiled, narrow-lined, pencil-written copy. To make a manuscript presentable, he should remember the following:

Paper. If the report is typed, unlined bond paper ($8\frac{1}{2} \times 11$) should be used rather than onionskin paper, which makes reading difficult. The type should be clean and the ribbon reasonably fresh. If a paper is in longhand, lined paper should be used; approved theme paper is usually available in college bookstores. Blue or black ink is preferable to green or purple, and though there is little or no correlation between penmanship and intelligence, everyone can make a supreme effort to write legibly.

Form. A paper should be written on one side of the page only. Typed papers should be double spaced except for long quotations, which are indented and single spaced but not put in quotation marks. Margins should be approximately one and one-half inches on the top and left-hand side, and one inch on the bottom and right-hand side. Narrow margins give a congested appearance, and excessively wide margins are wasteful. Paragraphs should be indented five spaces, and all end punctuation followed by two spaces. Arabic numerals should be used for pagination.

The final draft should be free from corrections, but few readers will object to an occasional last-minute revision. Such corrections are made according to accepted practices. Incorrect items are deleted by drawing a horizontal line through them ~~like this~~. Parentheses are

never used for this purpose (see pp. 248, 259). A caret (∧) is used to
indicate an insertion written above the line ∧ like this ∧ . A new paragraph in running text is shown by the symbol ¶ placed in the left-
hand margin before the appropriate sentence. Removal of a new
paragraph is signaled by "No ¶." Pages should be fastened together
by a paper clip, not folded and torn in the upper left-hand corner.

Title. A title is not a label or a filing index. Its purpose is to give an
overview of the topic, its range, and possibly its manner of treatment.
Omitting a title is like forgetting a black tie with formal attire. All
words in a title are capitalized, the only exception being determiners,
conjunctions, or prepositions not occurring initially. A title is not
placed in quotation marks or underlined. Finally, if the theme is on
a literary work, the title of the theme cannot be the title of the work.
Endorsement on a separate sheet usually contains the following
information:

Student's name and course number.
Title of the paper.
Date of submission.
Number of the paper.

EXERCISES

NOTE: The following problems can serve as a guide in the preparation
of a library paper if such an assignment constitutes part of the
course.

1. Explore a topic appropriate for a research project. Consider the fitness
of the topic for library research, your interest in it, and the knowledge
you already have of the subject. The most promising kind of topic is
one with which you already have some familiarity, so that the time
available to you for research can be more efficiently utilized than would
otherwise be possible. For example, if in one of your classes you are
devoting a month to the study of the *Odyssey*, it would seem reasonable
to explore some aspect of Homeric civilization, or, if you are acquainted
with James Joyce's *Ulysses*, to examine a significant parallel between
the two works. But to read Joyce's work first would hardly allow much
penetrating research in the time you can allot to this project.

After you have decided on a general topic, you should attempt to
limit it. Consider whether the topic meets the requirements set forth

in Chapter 13. The best test for weighing the soundness of a topic is to formulate it as a question, with the answers hopefully provided by your research.

2. After limiting your topic for effective handling in 1,500 words (or whatever length your instructor suggests—1,500 words is equivalent to about 6 double-spaced typewritten pages), consult your library for the availability of materials, and do some preliminary reading. Chapter 16 should be read carefully before you undertake this step.

    Remember that a scholarly treatment of a subject almost always contains an exhaustive bibliography, often annotated, that can save you hours of work. Unless you are certain of enough sources—perhaps 10 to 15—you should abandon your subject. Keep in mind that the availability of, let us say, a dozen items on your topic, by no means is a guarantee of their immediate usefulness and relevance to your needs. (See also Chapter 16, Exercise 5.)

3. Formulate a hypothesis or a guiding statement to provide a frame of reference for your research. The hypothesis is not something to be "proved" in the sense that one demonstrates a Euclidian problem in geometry. Rather, it should serve as a guide, which may itself have to undergo some reshaping after the commencement of actual research.

4. Write a sample note card for each of the following. As a source, use one of the paragraphs in Chapter 12, Exercise 1, or some other item to which your instructor has ready access, such as a textbook or a book of supplemental readings.

    1. A summary.
    2. A quotation.
    3. A paraphrase.
    4. Any combination of two of the three preceding items, including an editorial comment.

5. After completion of a substantial amount of research on your topic, prepare a preliminary, or working, outline to be handed in. Retain a carbon copy of the outline for revision while the working outline is being read by your instructor.

6. Put the following items into proper footnote form:

    1. A reference to page 11 of a book by Charles C. Fries entitled Linguistics and Reading, published by Holt, Rinehart and Winston, Incorporated, in New York in 1962.

2. A reference to Albert H. Marckwardt's Dictionaries and the English Language, an article on pages 336 to 345 in volume LII of The English Journal, which appeared in 1963.

3. A reference to pages 63 to 68 of the book cited in item 1.

4. A reference to an unsigned article with the title Language Crisis in Ceylon on page 12 of the Christian-Science Monitor on Friday, October 4, 1963.

5. To page 435 of an essay entitled The Freshman and His Dictionary by Mitford M. Mathews in Readings in Applied English Linguistics, edited by Harold B. Allen and published in New York in 1964 by Appleton-Century-Crofts in a second edition.

6. To pages 698 to 703 of an essay entitled Language written by George L. Trager for volume 13 of the Encyclopaedia Britannica, published in 1956.

7. To an article by Dwight Macdonald entitled The String Untuned in The New Yorker on March 10, 1962. The article runs from pages 130 to 160, but the specific reference is to page 133.

8. To an essay by Edward Sapir entitled Dialect on pages 83 to 88 in Selected Writings in Language, Culture and Personality. The collection, edited by David G. Mandelbaum, was published in Berkeley in 1949 by the University of California Press.

9. To page 16 of Sapir's essay Language in the same volume as item 8.

10. To page 465 of American English in its Cultural Setting, a book co-authored by Donald J. Lloyd and Harry R. Warfel, and published in New York in 1956 by Alfred A. Knopf.

7. Arrange pertinent items in Exercise 6 in bibliographical form.

8. After writing a rough draft of your paper and thoroughly reviewing Chapter 15, copy the equivalent of a typewritten page (include a carbon) and make intensive revisions. Then prepare a clean copy of the revised version. Hand in copies of both versions to your instructor.

9. Write a summary of your paper not to exceed one paragraph. If the summary reveals any obvious defects in organization or logic, check your paper for possible flaws and make appropriate changes.

10. Hand in your library paper, including a final outline and summary, as your instructor may specify.

16) The Library

The resources of a library collection are of greatest usefulness to the person who knows what material to look for and how to find it. That is why any serious student should become thoroughly acquainted with the facilities of his college or university library. He should, first of all, study its physical layout, the arrangement of its book holdings, reference services, and newspaper and periodical collections. He should learn whether his library maintains its permanent book collection as a unit or whether it separates it into divisional collections such as natural science, humanities, education, and social science. In addition, he should inquire if any special services or facilities are offered, such as microfilm collections and thermofax or photoduplication services that reproduce printed material for a few cents a page.

A college library offers these major services: (1) its permanent collection of books that may be borrowed; (2) its reference collection for use in the library; (3) its periodical collection, which may be borrowed in some libraries after current issues have been bound in a volume. In addition, a college library provides reserve shelves for books used frequently in courses. It may also hold rare book collections and microfilms of dissertations, newspapers, and rare books.

The principal means of access to the major collections are the card catalog for books, bibliographical guides to reference works, and indexes to periodicals. This is perhaps an oversimplification, for a distinction must be made between finding a book in a given library and the bibliographical problem of finding the existence of a book or an article. In small libraries, for example, the card catalog serves chiefly as a finding tool, but in large libraries and special collections, it functions as a bibliographical tool as well. In this sense, then, the card catalog is comparable to guides to reference books and indexes to periodicals.

THE CARD CATALOG

The card catalog is an alphabetically arranged file of 3×5 cards with author, title, and subject cards interfiled, or, less commonly, divided into two categories: the author-title catalog and the subject catalog. A typical card contains much useful information about a book:

PN
3335 (1) **Maugham, William Somerset, 1874–**
.M35 (2)   The art of fiction; an introduction to ten novels and their
1955   authors. ₁1st American ed.₎ Garden City, N. Y., Double-
          day, 1955 ₁°1954₎

(3)   818 p. 22 cm.

(4)   "A revised and enlarged version of a collection of Prefaces pub-
           lished in 1948. The present book appears in England under the title:
           Ten novels and their authors."

(5)   1. Fiction—Hist. & crit. 2. Authors.   I. Title.

(6)   PN3335.M35   1955   808.3   (7) 55—7011

(8)   Library of Congress   ₁62b*2₎

In the sample author card, the typed numbers at the left indicate the Library of Congress call number of the book (see p. 208). Item (1) gives the author's full name and date of birth. The title and subtitle of the book, as well as pertinent data about its publication, are shown in (2). These include a reference to its edition, the place of publication, the publisher, and the date of publication. The two dates refer to its copyright date, 1954, and the year of publication of the American edition. Item (3) gives the number of pages of the book and its size. Item (4) includes notes of all kinds, in this instance showing that the book is a revised and enlarged version with a new title. A statement about the publication of the book in England follows. Item (5) gives two subject headings under which the book would be listed in the subject catalog; "Title" refers to the title of the book under which it would appear in the title catalog. Item (6) gives both the Library of Congress call number and the Dewey Decimal call number. Item (7) shows the order number for the card. Item (8) indicates the printer's serial number.

An author card may list one or more authors, or a corporation or institution if it qualifies as author:

N
5963
. B7
1955

British Museum. *Dept. of British and Mediæval Antiquities.*
Early medieval art in the British Museum, by Ernst Kitzinger. ₍2d ed.₎ London, Trustees of the British Museum,
1955.

ix, 114 p.   illus., 48 plates.   21 cm.

1. Art, Medieval.   ɪ. Kitzinger, Ernst, 1912–   ɪɪ. Title.

N5963.B7   1955   56–26837

Library of Congress   ₍8₎

Title cards are similar to author cards except that the title of the publication is typed above the author's name. Bound journals, if they are listed in the card catalog at all, appear under the title and include a call number. A checklist sometimes follows the title card of a bound journal, showing the volumes owned by the library.

Subject cards are useful because they often give the range of material on a specified topic. They are similar to author cards with the subject typed across the top of the card. A particular publication may have one or more subject cards, or none at all if the title begins with such phrases as "The life of . . . ," "Principles of . . . ," or "A history of . . . ." It is obvious therefore that the holdings of a library on a particular subject may not all be found in the same place. The investigator must often use his ingenuity in locating material on a specific subject.

But aids are available. Cross references marked "see" indicate that a topic is listed elsewhere in the catalog:

Drama—Copyright		Drama—Biography
see	*or*	see
Copyright—Drama		Dramatists

Another type of cross reference is the "see also" card which refers the investigator to one or more additional subject headings:

DRAMA

   see also

ACTING	COLLEGE AND SCHOOL DRAMA
BALLET	COMEDY
BURLESQUE	DETECTIVE AND MYSTERY
CARNIVAL PLAYS	PLAYS
CHARACTERS AND	DIALOGUE
CHARACTERISTICS	DRAMATISTS
IN LITERATURE	FARCE
CHILDREN'S PLAYS	FOLK-DRAMA
CHRISTMAS PLAYS	GHOST PLAYS
CLASSICAL DRAMA	

To use the card catalog efficiently, one should know certain rules that libraries follow in alphabetizing cards. Initial function words in English and other languages, such as *a, an, the, der, das, le, la,* are disregarded in filing title cards. Abbreviations like *Dr., U.S.,* or *S.* are filed as though they were fully spelled out; thus, *Doctor, United States, San* or *Sanctus.* Numerals are treated similarly with "and" omitted: *two hundred* instead of *200; three hundred fifty* instead of *350.* Hyphenated words are treated as separate words:

Bridges, Robert S.
Bridges-Adams William
Bruehler, Paul

Words with hyphenated prefixes are treated as a single word if spelled as a single word, but as two words if they are spelled as two words:

Pan-American
Pan-German
Panama
Pangermanism

Alphabetization is letter by letter for the first word and then for the second word. That is why *Panama* follows *Pan-German* and *Pan-American*.

Since alphabetization proceeds letter by letter and abbreviations are filed as if fully spelled out, an arrangement like the following may be found in a large catalog:

Machorro	Machray
McHose	Macht
McHoul	Machu
Machover	Machuca
Machowinski	McHugh
	MacHuisdean

When the name of a person, place, and title is identical, the arrangement follows in that order. For example:

Names of persons	Lincoln, Abraham
	Lincoln, Edward F.
	Lincoln, James Finney
Names of places	Lincoln, *Eng.* (Diocese)
	Lincoln, Mass.
Titles	*Lincoln among his friends*
	Lincoln and California
	Lincoln and Douglas

Although the alphabetical arrangement is basic, there are some departures in form. Historical events, for example, are arranged chronologically within the larger alphabetical framework:

U.S.   History—Civil War
U.S.   History—1865
U.S.   History—1865–1898
U.S.   History—War of 1898
U.S.   History—20th Century
U.S.   History—European war 1914–1918

A geographical location has its subdivisions arranged alphabetically:

London   Royal academy
               Royal college
               Royal dental hospital
               Royal English opera house
               Royal exchange
               Royal horticultural society
               St. Paul's cathedral
               School of Economics

Finally, publications by an author precede those about him. This is useful to know when looking under such names as Shakespeare, Milton, and Lincoln.

SUPPLEMENTS TO THE CARD CATALOG

In order to augment information from the card catalog, the investigator will find it useful to examine bibliographies, such as the following:

Besterman, Theodore. *A world bibliography of bibliographies*, 1955, 4 vols.
Bibliographic Index, 1938—

A detailed listing of the contents of collections and anthologies may be found in the *Essay and General Literature Index*, 1900—. The

Maugham, William Somerset
  Art of fiction
     Contents
    Art of fiction
    Balzac and "Le père Goriot"
    Charles Dickens and "David Copper-
      field"
    Dostoevsky and "The brothers Kara-
      mazov"
    Emily   Brontë   and   "Wuthering
      Heights"
    Flaubert and "Madame Bovary"
    Henry Fielding and "Tom Jones"
    Herman Melville and "Moby Dick"
    In conclusion
    Jane Austen and "Pride and prejudice"
    Stendhal and "Le rouge et le noir"
    Tolstoy and "War and peace"
  How I write short stories
    In Saturday review (Periodical) Satur-
      day review Treasury p81-88

From *Essay and General Literature Index, 1900–*.
Reproduced by permission of The H. W. Wilson Company.

sample entry from the *Essay and General Literature Index* gives more complete information on the contents of Somerset Maugham's *The Art of Fiction* than the author card for the same item shown earlier in this chapter. Some libraries, however, prepare "analytical" cards for each item in a collection.

To borrow a publication from the library, the reader may have to fill out a call slip, which requires the author and title of a book (volume if pertinent), its call number, and the borrower's name and address. The call number shows the precise location of the book and must therefore be copied exactly.

The two systems of classification generally used in American colleges and universities are the Dewey Decimal system and the Library of Congress system. The Dewey Decimal system classifies knowledge into ten principal categories with subdivisions, each digit and decimal point indicating a more specific part of the subject than the next larger division. The 300–399 class, for example, lists the social sciences; 320–329, political science; 327, foreign relations. An item containing the call number 320.1, for example, would be concerned with political theory. Additional symbols below the classification number identify the author. The Library of Congress system uses letters of the alphabet as its major categories, thus making possible a more detailed general classification. Each letter represents a principal division of knowledge: H represents social science; N, fine arts; P, language and literature. Like the major categories of the Dewey Decimal system, the lettered classes in the Library of Congress system are extensively subdivided.

THE STRUCTURE OF A BOOK

The intelligent researcher can learn much about a book by knowing how to interpret its main parts. The title, especially the subtitle if the book has one, indicates the range of a subject. Charles C. Fries's *American English Grammar*, followed by the subtitle *The Grammatical Structure of Present-Day American English with Especial Reference to Social Differences or Class Dialects*, clearly indicates a descriptive treatment of present-day American English, notably of usage, rather than a historical account. The author's reputation is of course important, and his stature can often be ascertained in a biographical dictionary. But his eminence in one field is not always a guarantee of his qualifications in another. A tourist is not necessarily a competent analyst of American foreign policy simply because he has been around the world.

Besides author and title, the title page lists the publisher and the edition of a book. Reputable publishing houses are unlikely to produce a work unless its quality has been judged by experts. The copyright date of a book indicates its first publication or latest revision. In a field where progress and change are significant, revision may be crucial.

The preface makes acknowledgments and justifies a book's existence. Usually it also explains the author's approach to his subject. For example, in his preface to *English Sentences* (New York: Harcourt, Brace & World, 1962), Paul Roberts says:

> That which is new in this book derives mainly from the work of Professor Noam Chomsky and his collaborators at the Massachusetts Institute of Technology. Chomsky's transformational, or generative, grammar is certainly one of the major developments in linguistics in recent years.

The preface must be distinguished from the introduction, which is an integral part of the body, or text, of a book. The introduction often presents the necessary background to a subject and defines its treatment.

The table of contents, which precedes the introduction, gives the reader a quick overview of the range of a book, so that the skilled investigator can often tell at a glance whether or not a work is likely to be useful to him. Closely related to the table of contents is the index, an alphabetically arranged list of the topics treated in a book with appropriate page references. Comparison reveals that an index usually has a more detailed listing of topics than a table of contents. For example, Chapter 5 of the paperback edition of Frederick L. Allen's *Only Yesterday* (New York: Bantam, 1959), "The Revolution in Manners and Morals," pp. 61–86, contains a discussion of "Suffrage, feminine independence, jobs for women," according to a subhead in the table of contents. The index, however, gives other references (in italics) under "women," as the following table shows:

Women, and short skirts, 62, 64–65, *249*
   bobbed hair, *2*, 74, *248*
   and drinking, 63
   fashions, *1*, *248–249*
   influence of suffrage, 67

The index lists references that would elude the investigator if he relied solely on the table of contents.

Other important parts of a book are the appendix, or appendices, which may contain important explanatory notes, reproductions of original documents, tables of statistics, and bibliographies, either with annotations (brief comments on the contents of a book) or with critical comments (judgments on the merits of a book). Robert A. Hall's *Linguistics and Your Language* (New York: Doubleday Anchor Book, 1960), for example, contains a small critical bibliography for beginners in linguistics and specifically cites two books that the reader should avoid. H. A. Gleason's *An Introduction to Descriptive Linguistics*, rev. ed. (New York: Holt, Rinehart & Winston, 1961), has a more extensive bibliography than Hall's, followed by a six-page analysis of the most important books in the list. Thus, unless the student gathering a bibliography in modern linguistics is aware of Hall and Gleason, he could waste hours in the library when carefully selected and up-to-date bibliographies are readily available. Skill and ingenuity are often necessary in finding the right information. And in a research project, finding the right information is usually half the battle.

INDEXES AND GUIDES TO PERIODICALS AND BOOKS

Periodical indexes are guides to articles in journals, much as a card catalog is a guide to books. The most commonly used magazine and newspaper indexes are the following:

Readers' Guide to Periodical Literature, 1900–
International Index to Periodicals, 1907–
   [Since June, 1965, known as *Social Science & Humanities Index.*]
The New York Times Index, 1913–

Over 100 magazines are indexed in the *Readers' Guide* as against approximately 150 more scholarly and specialized journals in the

International Index. A list of periodicals indexed in each, as well as a key to abbreviations and symbols, appears in front of each volume. Items are indexed under subject and author, as the examples show.

Subject entry: **MAU MAU**
After one year, worse. Time 62:30-1 N 2 '53
Anti-whites. il Life 34:35 Ap 13 '53
Atlantic report on the world today. Atlan 193:16-19 Ja '54
Background. Time 62:35 D 7 '53
Behind the blood oath of the Mau Mau. L. S. B. Leakey. il N Y Times Mag p 14-15+ My 3 '53
Blood brother. Time 64:38 N 1 '54
Burning spear. il Newsweek 41:53 Ap 20 '53
Challenge, then shoot. Time 61:38 Ap 13 '53
Conversions reported ending Kenya's Mau Mau terror. Christian Cent 72:3 Ja 5 '55
Court-martial; Spark of hope. Time 63:37 Mr 22 '54

● ● ● ● ● ● ● ● ● ● ● ● ● ● ● ●

Author entry: **MAUGHAM, Somerset.** See Maugham, W. S.
MAUGHAM, William Somerset
Looking back on eighty years: we are freer. Reporter 10:32-4 My 25 '54
Remembrances of H. G. Wells. por Sat R 36:17-19+ Ap 11 '53

about

Dean of the smoothies. H. Alpert. por Sat R 36:21 Ap 25 '53
Eighty years of Mr Maugham. T. F. Brady. pors N Y Times Mag p 12+ Ja 24 '54
Maugham and the young idiot. D. Taylor. Vogue 122:172+ S 1 '53
Maugham at eighty. F. Swinnerton. pors Sat R 37:13-14+ Ja 23 '54
Maugham the artist. S. Krim. Commonweal 61:284-7 D 10 '54
Maugham's Of human bondage; reprinted from December 25, 1915 issue. T. Dreiser. New Repub 131:58 N 22 '54
Mr Maugham's magic cup. J. Chambrun. por Read Digest 65:10 D '54
New Somerset Maugham. N. Barber. il por Holiday 15:16+ F '54
Plush stuff. por Newsweek 42:114 O 19 '53
Portrait
    Sat R 36:65 N 28 '53
    Time 64:34 Jl 26 '54
    Womans Home C 81:9 Je '54
Somerset Maugham. S. Krim. Commonweal 61:245-50 D 3 '54
Somerset Maugham at eighty. pors Look 18:90-1 F 9 '54
Ten who know the secret of age. M. Gumpert. por N Y Times Mag p 10-11 D 27 '53
Voices of authors; recordings. por Life 35:134 O 12 '53

From *Readers' Guide to Periodical Literature, 1900–.*
Reproduced by permission of The H. W. Wilson Company.

As in the card catalog, works by an author precede those about him. The entries in the *Readers' Guide* under William Somerset Maugham include an article, "Looking Back on Eighty Years: We Are Freer," in volume 10 of *The Reporter* (May 25, 1954), from pages 32 to 34. Another article, "Remembrances of H. G. Wells," including a portrait, appears in volume 36 of the *Saturday Review* (April 11, 1953), from pages 17 to 19 and on later pages of the same issue (+).

Subject entry: **MAU MAU**

Anthropological approach to the Mau Mau problem. A. Rosenstiel. bibliog f Pol Sci Q 68:419-32 S '53

Anti-Mau Mau drive; and a Kikuyu registration scheme [photographs with text] Illus Lond N 222:149 Ja 31 '53

Any solution for Kenya? New Statesm 46: 170 Ag 15 '53

Behind the Mau Mau. G. Padmore. bibliog f Phylon 14:355-72 D '53

Case against Jomo Kenyatta. New Statesm 44:590 N 22 '52

Charged with managing the Mau Mau subversive movement: Jomo Kenyatta. il Illus Lond N 221:908 N 29 '52

Conflict of culture in Africa. P. Abrahams. Int Affairs 30:304-12 Jl '54

● ● ● ● ● ● ● ● ● ● ● ● ● ● ● ●

Author entry: **MAUGHAM, Frederic Herbert Maugham, 1st viscount**

U.N.O. and war crimes. Int Affairs 28:410-12 Jl '52

U.N.O. and war crimes. Review Int Affairs 28:207 Ap '52. F. Honig

MAUGHAM, William Somerset

Dorothée [adaptation of dramatization] See Wall, J.

[Colored portrait by G. Sutherland] Illus Lond N 221:IV Ag 16 '52

Maugham effect. J. D. Scott. Spec 192:129 Ja 29 '54

Maugham enigma, ed. by K. L. Jonas. Review

New Statesm 47:101-2 Ja 23 '54. J. Raymond; Reply. R. Lehmann. 47:131 Ja 30 '54

MAUGHAM, William Somerset—*Continued*
Portrait

Illus Lond N 224:163 Ja 30 '54
Illus Lond N 224:194 F 6 '54
Illus Lond N 224:1038 Je 19 '54
Illus Lond N 225:149 Jl 24 '54

Survival of Mr Maugham. T. C. Worsley. New Statesm 45:147-8 F 7 '53

Ten novels and their authors. Review
Illus Lond N por 225:896 N 20 '54. J. Squire
New Statesm 48:617 N 13 '54. N. Annan

Vagrant mood. Review
Illus Lond N por 221:802 N 15 '52. J. Squire

W. Somerset Maugham and the Christian preacher. J. J. Bunting, jr. bibliog f Relig in Life 21 no3:401-10 '52

From *International Index to Periodicals, 1907–*.

Reproduced by permission of The H. W. Wilson Company.

Articles about Maugham are more numerous and include items from the *Saturday Review, The New York Times Magazine, Vogue, Commonweal, New Republic, Reader's Digest, Holiday, Newsweek,*

Look, and *Life.* In addition, portraits of Maugham can be found in the *Saturday Review, Time,* and *Woman's Home Companion,* as well as in a number of other articles cited.

The *International Index,* which is arranged like the *Readers' Guide,* is particularly useful in the social sciences and humanities. Though the sample covers approximately the same period as that of the *Readers' Guide,* its listings under Maugham are less extensive, showing how effectively the two indexes complement each other.

The New York Times Index summarizes and classifies news alphabetically by subject, person, and organization. Published semimonthly and cumulated annually, it is useful chiefly as a reference to daily events in *The New York Times* and Sunday supplements, as well as to those newspapers that are not indexed. In this sense it is indeed a master key to the news. A sample entry from the 1960 volume shows its value both as an index and as a guide to capsule news:

> Maugham, W. Somerset. See Books-Awards Ag 24 Int. on eve of 86th birthday, Bangkok; por, Ja 25, 29:2; comment on int, F 3, 32:3; leaves Singapore for London, F 17, 31:2; nephew Lord Maugham hurt in quake, Agadir, Morocco, Mr 2, 18:3; Maugham in Marseilles after Asian tour, Mr 6, 8:1; ordered to rest, Ag 6, 12:8.
>
> © 1960 by The New York Times Company. Reprinted by permission.

The classification proceeds from heading to subheading, entry (summary), date, page, and column. Sections in the Sunday edition, except the first, are indicated by Roman numerals following the date.

Besides *The New York Times Index, The Times Index* (London) and *The Wall Street Journal Index* are helpful in locating items in newspapers.

Other general indexes include the following:

Poole's Index to Periodical Literature. 1802–1906.
   Subject index to 19th century periodicals.
Nineteenth Century Readers' Guide to Periodical Literature.
   Index to periodicals 1890–1899.
Vertical File Service Catalog. 1932–.
   Annotated subject catalog of brochures, pamphlets, circulars, etc.
Book Review Digest. 1905–.
   Summaries and quotations of critical opinions expressed in book reviews; full references to the sources cited.

An indispensable tool listing the vast variety of material published by the U.S. Government is the *Monthly Catalog: United States Government Publications*, 1895 to the present. Government publications, or documents, as they are called, are not normally included in the card catalog. An introduction to the use of government publications is found in Lawrence F. Schmeckebier and Roy B. Eastin, *Government Publications and Their Uses*, rev. ed. (Washington: Brookings Institution, 1961).

Many other specialized indexes are available to the researcher, and some of these are included in the list of general and specialized references below. Anyone wishing to gain a more comprehensive knowledge should consult one of these guides to reference books:

Barton, Mary Neill. *Reference Books.* 5th ed. Baltimore: Enoch Pratt Free Library, 1962.

Murphey, Robert W. *How and Where to Look It Up.* New York: McGraw-Hill, 1958.

Shores, Louis. *Basic Reference Books.* Chicago: American Library Assoc., 1954.

Winchell, C. M. *Guide to Reference Books.* American Library Assoc., 1951. Supplements to June 1962.

A list of books in print in the United States may be found in the *United States Catalog* (1928) and the *Cumulative Book Index* (New York: H. W. Wilson Co., 1928-date). These two guides are especially useful for verifying the names of authors, titles, and facts of publication.

GENERAL AND SPECIALIZED REFERENCE WORKS

The function of reference works is to give the reader an overview of a subject, to answer specific questions about it, and to guide him to other, more detailed, treatments. Though written by experts, reference works should be used with caution because they may be out of date. There are certain exceptions, such as the eleventh edition of the *Encyclopaedia Britannica*, which has gained a reputation for its authoritative discussions in the humanities. But in the social or natural sciences, the most recent references are generally the most pertinent.

Reference works include bibliographies, dictionaries, encyclopedias, periodical and newspaper indexes, yearbooks, and pamphlets. Following is a list of useful and reliable sources:

General Encyclopedias

> *Collier's Encyclopedia*
> *Encyclopedia Americana*
> *Encyclopaedia Britannica*

Articles in these encyclopedias, often with selective bibliographies, are written by specialists. Annual supplements keep each reference up to date:

> *Collier's Year Book.* 1939–.
> *The American Annual.* 1924–.
> *Britannica Book of the Year.* 1938–.

The investigator often finds it helpful to consult the index volume of an encyclopedia because specific points of information may appear under different subject headings.

Reference works in a variety of specialized subjects are listed in the remainder of this chapter.

Biography

> *American Men of Science.* 11th ed. 1965. 6 vols.
> *Biography Index,* 1946–.
> A quarterly index to biographical material in 1500 periodicals and books published in English.
> *Chamber's Biographical Dictionary,* 1961.
> *Current Biography.* 1940–.
> Monthly, cumulated annually.
> *Directory of American Scholars.* 4th ed. 1964.
> *International Who's Who.* 1935–.
> *Who's Who.* 1849–. Annual.
> *Who's Who in America.* 1899–. Biennial.

These sets list distinguished American and British persons of the past and include bibliographies:

> *Dictionary of American Biography.* 1928–1944. 20 vols. and supplements.
> *Dictionary of National Biography.* 1885–1940. 22 vols. and supplements.

Specialized biographical references listing prominent persons in aviation, business, labor, engineering, medicine, etc., are available in almost any library.

Unabridged Dictionaries, Books on Usage, Synonyms

Webster's New International Dictionary (Unabridged). 3rd ed., 1961.
Dictionary of American English on Historical Principles. Ed. Sir William
Craigie and J. R. Hulbert. 1936–1944. 4 vols.
A Dictionary of Americanisms on Historical Principles. Ed. Mitford M.
Mathews. 1951. 2 vols.
Oxford English Dictionary. Ed. Sir James Murray. 1888–1933. 10 vols.

The third edition of *Webster's New International Dictionary*, guided
by principles of modern linguistic science, is noted for its liberal point
of view. The amateur lexicographer will find it fruitful to compare it
with its predecessor, the second edition, published in 1934. The
Oxford English Dictionary, or *OED*, sometimes also referred to as the
New English Dictionary (*NED*), is a historical dictionary, listing
meanings of words from their inception in the language and illus-
trating changes of meaning and usage by quotations from representative writers. A two-volume abridgment of the *OED*, the *Shorter
Oxford English Dictionary*, has been available in its third revised
edition since 1955. The *Dictionary of American English* and *A
Dictionary of Americanisms*, like the *OED*, are based on historical
principles and trace the meanings of words from their first use in the
United States to the present.

Specialized dictionaries in law, medicine, chemistry, psychology,
etc., are meeting the needs of rapidly growing terminologies in these
fields.

Reference works on usage, synonyms, etc., are helpful supplements
to dictionaries. The best known include the following:

The American Language (Mencken). 4th ed. Supplements I and II.
1936–1948. (One-vol. abr. ed. by Raven I. McDavid, Jr., 1963).
Dictionary of American-English Usage (Nicholson). 1957.
A Dictionary of Contemporary American Usage (Evans). 1957.
Dictionary of Slang and Unconventional English (Partridge). 5th ed. 1961.
Roget's International Thesaurus. 3rd ed. 1962.
Webster's Dictionary of Synonyms. 1951.

A word of caution is in order for the student using a thesaurus or a
dictionary of synonyms. *Webster's Dictionary of Synonyms*, for
example, lists synonyms (that is, words having "the same or very
nearly the same *essential* meaning") in alphabetical order and dis-
criminates and illustrates them with citations from past and present

authors. In addition, it includes antonyms and near synonyms and antonyms. *Roget's Thesaurus*, on the other hand, classifies words and expressions into major categories (such as abstract relations, space, matter, intellect, volition, and affections), each of which is further

> **relieve.** Relieve, alleviate, lighten, assuage, mitigate, allay agree in meaning to make something tolerable or less grievous. Though they are often used interchangeably, they are clearly distinguishable. **Relieve** implies a lifting of enough of a burden to make it definitely endurable or temporarily forgotten; as, drugs that *relieve* pain; to *relieve* the misery and suffering caused by a disaster. Occasionally *relieve*, when used in the passive, implies a release from anxiety or fear; as, they were greatly *relieved* when her letter came: sometimes, it suggests a break in monotony or in routine. "I've had some trouble to get them together to *relieve* the dullness of your incarceration" (*Meredith*). **Alleviate** stresses the temporary or partial nature of the relief and usually implies a contrast with *cure* and *remedy;* as, oil of cloves will *alleviate* the toothache. "It has always been considered as an *alleviation* of misery not to suffer alone" (*Johnson*). **Lighten** implies reduction in the weight of that which oppresses or depresses; hence it often connotes a cheering or refreshing influence; as, his interest in his work *lightened* his labors. "That blessed mood... In which the heavy and the weary weight Of all this unintelligible world Is *lightened*" (*Wordsworth*). **Assuage** suggests the moderation of violent emotion by influences that soften or mollify or, sometimes, sweeten. "The good gods *assuage* thy wrath" (*Shak.*). "My sorrows I then might *assuage* In the ways of religion and truth" (*Cowper*). **Mitigate** also suggests moderation in the force, violence, or intensity of something painful; it does not, as *assuage* does, imply something endured but something inflicted or likely to inflict pain; as, "to *mitigate* the barbarity of the criminal law" (*Inge*); to *mitigate* the rigors of an explorer's life; to *mitigate* the severity of a winter. **Allay,** though it seldom implies complete release from that which distresses, disquiets, or the like, does suggest an effective calming or quieting; as, the report *allayed* their fears; to *allay* one's thirst; his suspicions were *allayed*. "These...words....were of sobering tendency; they *allayed* agitation; they composed, and consequently must make her happier" (*Austen*).
> **Ana.** *Comfort, console, solace: *moderate, qualify, temper, attemper: diminish, reduce, lessen, *decrease.
> **Ant.** Intensify: embarrass: alarm.

subdivided. No discriminations between terms are made, nor are any citations given. Entries are arranged in parallel columns, with words in the second column usually contrasting in meaning with those in the first column. An important assumption underlying a compilation like the thesaurus is that the reader already has an idea about the word he wants but merely lacks the right word. The thesaurus helps him select the word with the exact sense or right nuance, provided he is already familiar with a synonym or near synonym. *Roget's Thesaurus*, then, serves primarily as a word finder, whereas *Webster's Dictionary of Synonyms* offers additional features, principally its extensive discriminations among synonyms. The distinction made between synonyms and near synonyms offers another refinement not found in the thesaurus. For example, *stoop* and *deign* are cited as synonyms for *condescend*, with *favor, accommodate, oblige,* and *vouchsafe, concede,* and *grant* as near synonyms. Similar practice governs the treatment of antonyms and near antonyms in the *Dictionary of Synonyms*. Its handling of an entry, therefore, is at once more restrictive but more detailed than in *Roget's Thesaurus*, whose listings under a particular entry are more inclusive (see illustration).

884. RELIEF

NOUNS 1. **relief, easement,** easing, ease; **reduction,** diminishment, lessening; **alleviation, mitigation, palliation,** softening, assuagement, allayment, appeasement, mollification, subduement; soothing, salving; dulling, deadening.

2. **release, deliverance, freeing,** removal; reprieve; catharsis, emotional release.

3. **lightening, disburdening,** disencumbrance, disembarrassment; a load off one's mind.

4. **sense** or **feeling of relief,** sigh of relief.

VERBS 5. **relieve,** give relief; **ease,** ease matters; **reduce,** diminish, lessen; **alleviate, mitigate, palliate,** soften, assuage, allay, lay, appease, mollify, subdue, soothe; salve, pour balm into, pour oil on; poultice, foment, stupe; slake, slacken; **dull, deaden,** dull or deaden the pain; temper the wind to the shorn lamb, lay the flattering unction to one's soul.

6. **release, free, deliver,** reprieve, remove, free from.

7. **lighten, disburden,** disencumber, disembarrass; **set one's mind at ease** or rest, set at ease, **take the load off one's mind,** smooth the ruffled brow of care.

8. **be relieved, feel relief,** feel better about it; **breathe easy** or **easier,** breathe more freely, breathe again; **heave a sigh of relief,** draw a long or deep breath.

ADJS. 9. **relieving, easing, alleviative,** alleviating, **mitigative, mitigating, palliative,** lenitive, assuasive, softening, subduing, soothing, demulcent, **emollient, balmy,** balsamic; dulling, deadening.

Both Webster's *Dictionary of Synonyms* and *Roget's Thesaurus* can be invaluable guides if used properly. In almost all contexts, words can be substituted for other words, and both references can help in selecting the word that fits best. Sometimes an idea may even be suggested by a particular word or expression. But each word has a unique shade or subtlety of meaning not shared by any other word, however similar to that word it may be in its essential sense. For the apprentice writer especially, for whom "variety" has become a demon, who has not yet come to feel any difference between desirable repetition and dull repetitiousness, who may have been told "don't repeat" over and over again, such a student, trying to describe a theater audience quieting down, might choose an inappropriate noun like *throng*, *multitude*, or *congregation* simply to avoid *audience*. Describing a cumulus cloud, he might call it, among other things, *fat*, *obese*, or *corpulent*. Grotesquely and often hilariously wrong combinations are therefore possible if a thesaurus or a dictionary of synonyms is used without care.

Abridged or Collegiate Dictionaries[1]

Because unabridged dictionaries are expensive, bulky and impossible to carry under one's arm—not to speak of the prohibitive cost of frequent revisions—abridged or collegiate dictionaries have become an indispensable tool of business and professional people, of students—of anyone, in fact, whose work involves the use of language. The best-known collegiate dictionaries include the following:

American College Dictionary (Random House, 1964).
Funk & Wagnalls Standard College Dictionary (Funk & Wagnalls, 1963).
Standard College Dictionary (Harcourt, Brace & World, 1963).
Webster's New World Dictionary (World, 1964).
Webster's Seventh New Collegiate Dictionary (Merriam-Webster, 1963).

Entries in these dictionaries vary from 90,000 to 150,000 in contrast to the approximately half a million in an unabridged dictionary. Each of the collegiate dictionaries has its distinctive merits, and the choice of one over another is frequently a matter of personal taste. A discussion of the uses of dictionaries, however, and suggested points of comparison may lead to a more critical awareness of each.

Modern standard college dictionaries are compiled and edited by large staffs of specialists who examine the vast amounts of materials published in English-language newspapers, magazines, trade journals, pamphlets, and books. Thousands of words, each one in context, are

[1] Adapted from "Using the Dictionary," an unsigned article by William Schwab, *Communication Skills Syllabus*, 9th ed. (East Lansing, Mich.: Michigan State University Press, 1956) pp. 23–24. By permission.

recorded and filed; no word is rejected because it might seem offensive or degrading. The uses of both new and old words are examined, and in this way an exhaustive record of the living language is constantly kept up to date.

Recording the meanings of words is perhaps the central task of a lexicographer, though accurate recording of the spelling, pronunciation, etymology, usage levels, inflections, and parts of speech is equally important. A systematic comparison of several college dictionaries will show that complete agreement on the listings of entries does not always exist.

Lexicographers subscribe to certain guiding principles. First, a dictionary only records usage; it does not prescribe it. Language specialists define words in accordance with the ways in which words are used, not as they think words should be used in a particular environment. The authority of a dictionary, therefore, lies in the competence of its staff, that is to say, the accuracy with which the staff records and reports the facts of actual English usage. We should remember this whenever we consult a dictionary. And since there are several competently edited college dictionaries, none can really lay claim to be the final authority. Only when one dictionary excels another in clarity, accuracy, and completeness can one say that it is more authoritative than another.

Dictionaries are hardly ever up to date, since it takes a number of years to compile and edit them. Words such as *blitzkrieg, flying saucers*, and *strafe* are unlikely to be found in dictionaries published before World War II. On the other hand, the tendency of most people to follow the established convention of spelling and pronunciation helps to stabilize the bulk of our language.

Just as many of us have old-fashioned notions about the authority of a dictionary, believing this authority to be a kind of mysterious dispensation given to dictionaries to legislate usage, so many of us still believe that dictionaries are the final and absolute authorities on the definition of words. Strictly speaking, dictionaries do not define words; they give us only directions of meaning. We should not deceive ourselves into thinking that after looking up a term like *democracy* in a dictionary, we know what the term means. We can seldom expect more than brief explanatory statements, and these are usually on the same level of abstraction as the word to be explained.

This is not to belittle or condemn a dictionary. Rather, we want to clarify in our minds precisely what a dictionary does and does not do. If we wish to gain an accurate notion of democracy as a philosophical concept (as distinct from democracy as a form of government, for example), we had better start doing some reading on our own, perhaps even enroll in a philosophy or political science course.

Still another misconception about dictionaries is widely held. We tend to look for *the* meaning of a word as though a word had only one meaning. Some words do; but the more common a word, the more meanings it is likely to possess. (How many meanings does your dictionary list for *come, get, go, put, run*?) We would do well to stop thinking in terms of absolute meanings of words and begin to think in terms of areas of meaning and range of meanings. For example:

(1) The new model introduced *radical* changes.
(2) The new Cabinet introduced *radical* changes.

In both statements the common range of meaning of *radical* denotes the idea of fundamental changes. Indeed, the stem of the word *radical* is the Latin word *radix* meaning *root*. But to say that the word means *fundamental* in both statements is not really sufficient. *Radical* in (1) denotes the idea of sweeping changes in the new model, changes that may make it more attractive than an earlier model. *Radical* in (2) denotes the idea of extreme, drastic measures. What the measures actually were, we cannot tell from the sentence. What we are saying, in effect, is that without context the meaning of a word is incomplete. Indeed, it is the context of a word that determines its meaning and makes communication clearer, more accurate and forceful.

Humanities[2]

HISTORY

Cambridge Ancient History. 1923–1939. 12 vols.
Cambridge Medieval History. 1911–1936. 8 vols.
Cambridge Modern History. 1902–1926. 13 vols.
Dictionary of American History (Adams). 1940–1944. 6 vols.
An Encyclopedia of American History (Morris). Rev. and enl. ed., 1961.
An Encyclopedia of World History (Langer). Rev. ed., 1952.

[2] Based on "Reference Books," *Communication Skills Syllabus*, 9th ed. (East Lansing, Mich.: Michigan State University Press, 1956), pp. 109–115. By permission.

A History of American Life (Schlesinger). 1927–1948. 13 vols.
New Larned History. 1922–1924. 12 vols.

LITERATURE

Cambridge Bibliography of English Literature. 1941–1957. 5 vols.
Selective Bibliography for the Study of English and American Literature (Altick and Wright). 2nd ed. 1963.
Dramatic Index. 1909–.
Granger's Index to Poetry. 5th ed. 1962.
Annals of English Literature. 1961. A list of important books published from 1475–1950. 2nd ed.
Cambridge History of American Literature. 1917–1921. 3 vols.
Cambridge History of English Literature. 1907–1927. 15 vols.
Concise Cambridge History of English Literature (Sampson). 2nd ed. 1962.
Oxford Classical Dictionary. 1949.
Oxford History of English Literature (Wilson and Dobrée). 1945–. 14 vols. projected; 5 vols. published.
Oxford Companion to American Literature. 2nd ed. 1948.
Oxford Companion to Classical Literature. 1937.
Oxford Companion to English Literature. 3rd ed. 1946.
Oxford Companion to the Theatre. 1951.
A Literary History of England (Baugh). 1948.
Literary History of the United States (Spiller). 1948. 3 vols. incl. bibliography supplement.
The Oxford Dictionary of Quotations. 2nd ed. 1953.
American Authors 1600–1900 (Kunitz). 1938.
British Authors Before 1800 (Kunitz). 1952.
British Authors of the Nineteenth Century (Kunitz). 1936.
Twentieth Century Authors (Kunitz). 1942. Supplement 1955.

RELIGION AND PHILOSOPHY

American Theological Library Association. *Index to Religious Periodical Literature*. 1949–.
Catholic Periodical Index. 1930–.
Catholic Encyclopedia. 1907–1922. 17 vols.
Encyclopedia of Religion and Ethics. 1908–1927. 13 vols.
Masterpieces of World Philosophy in Summary Form (Magill). 1961.
Mythology of All Races. 1964 ed. 13 vols.
New Schaff-Herzog Encyclopedia of Religious Knowledge. 1908–1927. 13 vols. 2 vols. Supplement.
Universal Jewish Encyclopedia. 1939–1944. 12 vols.

Fine Arts

ART, ARCHITECTURE

Art Index. 1929–.
 Index includes 100 periodicals, museum bulletins, and annuals.
Cyclopedia of Painters and Painting (Champlin). 1886–1888. 4 vols.
Encyclopedia of World Art (15 vols. in process). 1959.
Harper's Encyclopedia of Art. 1937. 2 vols.
Index of Artists (Mallett). 1935. Supplement 1940.

MUSIC

Music Index. 1949–.
 Monthly cumulative index to approximately 80 journals.
Grove's Dictionary of Music and Musicians. 5th ed. 1954. 9 vols.
A Guide to Reference Materials on Music. 3rd ed. 1955.
International Cyclopedia of Music and Musicians. 9th ed. 1965.
Oxford History of Music. 2nd ed. 1929–1938. 8 vols.

Social Sciences

London Bibliography of the Social Sciences. 1931–.
Encyclopedia of the Social Sciences. 1935. 15 vols.

BUSINESS AND ECONOMICS

Industrial Arts Index. 1913–1957.
 A monthly subject index to selected business, technical, and engineering magazines and books. Since 1958, *Applied Science and Technology Index.*
Public Affairs Information Service *Bulletin.* 1915–.
 A weekly subject index to periodicals, books, pamphlets, and government documents in economics, commerce, finance, political science, and sociology.
Economic Almanac. 1940–.
Encyclopedia of Banking and Finance (Munn). 5th ed. 1949. Supplements.

EDUCATION

Education Index. 1929–.
 A monthly cumulative index to approximately 150 periodicals, books, and documents on teaching, educational philosophy, and administration.

Bibliographies and Summaries in Education to July 1935 (Monroe and Shores). 1936.

Cyclopedia of Education. 1911–13. 5 vols.

Encyclopedia of Educational Research. 3rd. ed. 1960.

POLITICAL SCIENCE

Student's Guide to Materials in Political Science (Burchfield). 1935.

Encyclopedia of Modern World Politics (Theimer). 1950.

Political Handbook of the World. 1962.

Yearbook of the United Nations. 1947–.

PSYCHOLOGY

Psychological Abstracts. 1927–.

A monthly abstract of books and articles with annual subject and author indexes.

Psychological Index. 1895–1936.

An annual index of books and articles of that period.

Professional Problems in Psychology (Daniel). 1953.

SOCIOLOGY

Social Work Year Book. 1929–.

Physical and Biological Sciences

Annotated Bibliography of Economic Geology. 1929–.

Guide to Geologic Literature (Pearl). 1951.

Biological Abstracts. 1926–.

Chemical Abstracts. 1907–.

Science Abstracts. 1898–.

Physics and electrical engineering.

U.S. Atomic Energy Commission. *Nuclear Science Abstracts.* 1948–.

Cambridge Natural History. 1895–1909. 10 vols.

Dictionary of Scientific Terms. 6th ed. 1957.

Guide to the Literature of Mathematics and Physics (Parke). 1958. 2nd rev. ed.

Handbook of Chemistry (Lange). 10th ed. 1961.

Handbook of Chemistry and Physics. 45th ed. 1965.

Larousse Encyclopedia of World Geography. 1965.

Standard Cyclopedia of Horticulture (Bailey). 1947. 3 vols.

Thorpe's Dictionary of Applied Chemistry. 4th ed. 1937–1954. 11 vols.

Van Nostrand's Scientific Encyclopedia. 3rd ed. 1958.

Applied Sciences

Agricultural Index. 1916–.
Applied Science and Technology Index. 1913–. (1913–57 *Industrial Arts Index.*)
Engineering Index. 1884–.
Technical Book Review Index. 1917–.
Cyclopedia of American Agriculture. 1907–1909. 4 vols.
Dictionary of Guided Missiles and Space Flight (Merrill). 1959.
Kent's Mechanical Engineer's Handbook. 12th ed. 1950. 2 vols.
The Space Encyclopedia. 2nd rev. ed. 1960.

Yearbooks, Almanacs

Facts on File. 1940–.
    A weekly digest of world events with a cumulative index.
Information Please Almanac. 1947–.
Statesman's Year-Book. 1864–.
    Statistical, political, economic information about governments of the world.
Statistical Abstracts of the United States. 1878–.
United Nations Yearbook. 1946–.
World Almanac. 1868–.

Atlases, Gazetteers

The Columbia Lippincott Gazetteer of the World. 1962.
Commercial Atlas and Marketing Guide (Rand McNally). 7th ed. 1966.
Goode's World Atlas (Rand McNally). 12th ed. 1964.
Historical Atlas (Shepherd's). 8th ed. 1956.
Webster's Geographical Dictionary. 1959.

EXERCISES

1. Locate and survey your library's permanent holdings in your field of interest, its reference and periodical collections, and the system of classification used.

2. What filing system is used in the card catalog of your library?

3. Make a list of the special facilities available at your library, such as microfilms or duplication services.

4. Select a book and analyze its main parts in a report of 300–500 words. Be sure to consult the preface, the table of contents, and the index, as well as other significant parts discussed in this chapter.

5. List two items each for future supplementary reading from the *Readers' Guide*, the *International Index*, *The New York Times Index*, and from any other two general or specialized indexes.

6. List ten references in a subject of your choice by consulting the bibliographies following pertinent articles in an encyclopedia or other reference work.

7. Study the keys to abbreviations and the symbols used in your collegiate dictionary, including those relating to etymology, syllabication, parts of speech, subject labels, and synonyms and antonyms. For a better understanding of lexicography, read Charles C. Fries's "Usage Levels and Dialect Distribution" in the preface to the *American College Dictionary*, and Harold Whitehall's "The Development of the English Dictionary" in *Webster's New World Dictionary*.

8. In order to develop an awareness of principles of lexicography, examine your dictionary and note your editor's handling of the following:

    1. Alternate spellings and the relative importance of the order of their listing.
    2. Alternate pronunciations and the relative importance of the order of their listing: the sound-values of symbols in the pronunciation key.
    3. The listing of senses in your dictionary in either chronological order or in order of frequency, with modern senses preceding earlier ones.
    4. Usage labels such as *colloquial, archaic, obsolete, slang, dialect,* and *illiterate.*
    5. Items of divided usage, like *shall—will, who—whom, like—as, isn't—ain't.*

9. Prepare a short report on one of the following words, tracing some of their changes in meaning as reported in a historical dictionary, such as the OED: *clip, farmer, fellow, gospel, lace, lumber, knave, meat, perfume, quell, silly, treasure.*

10. Compare an entry in an unabridged dictionary with one in a collegiate dictionary.

III] Mechanics

17) *The Role of Punctuation*

The main purpose of punctuation is to help the reader grasp written material better than he could without it. This may seem obvious until one is reminded that punctuation has not always had this purpose. In medieval English manuscripts, for example, punctuation served primarily to mark breath groups for oral delivery, and only incidentally to interpret meaning. The Pentateuch, written on parchment scrolls in ancient Hebrew letters, has no punctuation at all, nor do some Greek manuscripts before 300 B.C. The system of punctuation as we know it did not develop until the advent of modern printing.[1]

For convenience, punctuation will be examined under two major headings. The first consists of those marks that have structural or grammatical points of reference and that partially represent features signaled in speech by intonation. These include certain uses of the period (to indicate the end of a sentence, for example) and the comma (to set off a relative clause or to separate elements in a series). Other marks included in this group are the exclamation point, question mark, semicolon, colon, parentheses, dash, apostrophe, and hyphen. The second group consists of items whose use is strictly arbitrary, such as italics to indicate the titles of books or periodicals, or quotation marks to set off citations. This group also includes brackets, ellipses, as well as certain fixed uses of the period, comma, and parentheses.

1 See Charles C. Fries, "Shakespearian Punctuation," *Studies in Shakespeare, Milton and Donne* (Ann Arbor: University of Michigan Lang. and Lit. Series, 1925), I, 65–86.

INTONATION AND PUNCTUATION

Since punctuation partly performs the same function in writing as intonation in speech, a brief explanation of the features of intonation is in order. The intonational system of English consists of four contrastive levels of stress, pitch, and juncture. Thus, words like *import, permit, present* may be either nouns or verbs. With a heavy, or primary, stress (´) on the first syllable and weak stress (usually not marked) on the second, they are nouns; with primary stress on the second syllable and weak stress on the first, they are verbs:

N	V
ímport	impórt
pérmit	permít
présent	presént

Secondary (ˆ) and tertiary (`) stress are shown by the following contrasts:

wíldlìfe	wîld lífe
bláckbìrd	blâck bírd
Nèw Jérsey	nêw jérsey

Items in the first column have primary and tertiary stress; those in the second column, secondary and primary stress, respectively. Each item in the first column contrasts with one in the second column. Wildlife, for example, refers to flora and fauna; wild life, to fast living.

The four levels of contrastive pitch are symbolized by numbers: 1 represents low pitch; 2, normal; 3, high; 4, very high. In a naturally spoken utterance, such as the following, most speakers would begin on 2, rise to 3 on the syllable receiving primary stress, and then fall to 1:

^{2}He finished his ^{3}wórk^1

With high pitch at the end of *work*, we get an echo question:

^{2}He finished his ^{3}wórk^3

The utterance begins on pitch level 2, rises to 3 on *work* where it is sustained to the end. Still other contrasts are possible:

^{2}He ^{3}fínished^1 his work^1

^{3}Hé^1 finished his work^1

^{2}He finished his ^{4}wórk^1

The first utterance stresses the completion of the job by rising to pitch level 3 on the verb. The second utterance says that a particular person finished his work. The third utterance, rising to a very high pitch on *work*, could be an exasperated response to repeated questions.

Juncture refers to the manner of transition from one sound to another or to silence. Of the four contrastive junctures, the first, marked by plus (+) and usually called **plus juncture,** has to do with a variety of phonetic features that make it possible to distinguish pairs like *anointment, an ointment; an eel, anneal; nitrate, Nye trait, night rate.* The remaining three junctures, falling ($\searrow$), rising ($\nearrow$), and level ($\rightarrow$), called **terminal junctures,** are illustrated by the following utterances:

^{2}He finished his ^{3}wórk^1 $\searrow$

^{2}He finished his ^{3}wórk^3 $\nearrow$

^{2}He finished his ^{3}wórk^2 $\nearrow$

^{2}He finished his ^{3}wórk^2 $\rightarrow$

In the first sentence the falling juncture ($\searrow$) indicates a retardation on the last syllable, a slight drop below pitch level 1 and a fading into silence. In the second sentence the rising juncture ($\nearrow$) indicates a retardation on the last syllable, a slight rise in pitch above 3, followed by silence. Both junctures signal completion of the utterance. In the third sentence, the rising juncture, which occurs on pitch level 2 instead of on 3, signals incompleteness, and a continuation of the utterance is expected:

^{2}He finished his ^{3}wórk^2 $\nearrow$ ^{2}but he can't be ex^{3}cúsed^1 $\searrow$

In the fourth sentence, the level juncture indicates a retardation on the last syllable, but the pitch neither rises nor falls. The juncture signals incompleteness as in the third sentence:

^{2}He finished his ^{3}wórk^2 $\rightarrow$ ^{2}after getting ^{3}hélp^1 $\searrow$

It should be observed that each stretch of utterance containing one primary stress is bounded by a terminal juncture, which may be level, rising, or falling.

The terminal junctures in the preceding sentences are represented by punctuation marks as follows:

^{2}He finished his ^{3}wórk^1 $\searrow$ He finished his work.

^{2}He finished his ^{3}wórk^3 $\nearrow$ He finished his work?

²He finished his ³wórk² ↗ ²but he can't be ex³cúsed¹ ↘   He finished his work, but he can't be excused.

²He finished his ³wórk² → ²after getting ³hélp¹ ↘   He finished his work after getting help.

A falling juncture, usually heard at the end of a normally spoken utterance, is almost always represented by end punctuation. In the sample sentences it is marked by a period. A rising juncture, heard either within an utterance or at the end, may be indicated by a question mark, as at the end of the second sentence, or by a comma, as in the third sentence. A level juncture heard within an utterance is not usually marked by any punctuation.

The correlation of intonation with punctuation is by no means as regular as the examples so far would indicate. Rising or level junctures can be heard in the following utterances:

²The fra³térnity men¹ → ¹it may be ádded¹ ↗ ²won the ³cóntest¹ ↘

²The fra³térnity men² ↗ ²it may be ádded² ↗ ²won the ³cóntest¹ ↘

²The fra³térnity men² → ²it may be ádded² ↗ ²won the ³cóntest¹ ↘

Whatever the terminal junctures, the parenthetical clause is set off by commas in writing:

The fraternity men, it may be added, won the contest.

The correlation of intonation and punctuation is therefore only partial. Either one or two terminal junctures can be heard in the following:

²The fraternity men won the ³cóntest¹ ↘

²The fra³térnity men² → ²won the ³cóntest¹ ↘

The second utterance is slower and more deliberate than the first, but no punctuation is required to mark the level juncture. Indeed, a comma separating the subject and predicate would be a serious error.

Punctuation is sometimes the only feature that distinguishes the meaning of a sentence:

Have you studied, Johnson?
Have you studied Johnson?

In the spoken utterance, a terminal juncture is heard inside the first sentence but not inside the second:

²Have you ³stúdied³ → ³Jóhnson³ ↗

²Have you studied ³Jóhnson³ ↗

In a letter to the editor of the *Detroit Free Press* (Sept. 8, 1961, p. 8), a reader criticized the late President Kennedy's public speaking for lack of clarity, citing this instance:

> Well, every country operates under different systems and Mr. Khrushchev has done a good deal of brandishing of nuclear weapons, but I am hopeful, as I have said, that anyone—and I'm sure Mr. Khrushchev knows very well what the effect of this would be on the people of this world of ours if nuclear weapons were exchanged in a massive way between the countries which possess them—and I'm conscious of this and I'm sure Mr. Khrushchev is—and we won't have to wait and see now whether from that consciousness on both sides peace can be achieved, which is our objective.[2]

An analysis of the President's intonation would very likely have revealed which terminal junctures were misinterpreted by the newspaper's copy desk. Perhaps the President's intonation signaled this meaning:

> Well, every country operates under different systems and Mr. Khrushchev has done a good deal of brandishing of nuclear weapons, but I am hopeful, as I have said, that anyone—and I'm sure Mr. Khrushchev—knows very well what the effect of this would be on the people of this world of ours if nuclear weapons were exchanged in a massive way between the countries which possess them. And I'm conscious of this and I'm sure Mr. Khrushchev is. And we will have to wait and see now whether from that consciousness on both sides peace can be achieved, which is our objective.

The parenthetical element, separated by dashes in the revised version, seems clearly interpolated. However imperfect the correlation of intonation to punctuation may be, an awareness of their points of contact can often help to resolve problems of punctuation. All sample sentences in the following chapters should therefore be read aloud so that appropriate terminal junctures may actually be heard.

PUNCTUATION AND STYLE

The beginning student sometimes wonders why the same sentence may be punctuated in different ways. Choice operates in punctuation as it does in sentence structure, though not as much. In the following,

---

[2] The quotation, according to the editor of the newspaper, was "verbatim from the text approved by the White House."

for example, a comma, semicolon, or period may be used after the first clause:

> They flatly refused our first offer, but in the end they
> accepted our revised proposal.
> They flatly refused our first offer; but in the end they
> accepted our revised proposal.
> They flatly refused our first offer. But in the end they
> accepted our revised proposal.

A period before a conjunction is more emphatic than a semicolon. A semicolon, in turn, is more deliberate than a comma.

Punctuation tends to be sparser today than a century ago, reflecting the informality of the age. The following samples from John Ruskin's *Modern Painters* (1843) and Robert Spiller's *The Cycle of American Literature* (1955), respectively, offer a revealing contrast:

> And, first, I think it probable that many readers may be surprised at my calling Scott the great representative of the mind of the age in literature. Those who can perceive the intense penetrative depth of Wordsworth, and the exquisite finish and melodious power of Tennyson, may be offended at my placing in the higher rank that poetry of careless glance, and reckless rhyme, in which Scott poured out the fancies of his youth; and those who are familiar with the subtle analysis of the French novelists, or who have in anywise submitted themselves to the influence of German philosophy, may be equally indignant at my ascribing a principality to Scott among the literary men of Europe, in an age which has produced De Balzac and Goethe.—JOHN RUSKIN, *Modern Painters*

> There is a law in physics which proposes for every force an equal but opposite force; thus Nature retains her equilibrium. In literary history some such law seems to supply for every dynamic or romantic movement an equal and countermovement towards standards, forms, restraints. The literary movement which flowered in the United States in the twenties and thirties was no exception; it carried within it the seeds of reaction. Even before 1920, T. S. Eliot was calling for the depersonalization of poetry and the recognition of an ideal order in art. He and a few others were ready to apply the lash to unruly American authors and to bring them into line.—ROBERT SPILLER, *The Cycle of American Literature*

Ruskin's passage of 125 words consists of two sentences; Spiller's 112-word excerpt has five. Ruskin's prose is formal and balanced, with a long periodic sentence, that is, one whose meaning is suspended till the end. Spiller's writing is relaxed, giving the impression of careful, but informal, speech. Its five sentences are loosely constructed. *Modern Painters* has heavy internal punctuation that is now dated: commas separate coordinate elements and a subject from its predicate. In *The Cycle of American Literature* there is a minimum of internal punctuation: the semicolons separate clauses; the commas set off elements in a series and a sentence adjunct. These sample passages then show that punctuation can assist the writer as much in conveying his meaning as in helping the reader understand it.

EXERCISES

1. Pronounce each of the following with a primary stress on the first and then on the second syllable, marking the stress and word class of each item.

   EXAMPLE: íncrease (**V**) incréase (**N**)

1.	project	project	6. present present
2.	conduct	conduct	7. contest contest
3.	refuse	refuse	8. content content
4.	discharge	discharge	9. invert invert
5.	produce	produce	10. concert concert

2. Pronounce and mark the stress patterns of each of the following:

   EXAMPLE: take óff (**V**) táke-òff (**N**)

1.	shake up shakeup	6.	yellow tail yellowtail
2.	take over take-over	7.	bold face boldface
3.	hold over holdover	8.	blue stocking bluestocking
4.	cook out cookout	9.	acting director acting-director
5.	hand out handout	10.	a small executive's a small executive salad salad

3. Say each sentence and mark its intonation.

   EXAMPLE: ²We ate our ³lúnch¹ ↘
   1. Don returned the book [Meaning: Don returned the book, not a record.]
      Don returned the book [Meaning: Don didn't keep it.]
      Don returned the book [Meaning: Don, not anyone else, returned the book.]

2. After he entered the room he removed his coat
After entering the room he removed his coat
He removed his coat after he entered the room

3. Are you meeting John [Meaning: Someone is addressing a question to John.]
Are you meeting John [Meaning: Someone is asking a question pertaining to John.]

4. What are you doing tonight [Meaning: Someone is asking a straightforward question.]
Would you like to see a movie [Meaning: Someone is asking a straightforward question.]
Would you like to see a movie [Meaning: The person addressed has already rejected suggestions to attend a play and to go dancing.]
You would like to see a movie wouldn't you [Meaning: The speaker seeks information.]
You would like to see a movie wouldn't you [Meaning: The speaker seeks confirmation.]

5. We ate up our lunch
We ate it up
We ate up the hill

4. Punctuate the sentences in Exercise 3, indicating where punctuation represents intonation and where it does not.

18) *End Punctuation*

The end markers consist of the period, question mark, and exclamation mark.

PERIOD

A period indicates the end of a sentence and usually signifies a falling juncture:

The liner lay in its berth in the company pier.
The story reminds me of my home in northern Michigan.

The omission of a period at the end of a sentence results in a **run-on sentence**, that is, two successive sentences without any terminal punctuation between them:

UNACCEPTABLE:
The liner lay in its berth in the company pier it seemed even larger than I had imagined.

ACCEPTABLE:
The liner lay in its berth in the company pier. It seemed even larger than I had imagined.

The omission of the period is sometimes due to rapid scanning, with the result that a falling juncture is not heard where it should be heard in a deliberate, matter-of-fact reading.

237

Improper end punctuation may result in **sentence fragments,** that is, sentences lacking the basic subject-predicate structure, or word groups or included clauses punctuated as a sentence:

UNACCEPTABLE

The story reminds me of my home in northern Michigan where the trees in the fall are colored with different shades. The green of the evergreens and the red-and-yellowish colored maples. [Noun phrase punctuated as a sentence.]

UNACCEPTABLE:

The story reminds me of my home in northern Michigan. Where the trees in the fall are colored with different shades—the green of the evergreens and the red-and-yellowish colored maples. [Subordinate clause punctuated as a sentence.]

ACCEPTABLE:

The story reminds me of my home in northern Michigan, where the trees in the fall are colored with different shades—the green of the evergreens and the red-and-yellowish colored maples.

Sentence fragments result, in part, from a tendency to place a falling juncture at a point in a sentence where a falling juncture would not usually be heard, and to mark it, incorrectly, with a period.[1]

QUESTION MARK

A question mark follows a direct question, as in the following:

What did the survey reveal?
What broadcast followed the game?
He arrived, didn't he?
Were the students present?

A question mark at the end of a statement converts the statement into a question:

The Yankees won.
The Yankees won?

A rising juncture can be heard at the end of the last example. Both rising and falling junctures occur after so-called yes-or-no questions, such as "Were the students present?" Other question types usually have a falling juncture.

[1] See also pp. 285–287.

EXCLAMATION MARK

An exclamation mark follows a statement of strong emotion or force:

The Yankees won!
"It's the truth!" he shouted.

The exclamation point is used sparingly, because most writers prefer to express strong emotion through other means.

Note: For exercises, see the end of Chapter 21.

19) *Internal Punctuation*

Internal markers like the comma, semicolon, colon, and dash are used to signal various grammatical relationships.

COMMA

Uses of the comma can be divided into two major categories. The first has to do with the punctuation of coordinate elements, those that have equivalent grammatical rank. Coordinate elements consist of words, phrases, or clauses, either in pairs or in a series:

He entered the course late, but he made up the work within a month.
The foreign countries represented in the English class were Ecuador, Thailand, and India.

A comma separates two grammatically equivalent clauses in the first sentence, and items in a series in the second sentence.

The second category has to do with the punctuation of non-coordinate elements, those that have different grammatical rank and function. Noncoordinate elements set off by a comma also consist of words, phrases, or clauses at the beginning, in the middle, or at the end of a sentence. However complex the total pattern, its punctuation can be reduced to a simple scheme:

240

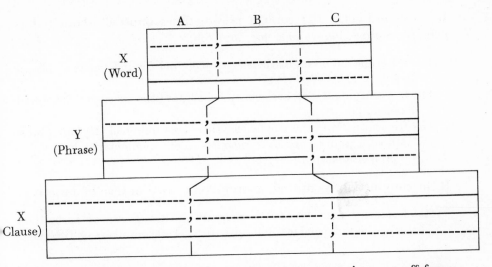

The broken lines in the diagram represent constructions set off from the rest of the sentence (unbroken line) by a comma or commas. These constructions, which may consist of words, phrases, or clauses, occur at the beginning, in the middle, or at the end of a sentence. The following, for example, fits into vertical slot (*A*) and horizontal slot (*Y*):

> After one semester of intensive drill, he developed an acceptable pronunciation of French.

The comma sets off a sentence adjunct, a prepositional phrase, at the beginning of the sentence. The next example fits into slots (*C*) and (*Z*):

> He comes from Chicago, I believe.

The comma sets off a parenthetical clause at the end of the sentence.

With Coordinate Elements

A comma is used between coordinate clauses if the second clause is preceded by a conjunction:

> The fraternity men began the program with a group of barbershop ballads, and the independents followed with several numbers of Dixieland jazz.

In short sentences the comma is sometimes omitted, though it is usually retained before *but*, *nor*, and *for*:

> The fraternity men sang barbershop ballads and the independents played Dixieland jazz.
>
> The fraternity men sang barbershop ballads, but the independents played Dixieland jazz.
>
> The fraternities won the trophy, for their ensemble had the best voices. [Without a comma, *for their ensemble* might momentarily be grasped as a prepositional phrase.]

If the conjunction is omitted, a semicolon is used instead of a comma:

> The fraternity men began the program with a group of barbershop ballads; the independents followed with several numbers of Dixieland jazz.

A comma is used to separate items in a simple series:

> The fraternity men acted, sang, and danced their way to victory.
>
> The fraternity men sang barbershop ballads, danced their way to victory, and accepted the trophy.

The preferred practice is to use a comma before the last member of a series, but usage is divided and the comma is sometimes omitted before the conjunction:

> The fraternity men acted, sang and danced their way to victory.
>
> The fraternity men sang barbershop ballads, danced their way to victory and accepted the trophy.

When the conjunction is not used, a comma or semicolon must follow each member of a series:

> The fraternity men sang barbershop ballads; the independents followed with the Dixieland jazz; the sororities finished with their rendition of Negro spirituals.

A comma may be used to indicate the omission of a word or phrase:

> The fraternity men presented a group of barbershop ballads; the independents, several numbers of Dixieland jazz.
>
> CONTRAST: The fraternity men presented a group of barbershop ballads, and the independents several numbers of Dixieland jazz. [More informal.]

With Noncoordinate Elements

A sentence adjunct at the beginning of a sentence may consist of a word, phrase, or clause. Words functioning as sentence adjuncts are usually adverbs or conjunctive adverbs:

Happily, the fraternity men won.
However, the fraternity men won.
Therefore, the fraternity men won.
CONTRAST: Happily the fraternity men won. [More informal.]
CONTRAST: Therefore the fraternity men won. [More informal.]

There may be different kinds of phrases:

Chosen best in the revue, the fraternity men won.
To maintain their record, the fraternity men were determined to win.
Having won, the fraternity men celebrated.
To the delight of the audience, the fraternity men won.
Last evening, the fraternity men repeated their feat of a year ago.
Or: Last evening the fraternity men repeated their feat of a year ago.

Subordinate clauses at the beginning of a sentence are usually set off by a comma:

Because they worked hard, the fraternity men won.
CONTRAST: The fraternity men won because they worked hard.
Or: The fraternity men won, because they worked hard.

Sentence adjuncts inside a sentence are set off by commas. The adjunct may consist of a word:

The fraternity men, however, won the trophy.
The fraternity men, overwhelmed, accepted the trophy.

A phrase:

The fraternity men, having won, celebrated.
The fraternity men, to celebrate their victory, sang an encore.
The fraternity men, overwhelmed by their victory, sang an encore.
The fraternity men, to the delight of the audience, sang an encore.
The fraternity men, a group of excellent singers, claimed the trophy.

Or a clause:

The fraternity men, it may be added, deserved to win.
The fraternity men, who were overwhelmed by their victory, sang an encore.[1]

[1] See the next section for punctuation of restrictive and nonrestrictive elements.

Sentence adjuncts are set off by a comma at the end of a sentence. The ajdunct may be a word:

The fraternity men won the trophy, however.
The fraternity men won the trophy, sadly.

A phrase:

The winners were the fraternity men, a group of excellent singers.
The fraternity men sang an encore, to the delight of the audience.
CONTRAST: The fraternity men sang an encore to celebrate their victory.

Or a clause:

The fraternity men deserved to win, it may be added.
The independents placed second, though they had made every effort to win the trophy.
The fraternity men sang an encore, which received overwhelming applause.

The comma is optional before a short subordinate clause at the end of a sentence:

A student will do better in college if he prepares himself in high school.
CONTRAST: If a student prepares himself in high school, he will do better in college.

The comma is retained before subordinators like *although, since* (meaning *because*):

He spoke the truth, although many in the courtroom doubted his testimony.
The fraternity men won, since they had professionally trained singers in their group.
CONTRAST: The fraternity men had practiced steadily since they moved into their new house.

With Nonrestrictive and Restrictive Elements[2]

The punctuation of nonrestrictive and restrictive elements can be illustrated by the following:

Sam Jones, a fraternity man, sang in the ensemble.
Sam Jones, who is a fraternity man, sang in the ensemble.
Fraternity man Jones sang in the ensemble.

In the first two sentences, commas set off an appositive and a relative

[2] See pp. 70–71.

clause, which amplify or expand the subject of the sentence, Sam Jones. Their omission does not affect the basic meaning of the sentence. A word, phrase, or clause that amplifies another element in a sentence but is not essential to the meaning of the sentence is said to be **nonrestrictive.** The nonrestrictive appositive and the relative clause in the first two sentences function as sentence adjuncts and are therefore set off by commas. Level or rising junctures can be heard after *Jones* and *man* in each sentence.

In the third sentence, on the other hand, *Jones* limits and defines the subject *fraternity man.* The appositive *Jones* is an essential part of the subject and its omission changes the basic meaning of the sentence. It is the fraternity man Jones, not anyone else, who sang in the ensemble. A word, phrase, or clause that limits or defines another element in a sentence is said to be **restrictive.** No terminal junctures are heard after *man* in the third sentence.

Certain sentences may have either restrictive or nonrestrictive modifiers. In these sentences the punctuation will depend on the writer's intent:

The fraternity men who rehearsed won the contest.
The fraternity men, who rehearsed, won the contest.

The first sentence says that those who rehearsed, not any others, won the contest. The second sentence says that the fraternity men won the contest and that they rehearsed. The relative clause in the first sentence is restrictive; the relative clause in the second sentence, nonrestrictive. Sometimes the difference between restrictive and nonrestrictive modifiers will also depend upon what the writer knows the reader knows. For example:

The boat which sank had been Don's pride over the years.
The boat, which sank, had been Don's pride over the years.

The reader of the first sentence presumably knows that Don owned more than one boat. The reader of the second sentence may be expected to know that Don owned only one boat. The question here is not the punctuation but the facts.

Nonrestrictive elements are set off by commas; restrictive elements are not:

Dr. Valley, the young internist, watched the operation.
The new internist, Dr. Valley, watched the operation.
CONTRAST: The new internist Dr. Valley watched the operation.

The fraternity men sang an encore, which received overwhelming applause.

CONTRAST: The fraternity men sang an encore which received overwhelming applause. [Emphasis is on a particular encore.]

The following formula may help in remembering how to punctuate restrictive and nonrestrictive elements: It restricts; don't punctuate. It does not restrict, punctuate.

To Prevent Misreading

Misreadings can sometimes be avoided by the use of a comma to represent terminal junctures:

Whatever John does, does not make much difference to me.

CONTRAST: He said that that is his final offer.

Clever in its design originally it was used as a tool by the fishermen. [Ambiguous.]

Clever in its design, originally it was used as a tool by the fishermen. [Clear.]

As they enter the room as if by the pressure of their breathing distends. [Ambiguous.]

As they enter, the room, as if by the pressure of their breathing, distends. [Clear.]

SEMICOLON

A semicolon indicates a falling juncture and therefore functions much like a period with which it can be sometimes interchanged. Stylistically a semicolon is not as strong a mark of separation as a period, but stronger than a comma. The choice of a semicolon or a period often depends on the kind of break desired:

The judges were impressed; the fraternity men had won.

CONTRAST: The judges were impressed. The fraternity men had won.

A semicolon is often used to separate two clauses if the second contains a conjunctive adverb:

The judges were unimpressed; however, the fraternity men had won the contest.

The judges were unimpressed; the fraternity men, however, had won the contest.

The judges were unimpressed; the fraternity men had won the contest, however.

CONTRAST: The judges were unimpressed. The fraternity men, however, had won the contest.

The use of a comma rather than a semicolon or a period to separate two main clauses results in an error known as a **comma splice,** or **comma fault:**[3]

A semicolon is used to separate items in a series that is internally punctuated:

He sent letters to the full committee: Sam Jones, the chairman; Fritz Beagle, his fraternity brother; Liza Beagle, Fritz's sister; and Mitzi Hingebottom, the junior class secretary.

CONTRAST: He sent letters to the full committee: Sam Jones, Fritz Beagle, Liza Beagle, and Mitzi Hingebottom.

Short elements in a series are usually separated by commas rather than by semicolons, but either a comma or a semicolon may be used to set off longer elements.

COLON

The colon is a formal mark of anticipation. It is used to signal an explanation or a series:

I have one objection to their victory: the judges were biased.

He lacks one quality: intelligence.

CONTRAST: He lacks one quality—intelligence. [More informal.]

We have three requirements: the desire to learn, the willingness to persevere, and the determination to succeed.

CONTRAST: We require of students the desire to learn, the willingness to persevere, and the determination to succeed.

A colon follows an introduction containing a formal word or phrase such as *following* or *as follows:*

Prospective students must meet the following requirements: superior academic attainment, diversified interests, and good health.

CONTRAST: His favorite extracurricular activities were basketball, track, and student government.

[3] See pp. 287–289.

A colon follows a formal introduction to a quotation:

> This is what the dean told the committee: "Our foreign language requirements are too stiff."
> CONTRAST: The dean told the committee, "Our foreign language requirements are too stiff."

PARENTHESES

Various kinds of nonrestrictive phrases and clauses, normally separated from the rest of a sentence by a comma or commas, are sometimes set off by parentheses to enclose an observation, explanation, illustration, or detail that may be only peripheral to the rest of the sentence:

> This year's winners (the fraternity men) will receive an invitation to perform at the state fair.
> CONTRAST: This year's winners, the fraternity men, will receive an invitation to perform at the state fair.
> The fraternity men (there are sixty) won the contest.
> CONTRAST: The fraternity men—sixty in all—won the contest.
> Sam Jones (who is a fraternity man) sang in the ensemble.
> CONTRAST: Sam Jones, who is a fraternity man, sang in the ensemble.

Parentheses set off the enclosed material more pointedly than commas. (See also p. 259.)

DASH

A dash is used to set off elements from the rest of a sentence—sometimes more emphatically and sometimes more informally than other marks of punctuation—and to indicate abrupt changes within a sentence:

> Two choruses from *Aïda*, some patriotic songs, and one or two hit-parade numbers—these were the highlights of the evening's program.
> It was not long before I discovered how in England, as elsewhere—but in England particularly because there insouciance is a fetish—casualness so easily turns into callousness and into lack of seriousness.
> —IRWIN EDMAN, *Philosopher's Holiday*

> Man is a rational animal—so at least I have been told.
> —BERTRAND RUSSELL, *Unpopular Essays*

The sun was made to light the day, and the moon to light the night—
though the moon, by some oversight, only shines during half the
nocturnal hours.—BERTRAND RUSSELL, *ibid.*

The dash, one of those expository aids best monitored by restraint,
will serve many stylistic effects: emphasis, surprise, climax, reversal—
in short, a device to grip and arrest the reader. And as long as he is
not jolted too hard, he will not object.

Note: For exercises, see the end of Chapter 21.

20) *Word Punctuation*

The apostrophe and hyphen serve principally to mark structural contrasts at the word level (person, persons, person's, persons'). The apostrophe is used to indicate the possessive and the plural forms of letters, symbols, and words used as words. It also serves to mark contractions. The hyphen is used to mark compounds and to divide a word at the end of a line.

APOSTROPHE

Plural nouns ending in the sounds /-əz, -z, -s/[1] add an apostrophe to form the possessive. However, some proper nouns ending in /-əz, -z, -s/, especially those having only one syllable, add either (') or *'s*:

the jud*ges'* decision /-əz/
the boy*s'* books /-z/
the student*s'* prerogatives /-s/
the Jones*es'* children /-əz/

Jones' children *or* Jones's children /-z/
Miles' briefcase *or* Miles's briefcase /-z/

Most singular nouns, plural nouns that do not end in -*s*, and pronouns like *anyone, everyone, someone*, add *'s*:

[1] For a simplified phonemic chart, see Chapter 22.

the judge's decision
the boy's books
the student's prerogatives
children's games
men's votes
anyone's guess

N's N constructions should be distinguished from **N N**:

a teacher's car (a car belonging to the teacher)
a teachers college (a college for training teachers)
a veteran's privilege (the privilege of a veteran)
the Veterans Administration (a bureau for veterans)

Possessive forms of compounded nouns and noun groups add *'s* to the last item:

This is my grandmother-in-law's house.
This is George and Jim's tent. (George and Jim own the tent jointly.)
CONTRAST: These are George's and Jim's tents. (Each owns a tent.)

"Possession" is sometimes shown by a prepositional phrase rather than by inflection:

He polished the buttons of his coat.
(*He polished his coat's buttons.)
But: It is a day's journey from Genoa.

The apostrophe is used to indicate contractions:

I don't like it.
She doesn't think so.
It isn't proper.
It's reason enough for leaving town.
CONTRAST: Its reason is simple to understand.

The apostrophe is used to indicate plural forms of numerals, special symbols, or words used as words:

Her telephone number had three 6's.
There are two *m*'s in accommodate.
His writing was full of *however*'s.

Possessive forms of pronouns, which have no apostrophe, are sometimes confused with determiners and pronouns contracted with forms of *be*:

Pronoun	Determiner	Contraction
yours	your	you're
its	its	it's
theirs	their	they're
whose		who's
hers	her	

Observe these contrasts:

Their books were stolen.
Theirs were stolen.
They're stolen.

The nation will bide its time.
It's time for a decision.

The victory is Lena's.
The victory is hers.

HYPHEN

Conventions governing the hyphenation of compounds are complex, and no strict rules can be laid down. New compounds constantly appear in print, and the spelling of an item as one or two words is quite arbitrary. A few generalizations are nevertheless useful.

Words, phrases, and clauses that function as a modifier preceding a noun are hyphenated:

well-known artist (*But:* That artist is well known.)
dark-blue sky (*But:* The sky is dark blue.)
face-to-face interview
door-to-door calls
I-don't-care attitude

Note: When the first word is an adverb ending in *-ly*, the hyphen is not used:

a widely discussed book
a poorly equipped house

A hyphen is used in compound words beginning with *self*:

self-appointed
self-conscious
self-denial

A hyphen is also used in compound words containing a proper name:

anti-American
ex-President
post-Sputnik
pre-Columbian

The hyphen is used between the prefix *re-* and the root of a word to convey a meaning different from a word having the same root combined with *re-* and written without a hyphen:

re-collect (collect again)
recollect (remember)
re-act (act again)
react (respond)

The hyphen is used between a prefix and the root of a word to avoid a confusing form of the word:

anti-inflation (*but* antislavery)
semi-invalid (*but* semisweet)

But the tendency is to omit the hyphen between a prefix and a word beginning with the same vowel:

cooperation (*or* co-operation)
coordinate (*or* co-ordinate)
reenlist (*or* re-enlist)
reestablish (*or* re-establish)

A hyphen is used in some compound nouns showing family relationships:

father-in-law
brother-in-law
half-sister
great-grandfather (*But:* grandfather)

Fractions used as modifiers are always hyphenated:[2]

a two-thirds majority
one-half higher
He swam three-fourths the length of the pool.
The manuscript was nine-tenths completed.

[2] Fractions used in noun positions do not require a hyphen (Two thirds were present), though some writers and editors still prefer one (Two-thirds were present).

Numbers from twenty-one to ninety-nine when written out are usually hyphenated, but some writers prefer no punctuation:

He borrowed twenty-two dollars.
He borrowed twenty two dollars.[3]
CONTRAST: He borrowed two hundred dollars.

Words of two or more syllables may be divided at the end of a line. Division usually occurs between affixes and roots (oc-cur, ac-com-mo-date, com-mit-ment, in-con-ven-ien-cy) and at points already hyphenated (low-priced, slow-moving, self-rule). A word is not divided if one of the syllables consists of a single letter (*a-gree, *o-bey, *u-nite).

Note: For exercises, see end of Chapter 21.

[3] The general practice in the use of words or figures to express numbers is to restrict words to round numbers and numbers that can be expressed in two words (twelve yards, a thousand dollars, forty-six boxes), and to use figures elsewhere (112 yards, $637.50, 1,169 boxes). But figures are preferred in informal writing (12 yards, $1,000, 46 boxes).

21) *Fixed Punctuation and Capitalization*

Certain uses of punctuation marks are entirely arbitrary, and any departure from standard practice constitutes an error.

PERIOD

A period is used after certain abbreviations: Dr., Prof., Mr., Messrs., Mrs., Sgt., Lt., R.N., Pres., Ph.D., M.D., U.N., govt., Pfc., ft.

Some abbreviations, especially those of learned journals or societies, do not use a period: PMLA (*Publication of the Modern Language Association*); LSA (Linguistic Society of America); SAA (Speech Association of America). Acronyms, words formed from the initial letters or syllables of compounds or strings of words, and abbreviations for certain governmental or international agencies, also omit the period: SHAEF; NATO; SEATO; UNESCO; Sunoco; CARE; radar.

COMMA

A comma is used to set off items in addresses, dates, and geographical names:

She arrived on Friday, August 13, 1961.

CONTRAST: We expected shipment on 23 March 1961. [A form used by the military and gaining wider acceptance.]

He lives at 303 S. 13th St., Vincennes, Indiana.

He spent the summer in London, Ontario.

CONTRAST: He spent the summer in London. [One may assume that the reference is to the British capital.]

A comma is used after the salutation and the complimentary close in personal letters:

Dear George,
Dear Mr. Faber,
CONTRAST: Dear Mr. Faber: [A colon is required after the salutation in a formal letter.]

Yours very truly,
Sincerely yours,

QUOTATION MARKS

Double quotation marks are commonly used to enclose direct quotations:

"Few parents now-a-days pay any regard to what their children say to them," said Oscar Wilde. "The old-fashioned respect for the young is fast dying out."—*The Importance of Being Earnest*, Act I

Single quotation marks are used to enclose a quotation within a quotation:

"In the theatre of Ibsen," said Shaw, "we are not flattered spectators, killing an idle hour with ingenious and amusing entertainment: we are 'guilty creatures sitting at a play.'"
—ARCHIBALD HENDERSON, *George Bernard Shaw*

Titles of articles, poems, short stories, etc., found in longer works are enclosed in quotation marks:

James A. Michener's "Should Artists Boycott New York?" appeared in the August 26, 1961, issue of the *Saturday Review*.

"Deaths and Entrances" is the title poem of a volume by Dylan Thomas.

Long quotations are single spaced and indented, and quotation marks are omitted:

There is a close parallel between acceptable usage in language and "correct" behavior in other social customs, such as personal garb or table manners. What is it that makes it perfectly good manners to eat some things, such as bread-and-jam, with the fingers, and not others, like meat or vegetables? Certainly not the decree of any official or self-appointed authority; and certainly not any inherent feature or characteristic of what we eat or do not eat with the fingers. Some things that we eat with our fingers are much more messy than others that we would always take up with knife and fork. Here again, it is social acceptability that determines whether we may or may not eat a given item of food with our fingers, or wear a four-in-hand tie with a tuxedo.

—ROBERT A. HALL, JR., *Linguistics and Your Language*

Exactly what constitutes a "long" quotation has to be decided by the writer. A rule of thumb is to single-space and indent a quotation of four lines or longer.

Quotation marks are sometimes used to enclose words used in a special sense, such as "correct" in the first sentence of the last citation. Their use by Hall to describe "behavior in other social customs" but not in language is deliberately ironic. Correctness, Hall implies, is a relative concept. In language, as in table manners or dress, correctness is determined by social acceptability.

The overuse of quotation marks to emphasize a word or phrase, or to apologize for the use of a slang expression, proclaims the amateur and should be avoided.

QUOTATION MARKS WITH OTHER MARKS

A comma is used to set off introductory or explanatory words from quotations:

Jesus asked, "Who is my mother? and who are my brethren?"
   —Matthew xii. 48.

CONTRAST: He said he was sorry. [Indirect statements are not set off by any punctuation.]

CONTRAST: He concluded his address as follows: "Perseverance is the mark of a mature mind." [Formal introductions are followed by a colon. See pp. 247–248.]

"I regret the inconvenience," he said, "but we must make room for younger men."

CONTRAST: "I regret the inconvenience," he said. "We must make room for younger men."

Other marks are used with quotation marks as follows: (1) a period or comma is placed inside the quotation marks; (2) a semicolon or colon is placed outside the quotation marks:

> The poet continued "in his craft and sullen art."
> "Misspellings are hardly acceptable," the professor warned.
> He offered two sayings: "Absence makes the heart grow fonder"; and "Out of sight, out of mind."

(3) A question or exclamation mark is placed inside the quotation marks if it pertains only to the quotation; outside the quotation marks if it pertains to the entire sentence:

> Dr. Graham concluded, "O *ye* hypocrites, ye can discern the face of the sky; but can ye not *discern* the signs of the times?"
> Do you agree that it is "better to reign in Hell than serve in Heaven"?

ITALICS

Italics, slanted letters to set off words or word groups in print, are indicated in typewritten copy by underlining. Titles of books, whole works, names of newspapers and magazines are italicized:

> He read Eliot's *The Mill on the Floss.*
> CONTRAST: He read Poe's "The Raven."
> We particularly enjoyed "Don Juan in Hell" when we saw *Man and Superman.* ["Don Juan in Hell" is part of Shaw's play *Man and Superman.*]
> We particularly enjoyed *Don Juan in Hell.* [The excerpt from Shaw's play has been published and produced separately.]
> He reads *The New York Times* daily.
> He also subscribes to *The Times.* [The reference is to the London *Times.*]
> He likes his *Saturday Review.*

Foreign words and phrases are italicized unless they have been absorbed into the English language:

> She has a certain *savoir faire.*
> CONTRAST: World War II began with a blitzkrieg through Poland.

Names of ships, titles of films and of paintings are italicized:

> They sailed on the *Rotterdam* and returned on the *France.*
> *Exodus* was held over for a fifth month.
> We admired Michelangelo's *David.*

So are letters and words used as words:

John's *h*'s look like *n*'s.
The past tense of *worship* can be spelled with either one or two *p*'s.

Words, phrases, or sentences may be italicized for emphasis:

Symbolization in animals appears to be restricted to the higher primates, to be but a minor element in their total behavior, *and never to be connected with vocal behavior.*
—NELSON BROOKS, *Language and Language Learning*

Italics for emphasis should be used sparingly.

PARENTHESES AND BRACKETS

The chief use of parentheses is to set off an explanatory or illustrative item:

Whatever may be said of its meaning, the form of poetry could be reduced to a science (that is, broken down into fixed units that would lend themselves to analysis and classification) by treating it wholly as sound: heard, seen, or imagined.
—ROBERT E. SPILLER, *The Cycle of American Literature*

The material enclosed in parentheses is an explanatory rather than an editorial comment, which would require brackets. The writer of the parenthetical passage and the quotation are one and the same person.

Brackets are used to enclose editorial insertions to clarify a point, to indicate an error, an unusual construction, or misspelling in a quotation:

"He wanted to preserve its [Cooperstown's] heritage by recreating the old building."
The letter concluded: "The last decision was made by George Montgummery [*sic*] who should have known better than to trust his advisors."

The bracketed *sic*, Latin for *thus it is*, shows that the writer is well aware of the misspelling in the citation, retained for obvious humor.

Brackets and parentheses should be carefully distinguished. Brackets signal an editorial comment; parentheses are part of the quoted material, never an editorial insertion.

ELLIPSIS

In expository writing the ellipsis functions largely as an editorial mark indicating omission of a word or word group. The omission is indicated by three spaced periods. If the omitted material occurs at the end of a quoted sentence, the period for the sentence is used in addition to the three spaced periods:

> "What I call the Downfall of Europe," said Hesse, "is foretold and explained with extreme clearness in Dostoevsky's works and in the most concentrated form in *The Brothers Karamazov. . . .*"
> —J. ISAACS, *An Assessment of Twentieth-Century Literature*

In descriptive and narrative writing, an ellipsis often indicates unexpressed thoughts or hesitations, as in the following excerpt from Joseph Conrad's *Lord Jim*:

> "Deucedly tired she must have been—and all that kind of thing. And—and—hang it all—she was fond of me, don't you see. . . . I, too . . . didn't know, of course . . . never entered my head. . . ."

CAPITALIZATION

Although a student is very likely to have mastered the rules of capitalization, problems sometimes arise. Important personal titles, for example, are capitalized whether they appear before or after a name, but usage is divided when lesser titles come after a name:

General Eisenhower
President Kennedy, Chief of State
Professor William Jones
William Jones, Professor of Spanish
Or: William Jones, professor of Spanish

Titles of books, magazines, articles, etc., are capitalized except for medial prepositions and determiners:

Seven Types of Ambiguity
The Reporter
A Portrait of the Artist as a Young Man

Points of the compass are capitalized when they denote geographical location, but not when they denote direction:

She was born in the South.
CONTRAST: Drive seven miles south.

Words indicating family relationships are capitalized when used as titles or with proper names:

The family honored Grandmother Fisher.

I sent Mother a letter yesterday.

CONTRAST: My mother asked me to write immediately. We expected Aunt Fanny for dinner.

Titles of academic courses are capitalized:

She registered for Area Studies 104.

CONTRAST: She majored in area studies.

CONTRAST: He studied English, French, and history.

EXERCISES

NOTE: All sentences in the exercises below are from *Background and Foreground: The Best from Thirty Years of* The New York Times Magazine, ed. Lester Markel (New York: Dell, 1963).[1]

1. Internal punctuation consisting of commas only has been deleted from the following sentences. Supply a comma or commas where needed. Be ready to account for your punctuation.

    1. Gettysburg is a quiet market town and a place where all the roads meet and it is also a place where destiny laid its hand on the American people amid great noise and violence.—BRUCE CATTON

    2. We live by symbols and Gettysburg is as good a symbol as any of the stupendous price that America paid to break its way into the modern world.—BRUCE CATTON

    3. Togetherness is a friendly condition and no one likes to make a principle of unfriendliness. It is also a strenuous condition and no one likes to admit he cannot keep up the pace.—CHARLES FRANKEL

    4. One likes cats because they set standards of beauty dignity and deportment unequalled in the animal kingdom and yet tolerate the company of men.—JAMES MASON

    5. Without the language any attempt to see into the Japanese mentality must fail for it is a strange truth that the Japanese are unable to express their thoughts truly in English.
       —JOHN D. ROCKEFELLER IV

[1] © 1965 by The New York Times Company. Reprinted by permission.

6. Because Japanese classrooms are not heated numb feet and legs are an everyday problem.—JOHN D. ROCKEFELLER IV

7. As every child knows the secret of family life is a little separateness. —CHARLES FRANKEL

8. Many physicians especially those of us who are interested in physiology and health as well as in disease consider physical exercise just as essential for the best health as rest and sleep food one's job recreation and peace of mind.—PAUL DUDLEY WHITE

9. An intense mental worker needs exercise to keep his mind clear and it is well if mental concentration can be alternated frequently with exercise or even accompanied thereby as was the common custom of the peripatetic philosophers in Athens in the days of its prime.—PAUL DUDLEY WHITE

10. Well over seven hundred universities and colleges are now offering courses in courtship marriage and the family and the instructors who teach them are almost to a man hostile to romantic love holding it to be a deception a danger and even a disease. —MORTON M. HUNT

2. In the following sentences, semicolons, colons, dashes, and commas have been omitted. Supply whatever appropriate punctuation is needed. (*Note:* In certain instances, alternate punctuation may be possible.)

1. The value of a committee is that the people on it get to know each other they learn habits of patience and tolerance they get a sense of participation and usefulness most remarkable of all they learn to think as a group.—CHARLES FRANKEL

2. In short a committee exists to bring people together and when this process really takes the results are unmistakable a successful committee spawns more committees.—CHARLES FRANKEL

3. The Japanese share one problem that is common to all of Asia's students poverty.—JOHN D. ROCKEFELLER IV

4. If a nuclear war occurred there are again various different logical possibilities first the victory of one group second reversion to universal barbarism third the end of the human race. —BERTRAND RUSSELL

5. Sister playing records in her room Junior in the attic Father in the kitchen Mother in the city on these small lonely things a solid family life is built.—CHARLES FRANKEL

3. The following sentences contain restrictive and nonrestrictive elements. Supply whatever punctuation is needed and be ready to defend your choice.

   1. Few families have ever got along if their members did not occasionally have a chance to be alone.—CHARLES FRANKEL

   2. I do not see any way out of our vicious circle of poverty except by utilizing the new sources of power which science has placed at our disposal.—JAWAHARLAL NEHRU

   3. It is easy to follow in the sacred writings of the Jewish people the development of the religion of fear into the moral religion which is carried further in the New Testament.—ALBERT EINSTEIN

   4. Even as a student at the officers' academy where his record was superb he [De Gaulle] chose to isolate himself from others.
      —C. L. SULZBERGER

   5. Two-thirds of the human race to whom adequate medical care is inaccessible are sick and hungry.—THOMAS A. DOOLEY

4. In the following sentences, hyphens and apostrophes, in addition to other internal markers, have been omitted. Supply whatever appropriate punctuation is needed.

   1. The self respecting individual will try to be as tolerant of his neighbors shortcomings as he is of his own.—ERIC HOFFER

   2. Contemporaries knew nothing about George Washingtons false teeth or Catherine the Greats wig. Todays famous statesmen inhabit an aquarium.—C. L. SULZBERGER

   3. Mayor La Guardia like Governor Smith was a down to earth catch as catch can talker in the vernacular not a fine writer embalming immortal thoughts for future readers.—ROBERT MOSES

   4. Our experience has proved to us that a heart to heart person to person program however simple can be extremely powerful efficacious and appreciated.—THOMAS A. DOOLEY

   5. The word grandeur belongs to the environment of De Gaulles class the rural aristocracy of devout Catholics and firm patriots that has furnished so many of Frances great captains from the days of Du Guesclin La Hire and Bayard to De Gaulle himself with his highly evocative name.—C. L. SULZBERGER

5. Fixed punctuation and other internal markers have been omitted from the following sentences. Supply whatever appropriate punctuation is needed.

   1. The Allied invasion of France on June 6 1944 was both the emotional and strategic climax of World War II.
—HANSON W. BALDWIN

   2. Every despotism wrote the nineteenth century philosopher Amiel has a specially keen and hostile instinct for whatever keeps up human dignity and independence.—ERIC HOFFER

   3. More than a century ago Alexis de Tocqueville noticed the peculiar aptitude of Americans for forming associations. As soon as several of the inhabitants of the United States have taken up an opinion or a feeling which they wish to promote in the world he observed they look out for mutual assistance and as soon as they have found one another out they combine.—CHARLES FRANKEL

   4. The question of homing dogs was considered by Bergen Evans in his book The Natural History of Nonsense but he touched on these mysterious creatures in a gingerly fashion like a minister caught alone in a parlor with an irritable schnauzer.—JAMES THURBER

   5. Sometimes the argument is made as by Prof Israel M Kirzner in a letter to The New York Times on June 4 that private enterprise can provide more efficiently the very services which government is being asked to perform.—CHARLES F. DARLINGTON

6. End punctuation and internal markers have been omitted from the following groups of sentences. Supply whatever appropriate punctuation is needed.

   1. From the point of view of humanity in general the hostility between Russia and America is what threatens disaster and anything tending to mitigate this hostility is a service to man because of the destructive character of nuclear weapons it is no longer useful to point to the wickedness of the side to which we do not belong.
—BERTRAND RUSSELL

   2. It is a tough life for a cat to have to fend for himself as the condition of the New York alley cats testifies according to Dr. Camuti the cat specialist the adult cat requires not less than four ounces of meat per day.—JAMES MASON

3. What happened in Hungary was not essentially a conflict between communism and anticommunism it represented nationalism striving for freedom from foreign control.—JAWAHARLAL NEHRU

4. I heard of a prominent American who had much to do in Europe in trains he dictated letters to his secretary in automobiles he held his conferences his councils took place at dinner.—KAREL CAPEK

5. For Gettysburg was a beginning and not an ending what we hope to be what we can yet bring forth on this continent somehow dates from this place.—BRUCE CATTON

22) Spelling

Correct spelling is a point of etiquette. Unless one follows standard conventions of orthography, he risks being labeled "illiterate." This may seem unfair, particularly since nobody has yet established a correlation between native intelligence and ability to spell. But spelling errors are readily apparent, even to the most unsophisticated, and rightly or wrongly they evoke unfavorable judgments about a writer.

PROBLEMS IN ENGLISH SPELLING

The greatest problem in English spelling, as has been pointed out in the Introduction, is the imperfect relationship between the pronunciation of a word and its written form. A letter or sequence of letters may represent different sound units, or phonemes, such as the letter *i* in *wit* and *divide*, or *ough* in *tough*, *though*, *cough*, and *through*. Conversely, a phoneme may be represented by different spellings: /s/ in *see* and *certificate*, for example, is also represented by such combinations as *ss* (*aggressive*) and *sc* (*fascination*).

Spelling problems would be eliminated if there were a one-to-one relationship between the phonemes of English and the letters of the alphabet. A one-to-one correspondence between phoneme and letter, however, with one letter of the alphabet representing one phoneme, is impossible, because the thirty-three phonemes of modern English correlate with only twenty-six letters of the alphabet. Yet a writing system with a perfect correlation of phoneme to letter would compel everyone to learn new symbols, so that he could write as he speaks. Since each person's speech is unique, there would be as many different ways of "spelling" as there are speakers of the language, and a common standard would be difficult, if not impossible, to achieve. All documents using traditional spelling, moreover, would in time read like a foreign language.

However one may complain about English spelling, the writing system is not as chaotic as some think. To an overwhelming extent it is patterned, and its complexities can be explained in terms of foreign influence and historical changes. The Old English alphabet, for example, had two possible scribal symbols for the *th*, neither of which our present alphabet can handle. We now use the same letter sequence for the voiceless and voiced *th* in *thing* and *this*, respectively. The combination *æ* represented the vowel sound in *back*, *at*, and *that*. In modern English, the letter *a* has replaced the Old English symbol, but in addition to the vowel sound in *mad*, it represents the vowel sounds of *bake*, *war*, and *sofa*. The Old English combination *sc* signaled the initial phoneme, now spelled *sh*, in words like *ship*, *shield*, and *should*, but in modern English this phoneme is represented in more than fourteen different ways. The letter *c* still represents the initial sound of *come*, *candle*, and *cliff*, but it has other values in *cello* and *sentence*.

Foreign influence has added greatly to the complexity of English spelling. After the invasion of 1066, Norman scribes inserted a *b* into words like *debt* and *doubt*, which, they reasoned, would bring the writing system in line with that of Latin in *debitum* and *dubitare*, though spellings like *dette* and *doute* actually approximated the Old English pronunciation more closely. French influence also accounts for the introduction of *u* in *guess*, *qu* in *quick*, and the use of *o* in words like *son*, *love*, and *tongue*. To the Dutch background of early printers, we can attribute the letter *h* in words like *ghost* and *gherkin*.[1] Greek is responsible for combinations like *pn* (*pneumatic*), *mn* (*mnemonic*), *ps* (*psychic*), *pt* (*ptomaine*). Though the initial letters are not pronounced in English, they remain in our writing system.

---

[1] Stuart Robinson and Frederic G. Cassidy, *The Development of Modern English* (Englewood Cliffs, N.J.: Prentice-Hall, 1954), pp. 331–333.

Many proposals have been made to achieve a more consistent English orthography. In the seventeenth century, for example, James Howell criticized the lack of correlation between sound and spelling and proposed simplifications, all of which today's troubled speller would have favored:[2]

favor		favour
war		warre
business	*instead of*	businesse
Parlement		Parliament
tresure		treasure

Some of Howell's simplifications have since become standard practice.

In the United States, perhaps the most formidable effort in behalf of spelling reform was made by Noah Webster, who dropped the *u* in *honour, labour, humour*; the *k* in *logick, musick*. He wrote *check, risk,* instead of *cheque, risque,* and tried to eliminate the "silent e" in *determine, medicine,* and *examine.* He changed *defence to defense, gaol* to *jail, mediaeval* to *medieval,* and approved of *theater, program,* and *cigaret,* though some still believe that smoking a *cigarette* while scanning a *programme* in a *theatre* is more elegant.

In the twentieth century Andrew Carnegie gave money for the establishment of a Simplified Spelling Board, which has exerted but little influence on present-day orthography. Individual efforts to simplify spelling have had little success, and piecemeal reforms of certain newspapers, such as the replacement of *ph* by *f* (*filosofy*) or *ei* by *a* (*frate*) have gained no support.

The student who has problems in spelling has little choice but to accept the present system of orthography with its imperfections and abandon hope for immediate reforms. He should remember, however, that the ways in which a writing system represents the spoken language is no reflection whatsoever of the characteristic features of the language.

PATTERNS OF WORDS FREQUENTLY MISSPELLED

The remainder of this chapter contains patterns of words frequently misspelled by college students. Words are arranged according to sound (phoneme)-letter relationships in patterns of contrastive

[2] Albert C. Baugh, *A History of the English Language* (New York: Appleton-Century-Crofts, 1935), pp. 490–491.

spellings, so that attention can be properly focused on the spelling difficulty.[3]

SIMPLIFIED PHONEMIC CHART[4]

Consonants		Vowels	
/p/	*p*ill, s*p*ill, li*p*	/i/	p*i*t
/b/	*b*ill	/e/	pet
/t/	*t*ill, s*t*ill, li*t*	/æ/	p*a*t
/d/	*d*ill	/ə/	p*u*tt, loaf*e*r
/k/	*k*ill, s*k*ill, li*ck*	/a/	pot, f*a*ther
/g/	*g*ill	/u/	p*u*t
/č/	*ch*ill	/o/	in most American dialects usually occurs as part of a diphthong.
/ǰ/	*J*ill		
/f/	*f*ail	/ɔ/	b*a*ll, n*augh*t
/v/	*v*eil		
/θ/	*th*igh	Diphthongs	
/ð/	*th*y	/iy/	be
/s/	*s*eal	/ey/	b*ay*
/z/	*z*eal	/ay/	b*uy*
/š/	*s*ure	/oy/	bo*y*
(ž/	mea*s*ure	/aw/	no*w*
/m/	ra*m*	/ow/	no
/n/	ra*n*	/uw/	ne*w*
/ŋ/	ra*ng*		
/l/	*l*ame, mai*l*		
/r/	*r*ail, lai*r*		

/w/ *w*on, no*w* /w/ after a vowel indicates increased lip rounding and upward and backward movement of the tongue.

/y/ *y*am, ma*y* /y/ after a vowel indicates increased lip spreading and upward and forward movement of the tongue.

/h/ *h*ome

I. A phoneme is not always represented by the same letter in writing.

---

[3] The list has been compiled over a period of years. It includes items from Edna L. Furness and Gertrude A. Boyd, "335 Real Spelling Demons for College Students," *College English*, XX (March, 1959), 292–295. Reprinted with the permission of the National Council of Teachers of English and Edna L. Furness and Gertrude A. Boyd.

[4] The pronunciations in this chart are those found in the northern tier of states west of the Atlantic seaboard. The /ɨ/ has been omitted.

A. Some phonemes are represented by either a single or double letter:[5]

Phoneme	Spelling	
/f/	*f*	*ff*
	afraid	different
	deficiency	difficult
	prefer	sufficient
	professor	suffix
/g/	*g*	*gg*
	against	aggravate
	disgust	aggregate
/k/	*c*	*cc*
	across	accommodate
	icon	accomplish
		accord
		accurate
		occasion
		occur
/l/	*l*	*ll*
	almost	allocate
	already	allot
	balance	allow
	calendar	all ready
	color	all right
	excel	challenge
	fulfill	college
	helpful	excellent
	until	fallacy
		finally
		fill
		fulfill
		intelligent
		parallel
		syllable
		villain

[5] There are historical reasons for some differences in spelling, but they do not concern us here.

Phoneme	Spelling	
/m/	*m*	*mm*
	among	accommodate
	omit	committee
		grammar
		immediately
		recommend
		symmetrical
/n/	*n*	*nn*
	dining	annual
	personal	personnel
	until	questionnaire
/p/	*p*	*pp*
	apart	apparatus
	aptitude	apparent
	opera	appear
	opinion	appoint
	surprise	approach
		appropriate
		opportunity
		oppose
		supply
		suppose
		suppress
/r/	*r*	*rr*
	around	arrange
	arouse	curriculum
	during	embarrass
	harass	irrelevant
/t/	*t*	*tt*
	admit	attain
	atone	attend
	atrophy	attest
	permit	attitude
	regret	committee

B.   Some phonemes are represented by single or double letters, as well as by combinations of letters:

Phoneme	Spelling			
/s/	*s*	*ss*	*c*	*sc*
	bias	asset	advice	ascend
	consensus	assignment	bicycle	discipline
	consider	classmates	certain	fascination
	counsel	embarrass	chance	muscle
	emphasis	essential	choice	scene
	expense	necessary	concentrate	science
	sense	possible	concern	
		professor	criticism	
			cylinder	
			decide	
			difference	
			disgrace	
			exercise	
			facet	
			farce	
			license	
			practice	
			precede	
			sentence	
			since	
			sincere	
			specimen	
/z/	*z*	*s*	*ss*	
	analyze	advise	possess	
	criticize	advertise		
	emphasize	confuse		
	magazine	disease		
	organize	does		
	quiz	exercise		
		propose		
		surprise		
/š/	*s*	*ssi*	*sh*	*si*
	sure	possession	shibboleth	compre-
		profession		hension
				extension
				pretension

Phoneme	Spelling		
	sci	*ci*	*ti*
	conscience	deficiency	conscientious
	conscious	efficient	definition
		official	cultivation
		politician	description
		proficient	influential
		special	initiative
			organization
			preparation
			tuition

Phoneme	Spelling	
/ž/	*s*	*si*
	usual	decision
		persuasion

Phoneme	Spelling			
/ǰ/	*g*	*gg*	*gi*	*ge*
	angel	exaggerate	religious	sergeant
	college			
	imagination			
	original			
	privilege			
	rigid			
	tragedy			

	dge	*j*
	knowledge	prejudice

Certain vowels and diphthongs have variant spellings:

Phoneme			
/e/	*e*	*ea*	*ie*
	led	dealt	friend
	red	meant	
	schedule	read	
	stretch	jealous	
	together		

Phoneme			
/ey/	*a*	*ai*	*ei*
	grateful	avail	neighbor
	spontaneous	laid	outweigh
		paid	
		straighten	
	prepare		

Phoneme	Spelling		
/iy/	*e*	*ee*	*ea*
	complete	proceed	breathe
	precede	speech	repeat
	procedure	succeed	peace
	theme		speak
	interfere		realize

	ei	*i*	*ie*
	ceiling	machine	achieve
	conceive	magazine	believe
	leisure	routine	chief
	receipt		grief
	seize		niece
			piece
	weird		relieve

C. The vowel sound in an unstressed syllable is represented by different letters and combinations of letters:[6]

/ə/	*a*	*e*	*i*
	adequate	average	business
	amateur	cemetery	clarify
	comparatively	consequently	definitely
	explanatory	considerable	distinction
	fundamental	desperate	divide
	grammar	destroy	divine
	incidentally	different	easily
	preparatory	enemy	eligible
	pleasant	existence	estimation
	relatively	further	experiment
	separate (Aj)	generally	imaginary
	separate (V)	interest	medicine
	tradition	listener	optimism
		literary	origin
		mathematics	primitive
		occurrence	similar
		reference	technicality

[6] Certain speakers do not pronounce some of the unstressed vowels in these words and omit them in writing, thus accounting for misspellings like *reptition, *orgin, *labratory.

Phonemes	Spelling		
/ə/	*a*	*e*	*i*
		repetition	
		several	
		supplement	
		supposedly	
		temperament	
		tendency	
		undoubtedly	
		vegetable	
		veteran	

o	*u*	*ai*
actor	curriculum	villain
contemporary	faculty	
humorous	naturally	
laboratory	pursue	
opportunity	upon	
poison		
sophomore		

eig
foreign

D. Certain sound sequences are represented by different combinations of letters:

/-ər/	*-ar*	*-er*	*-or*	*-re*
	familiar	maneuver	actor	mediocre
	grammar	pretender	author	
	peculiar	teacher	counselor	
	similar	theater	governor	
			instructor	
	-eur		professor	
	amateur		surveyor	

/-əl/	*-al*	*-el*	*-le*
	beneficial	level	article
	comical	nickel	considerable
	controversial	panel	eligible

Phonemes	Spelling	
/-əl/	-al	-le
	detrimental	horrible
	essential	muscle
	fundamental	obstacle
	grammatical	possible
	personal	vegetable
	practical	
	technical	
	total	
/-əbəl/	-able	-ible
	available	contemptible
	considerable	responsible
	indispensable	suggestible
	peaceable	
	valuable	
/-əns/	-ance	-ence
	acquaintance	audience
	attendance	competence
	brilliance	confidence
	guidance	consistence
	importance	convenience
	maintenance	correspondence
	observance	dependence
	relevance	difference
	repentance	excellence
	resistance	existence
	significance	experience
	tolerance	independence
	vengeance	intelligence
		occurrence
		permanence
		precedence
		reference

Adjectives corresponding to nouns ending in *-ance* add an *-ant* suffix: *attendant, important, observant*; adjectives corresponding to nouns ending in *-ence* add *-ent*: *competent, confident, consistent*.

E. For many American speakers the following pairs or triplets are pronounced the same, but their spellings are different:

a lot	allot	
aisle	isle	
allowed	aloud	
bare	bear	
brake	break	
capital	capitol	
coarse	course	
complement	compliment	
dew	do	due
fair	fare	
for	fore	four
grate	great	
hole	whole	
holy	wholly	
hoarse	horse	
hour	our	
its	it's	
knew	new	
know	no	
knows	nose	
mail	male	
marry	Mary	merry
meat	meet	mete
one	won	
pail	pale	
plain	plane	
principal	principle	
role	roll	
stationary	stationery	
their	there	they're
throne	thrown	
to	too	two
way	weigh	
wait	weight	
weather	whether	
whose	who's	
your	you're	

II.   So-called "silent letters" are sometimes incorrectly omitted in writing.

A.   The "silent *e*," italicized in the following list, is required in standard orthography:[7]

accurat*e*ly	becaus*e*
adequat*e*ly	bor*e*
attentiv*e*ly	concentrat*e*
definit*e*ly	concret*e*
extrem*e*ly	creat*e*
for*e*see	deviat*e*
immens*e*ly	examin*e*
lik*e*ly	graduat*e*
lon*e*ly	jud*ge*
relativ*e*ly	ignor*e*
saf*e*ly	tru*e*
sincer*e*ly	
som*e*thing	
sug*ge*stiv*e*ly	
unfortunat*e*ly	
ther*e*fore	

B.   Other silent letters include the following:

b	*h*	*p*	*gh*
debt	ghastly	pneumonia	although
doubt	ghetto	psyche	height
undoubtedly	ghost	psychic	straight
	rhymed	psychology	thought
	r*h*ythm		weight

C.   Derived forms of words ending in a "silent *e*" drop the *e* before suffixes beginning with a vowel:

---

[7] The "silent *e*" serves a purpose in distinguishing certain consonant and vowel sounds as in the following:

lung	lunge
bit	bite
far	fare

	-*ing*	*Vowel*	*Consonant*
acquire	acquiring		
argue	arguing	arguable	argument[8]
care	caring		
choose	choosing		
come	coming		
conceive	conceiving	conceivable	
continue	continuing	continuance	
create	creating	creative	
desire	desiring	desirable	
examine	examining	examination	
have	having		
hope	hoping		hopeful
ignore	ignoring	ignorance	
improve	improving		improvement
live	living	livable (*also* liveable)	
make	making		
move	moving	movable (*also* moveable)	
outline	outlining		
require	requiring		requirement
use	using	usable (*also* useable)	useless
write	writing		

Derived forms of the following drop the *e* before *ing* and before suffixes beginning with a consonant:

	-*ing*	*Vowel*	*Consonant*
abridge	abridging		abridgment
challenge	challenging	challengeable	
change	changing	changeable	
judge	judging		judgment
notice	noticing	noticeable	

III.   Dialect differences account for certain misspellings.

A..   The natural tendency to spell words as they are sometimes

---

[8] A special case in which the *e* is dropped, even though the suffix begins with a consonant.

or always pronounced is responsible for many errors in spelling:[9]

an*d*	env*i*ro*n*ment	ne*c*essary
ans*w*er	Febr*u*ary	pa*r*tic*u*larly
Ar*c*tic	gover*n*ment	proba*b*ly
auxil*i*ary	gran*t*ed	pun*c*tuation
ba*ck*ground	greates*t*	quan*t*ity
contin*u*ous	interp*r*et	reco*g*nize
cul*t*ivation	len*g*th	sema*n*tic
*e*ntire	lib*r*ary	stren*u*ous
		stud*y*ing
		use*d* (He use*d* to go.)
a*th*letic		us*u*ally
disas*t*rous		W*ed*nesday
		wors*t*

B.   The following pairs are sometimes confused in writing because they are pronounced nearly alike (in the dialects of certain speakers, some of the pairs may be pronounced identically):

accept	except
adapt	adept
affect	effect
are	our
climactic	climatic
clothes	cloths
command	commend
department	deportment
half	halve
hardly	heartily
ingenious	ingenuous
later	latter
loose	lose
of	off
precede	proceed
quiet	quite

[9] A few speakers pronounce these and other words as they are spelled, with resulting "spelling pronunciations," that is, overcareful, overprecise speech, like the use of /n/ in *government*, or of /zd/ in *used to*, both of which seem affected. Spelling pronunciations should be avoided.

setting	sitting
statue	statute
vary	very
wear	were
went	when
which	witch

The following are especially troublesome:

four	forty
guard	regard
perform	prefer

The pairs below contrast in pronunciation and stress:

command	comment
enter	inter
inconstancy	inconsistency
moral	morale
pastime	pass time (They pass time sleeping.)
personal	personnel

IV. Special problems account for certain errors in spelling.

A. The spelling of grammatically related forms is sometimes confused:

Verb	*Noun*
advise	advice
analyze	analysis
believe	belief
explain	explanation
prove	proof
pronounce	pronunciation

Adjective	*Noun*
curious	curiosity
desperate	despair
handy	handicap
lazy	laziness
lively	livelihood
repeat	repetition
true	truth

B.   The doubling of consonants in the formation of *ed* and *ing* forms of verbs or of other derivative forms beginning with a vowel follow predictable patterns. Words of one syllable ending in a single consonant preceded by a single vowel (*drag*) double the consonant before adding the suffix (*dragged*), but words of two or more syllables double the final consonant only if the final syllable is stressed (*prefer*, *preferred*, but *preference*):

begin		beginning	
commit	committed	committing	
control	controlled	controlling	
drag	dragged	dragging	
drop	dropped	dropping	
fit	fitted	fitting	
incur	incurred	incurring	
infer	inferred	inferring	inference
prefer	preferred	preferring	preference
refer	referred	referring	reference
regret	regretted	regretting	
ship	shipped	shipping	
stop	stopped	stopping	stoppage
transfer	transferred	transferring	transference[10]
benefit	benefited	benefiting	
develop	developed	developing	development
differ	differed	differing	

C.   Certain prefixes and suffixes account for the doubling of consonants.

    1.   A consonant is doubled if the last letter of a prefix and the first letter of the word to which the prefix is added are the same:

	dis-
satisfy	dissatisfy
simulate	dissimulate
solve	dissolve
solution	dissolution

[10] A special case where the *r* is not doubled despite stress on the second syllable.

CONTRAST: appear   disappear
          appoint   disappoint

ir-

          reparable   irreparable
          refutable   irrefutable
          relevant   irrelevant
          rational   irrational

mis-

          spelling   misspelling
          shaped   misshaped
          state   misstate

CONTRAST: represent   misrepresent

un-

          necessary   unnecessary
          natural   unnatural
          numbered   unnumbered

2. A consonant is doubled if the first letter of a suffix and
    the last letter of the word to which the suffix is added
    are the same:

-ly

          comical   comically
          personal   personally
          practical   practically
          radical   radically
          real   really
          total   totally

CONTRAST: true   truly
          accurate   accurately

D. Some words have more than one acceptable standard
    spelling.

1. The first spelling is American, the second British:

esthetic	aesthetic
caliber	calibre
fulfill	fulfil
offense	offence
theater	theatre

2. The first spelling is the more conservative:

demagogue	demagog
dialogue	dialog
through	thru (*or* thro)

List additional items frequently misspelled and develop the habit of using a standard dictionary.

EXERCISE

If you have a spelling problem, you should, first of all, identify your difficulty, preferably with the help of your instructor, and then go about correcting the deficiency in a systematic way. You can usually do so by practicing patterns of contrastive spellings and focusing on the visual contrasts of words which are usually misspelled. The arrangement of words in this chapter should enable you to select those patterns that give you trouble. A good procedure is, first, to copy these patterns several times, and, after a lapse of a day or two, to have another person dictate them. The correctly spelled items can then be gradually eliminated from the list until no misspellings remain.

23) *Correct Sentence Structure*

The rules for writing grammatical sentences offer the beginner a broad range within which to establish clear communication between himself and his reader. To subscribe to these rules is not to yield freedom of expression, but to accept conventions that have worked for most writers. The expert feels free to suit them to his own purpose, and he can do so only because he is an expert. The beginner should remember that competence in observing rules had better precede his impulse to bypass them.

SENTENCE FRAGMENTS

The acceptable syntactic unit in written composition is the sentence. Both smaller and larger units than the sentence, but punctuated as a sentence, are used by professional writers for special reasons. Used by the beginner, such units are almost always objectionable, because they occur without intent. Strings of words smaller than a sentence but punctuated as a sentence are called **fragments.**

Sometimes subordinate and relative clauses are incorrectly punctuated as sentences:

A high school football player should not be subsidized through college. *When he proclaims his intention of becoming a professional player.

But a clause introduced by a subordinator is not normally punctuated as a separate sentence:

> A high school football player should not be subsidized through college when he proclaims his intention of becoming a professional player.

Subordinate clauses introduced by function words like *although, unless, because, while* [meaning "whereas"] are usually preceded by a comma:

> A high school football player hostile to learning should not be subsidized through college. *While a potentially capable but poor student is denied the opportunity to advance himself.

> A high school football player hostile to learning should not be subsidized through college, while a potentially capable but poor student is denied the opportunity to advance himself.

Relative clauses introduced by *who, which, that, whose, whom* are sometimes improperly punctuated as sentences when they occur at the end:

> He anticipated no delay or interruption in his itinerary. *Which he had carefully prepared.

> He anticipated no delay or interruption in his itinerary, which he had carefully prepared.

Almost any syntactic structure may be incorrectly punctuated as a sentence. In the following, an appositive is given sentence status:

> After being ushered into the Oval Room, we were introduced to the Philippine Ambassador. *A vigorous champion of close Filipino-American relations.

> After being ushered into the Oval Room, we were introduced to the Philippine Ambassador, a vigorous champion of close Filipino-American relations.

In the following, a prepositional phrase is incorrectly punctuated as a sentence:

> Language mechanics should be taught more intensively in the primary schools. *With high schools emphasizing the study of literature.

> Language mechanics should be taught more intensively in the primary schools, with high schools emphasizing the study of literature.

Acceptable syntactic units smaller than a sentence are shown in the following examples. In each, the writer seeks the effects of spoken language by appearing to address the reader directly. Clifton Fadiman first establishes a casual intimacy with the reader through the collo-quial phrase "a great deal" instead of the more formal "much":

> For almost half a century literature has meant a great deal to me. Not as a "subject," for it is not a subject as geometry or Sanskrit is a subject. But as a mode (a good one, but only one) of enhancing, clarifying and con-centrating whatever fugitive sense I have of my own existence.
> —CLIFTON FADIMAN, *Holiday*

Archibald MacLeish takes an apparently irreverent attitude toward his subject by fragmenting the last sentence:

> Everybody knows that "creative writing"—which means the use of words as material of art—can't be taught. Nevertheless hundreds of professors in hundreds of colleges go on teaching it. Which is absurd but not as absurd as it sounds.—ARCHIBALD MACLEISH, *Harper's Magazine*

The beginner should not break up his sentences unless he does so deliberately.

RUN-ON SENTENCES

Two sentences incorrectly punctuated as one are called **run-on sentences.** Unacceptable in expository writing, run-on sentences are usually caused by a failure to hear a terminal juncture at the end of a sentence:

> *There are special programs for men these include sports, dramatics, and languages.
>
> There are special programs for men. These include sports, dramatics, and languages.
>
> There are special programs for men; these include sports, dramatics, and languages.

Sometimes a comma is used between two sentences when there should be a semicolon or a period.[1] Though a less glaring fault than no

1 See pp. 246–247.

punctuation at all, a **comma splice,** or **comma fault,** is unacceptable in serious writing:

> *There are special programs for men, these include sports, dramatics, and languages.

Revision requires a semicolon or period after *men.*

Comma splices are sometimes due to failure to hear a falling juncture where a falling juncture is normally heard. For example:

> * Negotiations for passage of the bill began after all the parties had agreed to limit debate, nonetheless, passage was considered unlikely for at least two months.

A normal reading of the sentence should reveal a falling juncture on *debate,* indicated by a semicolon or a period:

> Negotiations for passage of the bill began after all the parties had agreed to limit debate; nonetheless, passage was considered unlikely for at least two months.

> Negotiations for passage of the bill began after all the parties had agreed to limit debate. Nonetheless, passage was considered unlikely for at least two months.

Proper use of conjunctive adverbs like *nonetheless, however, therefore* can often help to avoid the typical comma splice, such as the one just cited. If the conjunctive adverb connects two clauses, it is preceded by a semicolon:

> * My brother and I are enrolled in the School of Science, preparing for a career in pharmacy, however, my brother had two years of practical experience before coming to college.

> My brother and I are enrolled in the School of Science, preparing for a career in pharmacy; however, my brother had two years of practical experience before coming to college.

If the conjunctive adverb occurs inside the sentence, the use of a comma or commas to set it off is optional:

> My brother and I are enrolled in the School of Science, preparing for a career in pharmacy; my brother, however, had two years of practical experience before coming to college.

> My brother and I are enrolled in the School of Science, preparing for a career in pharmacy; furthermore we expect to graduate within three years.

However, nevertheless, nonetheless are more likely to be set off by a comma or commas than *therefore, consequently,* or *furthermore.*

REFERENCE OF PRONOUNS

A pronoun should have a clearly defined reference to a preceding noun, called its **antecedent.**[2] When a pronoun has more than one antecedent, ambiguity results:

> Miss Pringle told her sister that she should purchase more fashionable footwear.
>
> Joan's friend called her sister.

The first sentence fails to state clearly whether Miss Pringle or Miss Pringle's sister should buy a pair of shoes:

> Miss Pringle told her sister: "I should purchase more fashionable footwear."
>
> Miss Pringle said that her sister should purchase more fashionable footwear.

The second sentence fails to make clear whether a telephone conversation took place, whether Joan's friend called her own or someone else's sister, or whether Joan's friend addressed someone else as sister, either once or habitually.

Antecedents of pronouns, especially those of *this, that,* and the relative *which,* are not always clearly stated, so that the reader's train of thought is momentarily interrupted:

> My husband is a general practitioner. It is not surprising therefore that some of *this* has become part of my mode of speech, more so now that I am the receptionist in his office.

One can only guess what antecedent the writer had in mind, since no noun in the first sentence can be identified with *this* in the second:

> My husband is a general practitioner. It is not surprising therefore that some of his *medical terminology* has become part of my mode of speech, more so now that I am the receptionist in his office.

Sometimes the antecedent of a pronoun is improperly placed in a

---

[2] See also pronouns as sequence markers, pp. 125–126.

prepositional phrase. In the following sentence, it is unclear whether *he* refers to Gulliver or to the author of *Gulliver's Travels:*

> *In Gulliver's visit to Lilliput, he observes the habits of the little people, who are one-twelfth his size.
>
> In his visit to Lilliput, Gulliver observes the habits of the little people, who are one-twelfth his size.

Also:

> *During a child's education, he is taught to get along with others.
>
> A child's education includes training on how to get along with others.

The habit of using pronouns in conversation without a clearly defined antecedent is sometimes inappropriately transferred to serious writing:

> They say that there'll be four inches of snow before morning.

The subject should be explicitly stated:

> The weather bureau predicts four inches of snow before morning.

Sometimes the indefinite *you* is used with deliberate intent, as in the second of the following sentences:

> No man can "like" literature as a whole any more than he can like all the people he meets. *You* can force a man into Philistinism by insisting that he do the first just as you can force him into misanthropy by insisting that he do the second.—CLIFTON FADIMAN, *Holiday*

Again in the following, the italicized pronouns have reference to preceding sentences:

> Erect more school buildings, hire more teachers, endow more scientists, let Congress appropriate a few more billions and—rich as America is—we can't help winning the Cold War in general and the crisis in education in particular. *That* seems to be the cry today. *This* is indeed a superficial view of the current emergency.—CLAUDE M. FUESS, *Saturday Review*

That refers to the entire first sentence, and *this* to the two preceding sentences. As already pointed out, however, the use by professional writers of pronouns whose antecedent is a sentence rather than an explicit word or phrase does not imply unreserved endorsement of such practice by the beginning student.

AGREEMENT

The subject-predicate relationship in English sentences is signaled by agreement in number. A singular subject (*hat*, *book*) requires the -*s* form of a verb (*sits*, *writes*, *has*); a plural subject (*hats*, *books*) requires the simple form of a verb (*sit*, *write*, *have*). Only *be* has three forms for the present tense (*am*, *is*, and *are*) and two for the past (*was* and *were*). The following scheme represents what is usually called **subject-predicate** agreement:

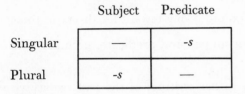

	Subject	Predicate
Singular	—	-*s*
Plural	-*s*	—

In basic patterns, subject-predicate agreement is observed without difficulty:

The *senate proposes* a committee for investigating student morale.
He proposes a committee for investigating student morale.
The *students propose* a committee for investigating student morale.
They propose a committee for investigating student morale.

With the exception of *be*, sentences with past-tense verbs do not observe subject-predicate agreement, since verbs are not inflected for number in the past tense:

He proposed a committee for investigating student morale.
They proposed a committee for investigating student morale.

Sentences containing forms of *be* observe subject-predicate agreement in both the present and past tense:

A *telephone is* indispensable to the businessman.
Telephones are indispensable to businessmen.
A *telephone was* a luxury not so long ago.
Telephones were a luxury not so long ago.

In sentences containing auxiliaries, *be* and *have*, not the verb, are inflected for number:

The *senate is* (*was*) proposing a committee for student morale.
The *students are* (*were*) proposing a committee for investigating student morale.

He has been a member of the committee on student morale.
They have been members of the committee on student morale.

Problems in subject-predicate agreement sometimes occur when the subject is separated from the verb by other constructions:

*The action of his plays point unmistakably toward his theory of time.

The sentence is ungrammatical because agreement is observed between *plays* and *point*. But *plays* is not the subject; it is part of a prepositional phrase expanding the subject, *action:*

The *action* of his plays *points* unmistakably toward his theory of time.

Agreement is observed between subject and predicate, no matter what words or phrases intervene:

The most memorable *moment* in her writings of the past twenty years *describes* her return to America after a self-imposed exile.

The parking *regulations* for salaried personnel of the company *are* subject to review by the board.

The greatest *pleasure* in visiting London both in summer and winter *is* its theatres.

Nonrestrictive phrases introduced by *together with, in addition to, as well as* do not affect subject-predicate agreement:

The *conductor*, as well as the stage manager and the chorus master, *has accepted* the principle of arbitration in the dispute.

The President, together with his family, *expects* to return to Washington Sunday evening.

Indefinite pronouns like *everyone, everybody, anyone, anybody, nobody* require the *-s* form of the verb:

Everyone in the seminar agree*s* that the readings are useful.

They may be replaced by a singular personal pronoun in writing, but in speech either a singular or plural pronoun can be heard:

Everyone agreed that *he* [not *they*] would continue the lessons.

Pronouns like *either, neither, one, none, any* may be followed by either the *-s* form or the simple form of the verb. The simple form of the verb is used when emphasis is on the idea of plurality:

Neither of the cars *was* in good shape. [Emphasis is on each separate unit.]

Neither of the cars *were* in good shape. [Emphasis is on the units as a whole.]

None of the students *is* present. [Emphasis is on each individual student.]

None of the students *are* present. [Emphasis is on the students as a group.]

Compound subjects may be followed by either the simple or the -*s* form of the verb:

The Greeks and Independents glare at each other balefully.
—DAVID BOROFF, *Harper's Magazine*

If the compounded items are thought of as one unit, the -*s* form of the verb [or *is* or *was*] is appropriate:

The tumult and the shouting over the motion of the earth *was* too violent to subside completely in three short centuries.
—BERGEN EVANS, *Natural History of Nonsense*

Fraternity and sorority row incurs a good deal of animus about UW's overdeveloped play habits, since the Greeks are the chief artisans of fun.
—DAVID BOROFF, *Harper's Magazine*

Compound subjects joined by *not, either . . . or, neither . . . nor* are followed by the -*s* form of the verb if the items compounded are singular; by the simple form of the verb if the items compounded are plural:

Neither pride nor humility shows itself in his work.
Observations, not prescriptions, are the basis of his contribution.

If one of the subjects is singular and the other plural, the verb agrees with the item closest to it:

Neither his later works nor his poetry is distinguished.
Neither his poetry nor his later works are distinguished.

Collective nouns like *faculty, group, committee, audience, government*, etc., are followed by the -*s* form of the verb if the noun is thought of as a unit; by the simple form of the verb if emphasis is on the individuals comprising the unit:

The faculty *believes* that freshman English should be mandatory. [Emphasis is on the faculty as a unit.]

The faculty *believe* that freshman English should be mandatory. [Emphasis is on the individuals comprising the faculty.]

The committee *passes* on all membership applications.

The committee *pass* on all membership applications. [British usage.]

Sentences beginning with the construction *there is (was)* or *there are (were)* observe agreement between the delayed subject and verb:

There *is* hardly enough *food* to avert a crisis.
There *are* two dozen *models* from which to make a selection.
There *were* several reasons for his anxiety.

Some nouns that are plural in form but singular in meaning are followed by the -*s* form of the verb (or *is* or *was*):

The political news *continues* to be disappointing.
Four months *was* enough vacation.
Freshman *mathematics is* taught each semester.

Some nouns that are plural in form but singular in meaning, like *scissors, trousers, pants*, are followed by the simple form of the verb (or *are* or *were*):

Bruce's white *trousers complement* his blue blazer.
Her *scissors were* her most effective weapon.

MISPLACED CONSTRUCTIONS

Since word order is a major grammatical device of modern English, words must be properly positioned in a sentence to convey the right meaning. A modifier placed too far from its head is sometimes responsible for illogical or unintentionally absurd meanings:

*All the metal was extracted through this process from the ore.
All the metal was extracted from the ore through this process.

*His exposition is difficult to follow at times, if not impossible.
At times his exposition is difficult, if not impossible, to follow.

*To prevent stretching or shrinking of the painter's canvas, it is fastened with wooden pegs to the frame.
The painter's canvas is fastened to the frame with wooden pegs to prevent stretching or shrinking.

A rule of thumb is to place a modifier as closely as possible to its head.
Sometimes an adverb can apply to either the preceding or following word or word group:

*The candidate was urged emphatically to deny his association with the group.

The candidate was emphatically urged to deny his association with the group.

The candidate was urged to deny emphatically his association with the group.

*They were instructed only to resolve one question.

They were only instructed to resolve one question.

They were instructed to resolve only one question.

Verbal phrases used as sentence adjuncts may be improperly related to the sentence. Usually they occur at the beginning, though they can also be found elsewhere in a sentence:

*Thinking of his future, the job was applied for at once.

The construction *thinking of his future* cannot logically expand *job*, since a job cannot think:

Thinking of his future, he applied for the job at once.

The two basic patterns from which the sentence derives have a common subject, *he*, which must be preserved in the transformation. Otherwise a dangling modifier will result.

He thought of his future.
He applied for the job at once.

Thinking of his future, he applied for the job at once.

Similarly:

*Having sailed from Bermuda and Haiti, our last stop was Nassau.

Clearly, a stop cannot sail from anywhere. In recasting the sentence, the writer must be certain that the subject of the sentence also identifies the performer of the action in the verbal phrase:

Having sailed from Bermuda and Haiti, we made Nassau our last stop.

Also:

*Opening the window, it was raining outside.
When he opened the window, he saw that it was raining outside.

*Being a married man, my wife has a great influence on my language habits.
My wife has a great influence on my language habits.

In the following, a prepositional phrase is improperly related to the rest of the sentence:

*By having a car, a sense of importance is gained by the teenager.

But *a sense of importance* can hardly own a car:

Having a car gives the teenager a sense of importance.

Misplaced constructions sometimes appear at the end of a sentence:

*Members of the rescue squad administered oxygen to little Jimmy Bellman after inhaling gasoline fumes.
—The Romeo *Observer Press* (Michigan)
Members of the rescue squad administered oxygen to little Jimmy Bellman after he had inhaled gasoline fumes.

SHIFTED CONSTRUCTIONS

The attitude of the writer toward his material, known as **point of view,** is expressed through person (I, we, you, he, she, it, they), number (singular or plural), or tense (present or past). Once the writer has made his choice, he must be consistent in his point of view, not only because this is logically sound, but because the reader expects it. In fact, an alert reader often anticipates the writer, and a sudden, unnecessary change in point of view violates his set of expectations. Such a violation is called a **shift.** Shifted constructions can be corrected by re-establishing consistency in point of view.

Shifts may occur in the use of person:

*What *one* hears hinted about him makes *you* want to know him better.
What *you* hear hinted about him makes *you* want to know him better.
What *one* hears hinted about him makes *one* want to know him better.

In the use of number:

An educated person is well-trained, likes people, and lives successfully with them. *They* also use proper etiquette and have an eye for beauty.
An educated person is well-trained, likes people, and lives successfully with them. *He* also uses proper etiquette and has an eye for beauty.

In the use of tense:

*Jonathan Swift's *Gulliver's Travels criticizes* mankind through simulated travel. The author *portrayed* man as he might be in contrast to what he really is.

Jonathan Swift's *Gulliver's Travels criticizes* mankind through simulated travel. The author *portrays* man as he might be in contrast to what he really is.

Or in the use of active and passive voice:

We attended a language seminar in New York, but *our evenings were spent* mostly going to the theater.

We attended a language seminar in New York but *spent* most of our evenings going to the theater.

No violation of grammatical convention occurs when the subject really requires a change in point of view. The writer of the following passage, for instance, uses both present and past tense forms: the present tense for references to the Declaration of Independence as a document, and the past tense for historically associated events:

It is often forgotten that the document which we know as the Declaration of Independence is not the official act by which the Continental Congress voted in favor of separation from Great Britain. June 7, 1776, Richard Henry Lee, on behalf of the Virginia delegation, submitted to the Continental Congress three resolutions, of which the first declared that "these United Colonies are, and of right ought to be, free and independent States, that they are absolved from all allegiance to the British Crown, and that all political connection between them and the State of Great Britain is, and ought to be, totally dissolved." This resolution, which may conveniently be called the Resolution of Independence, was finally voted by the Continental Congress on the 2 of July, 1776. Strictly speaking, this was the official declaration of independence; and if we were a nation of antiquaries we should no doubt find an incongruity in celebrating the anniversary of our independence on the 4 of July.

—CARL L. BECKER, *The Declaration of Independence*[3]

Professional writers sometimes vary their point of view for special reasons. MacLeish and Gellhorn both change from the third to the second person to deepen the reader's involvement in the subject:

One can argue that it is desirable to dilute the critical and scholarly atmosphere of a college community with a few artists but you won't get all the critics and scholars to agree.

—ARCHIBALD MACLEISH, *Harper's Magazine*

With the weather as an excuse, the English refuse to be tyrannized by fashion. Happily joining the population, one slops around in an aged suit,

[3] Footnotes in this quotation have been omitted.

a pair of slacks, a bandana, comfy shoes with thick rubber soles. If on occasion you defy the weather, or are sure of a taxi, and doll yourself up in spoilable clothing, a foolish hat, a piece of non-waterproof fur, everyone exclaims with delight and tells you how nice you look.
—MARTHA GELLHORN, *Harper's Magazine*

INFLECTIONAL FORMS

Inflection refers to formal changes in a word that signal grammatical relationships, such as the *-s* or *-es* suffix to indicate the written plural of nouns or the *-ed* suffix for the past tense and past participle of regular verbs. Modern English has relatively few inflections. Except for forms that constitute a problem of usage (*who, whom*), inflection is unlikely to be a source of difficulty for the writer. Most problems can be resolved by checking the appropriate inflectional forms of the four major word classes in an up-to-date standard dictionary.

Number: Nouns

Most nouns in modern English are inflected for number. The vast majority of nouns add *-s* (ritual*s*, source*s*) or *-es* (church*es*, process*es*); they seldom present a problem. Special plural forms, however, are sometimes confused.

Nouns ending in *-y* preceded by a consonant, change the *y* to *ie* before adding *-s*: *potency, potencies; sobriety, sobrieties; vanity, vanities; vulgarity, vulgarities.* But *standby, standbys; dry, drys; Carey,* the *Careys.*

Certain compounds add *-s* to the second noun: *foster parent, foster parents; landscape architect, landscape architects; post office, post offices.*

Some compounds add *-s* to the first noun: *brother-in-law, brothers-in-law; passer-by, passers-by.*

A few nouns ending in *-o* preceded by a consonant add *-es*: *hero, heroes; Negro, Negroes; tomato, tomatoes.*

A few plural suffixes are survivals of earlier forms: *ox, oxen; woman, women; louse, lice; knife, knives.*

Certain nouns are not inflected for plural number: *sheep, arithmetic, deer.* Others are always inflected: *goods, mathematics, scissors.*

In this group, nouns like *pants*, *goods* and *scissors* are followed by the simple form of the verb and nouns like *physics*, and *news*, by the *-s* form. Some, like *politics* and *athletics*, are followed by either the *-s* form or the simple form of the verb, depending on the meaning desired:

Politics is not an exact science.
American politics rise to a dramatic climax every four years.

Certain borrowed words retain their foreign plurals, though some of these have moved into the more productive *-s*, *-es* class:

cello	celli	cellos
concerto	concerti	concertos
curriculum	curricula	curriculums
datum	data	datas
index	indices	indexes
memorandum	memoranda	memorandums
phenomenon	phenomena	
virtuoso	virtuosi	virtuosos

Conservative writers prefer the borrowed forms; others use the Anglicized form.

Number: Pronouns

The formation of the plural number of pronouns depends on the subclass to which a pronoun belongs. Some pronouns have different forms for the singular and plural; a few are inflected like nouns; and some have no plural forms at all.

Personal Pronouns. Personal pronouns have different forms for the singular and plural, such as *I/we*, *mine/ours*, *me/us*. These are treated under case, pp. 302–303.

Demonstrative Pronouns. *This/these*, *that/those*, called demonstrative pronouns when pointing to something previously mentioned, have plural inflections:

> The record(s) cannot be moved.
> *This/these* cannot be moved.

CONTRAST: *It/they* cannot be moved. [The personal pronouns *it/they* have different forms for singular and plural number.]

> The children who are here will receive complimentary tickets.
> *Those* who are here will receive complimentary tickets.

Intensive and Reflexive Pronouns. Certain personal pronouns may be compounded with *-self* and *-selves*. They are called reflexive pronouns when they appear in the object position of a sentence; intensive pronouns when they appear elsewhere:

> REFLEXIVE: He offered himself as a candidate.
> INTENSIVE: He himself gave an interview.
> He gave an interview himself.

Personal pronouns in the possessive are not combined with *-self* or *-selves* in standard English. **Hisself* or **theirselves* are unacceptable in both educated speech and writing.

Indefinite Pronouns. Pronouns in this group include words like *somebody, nobody, anybody, everybody, no one, everything, few, most.* Some of these can be inflected for the plural as well as the possessive (*somebodies, nobodies, somebody's, nobody's*); others take only the possessive form (*anybody's, no one's*); still others are not inflected (*few, most*).

Number: Verbs

In the present tense, verbs are inflected only for the third person singular (*walk, walks; drive, drives; watch, watches*). In the past tense, verbs are not inflected for number. A special instance is *be* with three forms for the present (*am, is, are*) and two forms for the past (*was, were*).

The concept of number applied to verbs, moreover, differs altogether from that applying to nouns. The so-called plural form of a verb as in "we drive" or "we watch" does not mean that an action is being performed more than once or that there is more than one action. It is therefore more convenient—and more accurate—to speak of the simple and the *-s* form of a verb rather than of its singular and plural forms.

Tense

In writing, regular verbs add *-d* or *ed* to their stem (*condone, walk*) to form the past tense and past participle (*condoned, walked*). The suffix should not be omitted simply because it may not be heard:

> *They *use* to play outdoors constantly.
> They *used* to play outdoors constantly.

A small number of verbs have special forms, which must be learned as individual items. Those confused most commonly include:

blow	blew	blown
bring	brought	brought
come	came	come
draw	drew	drawn
fly	flew	flown
forget	forgot	forgotten
freeze	froze	frozen
go	went	gone
ring	rang	rung
prove	proved	proved, proven
show	showed	shown, showed
tear	tore	torn
wear	wore	worn

The following pairs are sometimes confused:

bid	bid	bid
bid	bade	bidden
hang	hanged	hanged
hang	hung	hung
lay	laid	laid
lie	lay	lain
raise	raised	raised
rise	rose	risen
set	set	set
sit	sat	sat

Forms such as *I seen it*, *I done it*, *I've went*, *I've tore it* are unacceptable in standard speech and writing.

Case: Nouns; Pronouns

Nouns. Nouns are inflected for plural number (*boy, boys*) and the possessive (*boy's, boys'*).[4] The possessive may be used before *-ing* verbs functioning as nouns, but so may the common form in standard

---

4 For punctuation of the possessive, see pp. 250–252.

English.[5] Both of the following are correct, the first of each pair being the more conservative:

There is little reason for his *students'* taking the examination early.
There is little reason for his *students* taking the examination early.

He heard of the *captain's* visiting the company.
He heard of the *captain* visiting the company.

The question of choice can be avoided by recasting each sentence:

There is little reason why his students should take the examination early.
He heard that the captain visited (would visit) the company.

Pronouns. Personal pronouns have subjective, possessive, and objective forms:

Subjective	Possessive[6]	Objective
I	my, mine	me
you (singular and plural)	your, yours	you
he, she, it	his, her, hers, its	him, her, it
we	our, ours	us
they	their, theirs	them

Selection of the appropriate form of the pronoun sometimes presents a problem. Taught never to use *you and me* in the subject position, a student is likely to write *you and I* in all noun positions. The use of one form because it is thought to be more nearly correct than another is called a **hyperform.** Here are some examples:

You and me are expected to pass.
You and I are expected to pass. [The subjective form is required.]

*There is no ill feeling between *you and I.*
There is no ill feeling *between you and me.* [The objective form is required after a preposition.]

*When she sees *John and I*, she becomes embarrassed.
When she sees *John and me*, she becomes embarrassed. [The objective form is required after a transitive verb.]

The following statement was made by a radio announcer at the end of the Michigan-Navy game on October 5, 1964:

[5] See Fries, *American English Grammar*, pp. 72–78.
[6] *My, your, his, her, our*, etc., also appear in the set of determiners. See pp. 19–21.

Seven more games for the Wolverines this season, folks; and they'll all be right here before you and I.

Among relative pronouns only *who* and *whom* are sometimes troublesome. *Who* replaces a subject, and *whom* replaces an object in a relative clause:

> *All the boys *who* the principal recommends may expect favorable treatment.
> All the boys *whom* the principal recommends may expect favorable treatment.
> *Send the names of boys *whom*, you think, will be successful.
> Send the names of boys *who*, you think, will be successful.

In the relative clause of the first sentence, *whom* replaces *boy*, the object of *recommends:*

> the principal recommends boys → the principal recommends whom → whom the principal recommends

In the relative clause of the second sentence, *who* replaces *boys*, the subject of *will be successful:*

> boys will be successful → who will be successful

The parenthetical clause *you think* does not affect the choice of the relative, as its deletion from the sentence shows:

> Send the names of boys who will be successful.

Interrogatives (*who, whose, whom, which,* and *what*) pattern like relatives: *Who* is required in the subject position and *whom* in the object position of a sentence. *Whose* replaces a determiner:

> *Who* is likely to succeed the President?
> *Whom* will the President support?
> *Whose* party will win?

Which and *what* are uninflected and should present no problem in writing.

Degree: Adjectives; Adverbs

Adjectives. Adjectives can be compared by the use of inflections or function words. One-syllable adjectives usually add *-er* to their regular form, called the **positive,** in order to form the **comparative,** and *-est* to form the **superlative** (*hard, harder, hardest; low, lower, lowest*). Two-syllable adjectives are compared either by the addition of the suffixes *-er* or *-est* or by the use of function words (*kindly, kindlier, kindliest; polite, more polite, most* [or *very*] *polite*). Adjectives of more than two syllables are compared by the use of function words (*beautiful, more beautiful, most* [*very*] *beautiful*). The forms of some adjectives are completely replaced (*good, better, best; bad, worse, worst*). A few (*dead, unique, perfect*) are not compared at all.

Common problems involving adjectives include the use of the superlative instead of the comparative when two items are compared:

*Francis is the *tallest* (*worst, most agile*) of the two brothers.

Although this form occurs commonly in speech, the comparative is preferred in standard writing:

Francis is the *taller* (*worse, more agile*) of the two brothers.

The superlative is used for comparison of three or more items:

Francis is the *tallest* (*worst, most agile*) member of the basketball team.

Another problem concerns those few adjectives that are not usually compared. One is either dead or alive, perfect or nearly perfect, unique or common. Editors therefore reject constructions like **very unique,* **rather unique,* or **more perfect,* though the writers of the Constitution, one may recall, were dedicated to the principle of forming a "more perfect Union."

Still another problem involves the confusion of adjectives with adverbs after linking verbs like *seem, appear, look, feel,* or *sound.* Linking verbs are followed by adjectives, and intransitive verbs by adverbs:

He seems safe.
He drives safely.

Verbs patterning as linking verbs and as intransitive verbs may be followed by adjectives or adverbs:

He looks cautious.
He looks cautiously.

Adverbs. Certain one-syllable adverbs can be inflected for comparison much like adjectives: (*soon, sooner, soonest; well, better, best*). Adverbs derived from adjectives by suffixation are usually compared by the use of function words (*quickly, more quickly, most* [*very*] *quickly*). Some adverbs are not compared in serious writing (*finally, uniquely, completely, perfectly*).

Words like *slow, well, fast* pattern as adjectives or adverbs:

He is a well man.
It is a well-written article.

Ambiguity sometimes occurs after verbs that function as either linking verbs or intransitive verbs:

The investigator looked well.

It is unclear whether the investigator appeared healthy or searched thoroughly. Since no formal difference separates this group of adjectives and adverbs, context must resolve the ambiguity in writing.

EXERCISES

Each of the following sentences is grammatically impaired. Identify the error and make appropriate corrections.

1. The fame of the *Mona Lisa* lies in her smile it is neither joyous nor flirtatious, but subtle and mysterious.

2. Having shown the old home to the buyer, the pending sale of the estate was announced.

3. The doctor explained to his patient what he could do.

4. I actually believe that if a person makes a firm commitment, they will not find it nearly as difficult to stop smoking as they think.

5. We invited only those of our friends whom, we thought, would appreciate Elizabethan music.

6. Even in the classroom he felt alienated from his friends. Although he was really an intelligent lad, according to his teachers.

7. The singer, together with her accompanist, expect to board the afternoon flight to London.

8. One of the greatest pleasures of European vacations are the culinary skills of Continental chefs.

9. Either his associates or his wife are responsible for his disagreeable attitude.

10. The senior class held its traditional "April Capers" in the Japanese "Petal Room," however, the affair was dampened by the absence of the Senior Queen.

11. He purchased his drawing set from the J. L. Hudson Company, which is made of German silver.

12. We were asked only to read the examinations.

13. Study of a foreign language leads to a firmer understanding of another culture, but some teachers say that you also learn to know your own language better.

14. English, like any other natural language, does not have an altogether logical structure, indeed, it is the product of fourteen hundred years of complex change and development.

15. The members of the College Accreditation Board visited over twenty high schools, but no reference was made in their report to secondary education.

16. In our senior year in high school we inevitably use to spend our Saturday evenings in a drive-in theater or a drive-in restaurant.

17. Personal relations have always been excellent between Professor Burdine and I.

18. In Pete Panther's set for Ibsen's *Ghosts*, he used very unique techniques of lighting.

19. In Macbeth's murder of Duncan, he obviously touches on the fundamental question of ends and means.

20. Being a bachelor, his neighbor's wife often invites him to dinner.

IV] Style

INTRODUCTION TO STYLE

Style has been much defined and described. Jonathan Swift, the author of *Gulliver's Travels*, believed its essence was "proper words in proper places." Shakespeare's contemporary, Ben Jonson, observed: "For a man to write well there are required three necessaries: to read the best authors, observe the best speakers, and much exercise of his own style." The Victorian critic Matthew Arnold thought that the "only secret of style" was to "have something to say and say it as clearly as you can." William Hazlitt, the nineteenth-century essayist, comes perhaps closest to the modern concept of what constitutes a good expository style: "To write a genuine familiar or truly English style, is to write as any one would speak in common conversation, who had a thorough command and choice of words, or who could discourse with ease, force, and perspicuity, setting aside all pedantic and oratorical flourish."

To the question then of what constitutes style there is no single answer. Certainly an experienced writer is sensitive to pattern and choice of words. He maintains integrity toward his material and his reader. He shapes his writing to his purpose, knows what fits and what is fitting. Elements of style can be isolated and exhibited for analysis, but a student should always remember that successful writing is a fusion of many qualities, all of which require attention. Certain characteristics, however, are found in all good writing. They are, besides grammatical correctness, which has been treated elsewhere, clarity, precision, and variety. To these one may add ethical requirements like accuracy and reliability.

The achievement of a good style depends greatly on revision, which inevitably strengthens a sentence:

> This paper has presented a complete picture of the methods used and the different steps followed in carrying this study to completion.

Imperfections seem to court one another, for this sentence, from an early draft of a thesis, suffers from wordiness, redundancy, mixing of levels, and self-conscious variation. "Methods used" and "steps followed" are repetitious. "Carrying this study to completion" is a cumbersome way of saying "to complete this study." "Has presented a complete picture" strikes the reader as presumptuous and represents a needless effort to be elaborate. The substitution of "study" for "paper" is an ill-advised attempt to avoid repetition, because a paper and a study are not necessarily the same. When the sentence is reduced from twenty-two words to nine, its meaning emerges more sharply:

> The procedures followed in this study have been described.

Or more informally:

> I have described the procedures followed in this study.

Imperfections not readily apparent before, are often discovered in revision.

In this, Part IV, style is treated under three chapter headings: (1) Diction; (2) Sentence Economy; and (3) Sentence Variety.

24) Diction

DENOTATION AND CONNOTATION

Experts agree that English has well over a million words. If the actual number is uncertain, it is only because an exact count would be wasteful, for new words constantly enter the lexicon. On February 21, 1962, the day of Colonel Glenn's space shot, *The New York Times* published a glossary of terms relating to the orbital flight. These included *apogee, altitude, booster, countdown, escape tower, orbit, pitch, roll, yaw, scrub, telemetry, T-time, umbilical, verniers, weightlessness.* What is interesting is that most of these words are not really new in the sense that they had to be coined. They are words or combinations with new meanings. The extension of meanings of words is a common process of linguistic change.

Clearly, the writer of English has an immense vocabulary at his service. There are several reasons for this: first of all English is rich in **synonymy,** that is, in words whose meanings are similar. Many of these words derive from the two mainstreams of English: the Germanic and the Romance languages. From the Germanic stock, for example, we have *house, home, abode;* from the Romance languages, *residence, domicile, villa, property.* Secondly, as has been pointed out, a language reflects the culture of its speakers.[1] English is the mother

[1] See Introduction, pp. 4–6.

tongue of speakers whose activities happen to be vitally important at present. Concepts like "space doctor," "go condition," or "aerospace" were inconceivable to the educated layman even a few years ago.

Thirdly—and this point requires some elaboration—almost all words have at least two kinds of lexical meaning. One is the **denotative meaning,** which is usually found in a dictionary. This meaning, presented in brief, explicit statements, contains the basic, literal sense of the word and represents the consensus of its users. For example, one sense of *dog* in Merriam-Webster's *Seventh New Collegiate Dictionary* is "carnivorous domesticated mammal (*Canis familiaris*), type of family Canidae." The definition is brief, elegant, and objective. It is unlikely to inspire either approval or disapproval like *mongrel*, *mutt*, or *cur*, though even *dog* may evoke pleasant associations among dog lovers and aversion among those who dislike dogs. The overtones of meaning, the attitudes a word inspires, the values associated with it—these are its **connotative meanings.** Whether to call a dog a "mongrel" or "mutt" depends on the response the writer seeks from his reader.

The borderline between the denotative and connotative meanings of a word is imprecise, because most words—even abstract numbers like *three, seven, eleven, thirteen*—convey both kinds of meanings to different persons. Certainly *dog* is more objective than *cur* or *mongrel*, but it would be foolhardy to claim that it is entirely so. At most, a writer can make intelligent choices based on thorough familiarity with his subject, for even the same word can evoke different responses from different readers. One may approve of *old-fashioned* pies but disparage *old-fashioned* clothes; sneer at *old-fashioned* furniture but write a large check for antiques. One may refer to a *date*, an *appointment*, or an *engagement*; to a *statesman, lawmaker, politician,* or *political boss*. This depends on context and intent. A *lakeside property* may be a *little lot* to a neighbor eager to snap it up at a bargain. As senator, Vice President Humphrey once proposed changing the name of the Senate Foreign Relations Committee to Committee on International Relations because he felt that *foreign* implied a patronizing attitude of the United States toward other nations—which indeed it does.[2] (Note that the substitution of *countries, states,* or *people* for *nations* changes the overall meaning of the preceding sentence.) Since World War II, U.S. government agencies have replaced the

[2] Lansing *State Journal*, March 12, 1957, p. 1.

term *backward nations* with *underdeveloped nations* and more recently with *developing nations,* surely the most tactful of the three. Even the schools know the importance of public relations, and bewildered parents may conceivably acclaim their Johnny for "producing minimally for his peer group" and "emerging as an underachiever," when he is, in point of fact, lazy and not very bright.[3] Exactly what defines a *socialist,* a *left-winger,* a *liberal,* a *middle-of-the-roader,* a *conservative,* a *right-wing conservative,* a *right-wing extremist,* or a *patriot* may be difficult or impossible to decide; yet these terms are often used indiscriminately to escape the inconvenience of thinking.

Making the right choice is not so much a matter of rules as a sense of what is proper, what is strategically right. For the writer of exposition this implies detachment and freedom from bias. But the emotional power of language should not be disparaged either. Indeed, without emotional appeals few ministers would stir their congregations to right thinking and right action; politicians would lose elections; consumers would buy less; and students would loaf more. Persuasion operates everywhere, as much in the demonstration of a hypothesis as in a poem, though differently. The writer can strive for control of his subject by choosing words that are ethically and strategically fitting.

PRECISION AND CONSISTENCY

A direct, specific word is preferable to a more general one. If one word does the work of many, so much the better, for the more precise the writer's diction, the clearer his meaning, and the more elegant his statement:

He assumed *a considerable amount* of responsibility.	He assumed (*partial, full*) responsibility.
As he continues, he shows how American culture fosters conformity.	*Then* he shows how American culture fosters conformity.
for reasons of the practical sort	*for practical reasons*
An example of their good intentions was revealed.	Their good intentions were revealed.
by the same token	*similarly*

3 See "The Hidden Meaning of Non-Meaning" (Guest Editorial), Detroit *Free Press,* March 13, 1965, p. 8–A.

Sometimes lack of familiarity with a term is responsible for circumlocution:

The persons of the nineteenth century enjoyed their magazines.	*The Victorians* enjoyed their magazines.
People trained in making a scientific analysis of language are in great demand.	*Descriptive linguists* are in great demand.
Here it is my duty to write *many letters which are of a collection nature.*	*My job* is to write *collection letters.*

Qualifiers and superlatives, however common in daily conversation, dissipate the strength of a written phrase:

exaggerated *quite a bit*	exaggerated
very strict and *very* precise	strict and precise
rather evident	evident
quite specific	specific
the most interesting person I have met	(doubtless an exaggeration)
my most exciting experience	(The reader should be allowed to judge whether the experience was exciting or not.)

Not every experience is "traumatic," not every movie is "fabulous," nor is every teen-ager "great"—at least not in writing.

Words like *character, quality, appearance, nature, activity* often sound pedantic:

of a helpful *character*	helpful
he had a pleasant *nature* about him	he was pleasant
the *field* of English	English
rain shower activity	showers

Effective diction is suited to its subject. Formal diction, for example, is more appropriate to an analysis of Milton's concept of free speech than to a book review of a detective story. Colloquial expressions are inappropriate in a formal presentation; so is formal diction in a casually treated subject:

The layman lets the scientist *figure out* new theories.	*develop*

Only a few *have the nerve* to express their feelings.	*have the courage*
He *related to* his family how he stole the pen.	*told*
The speaker should *try to get* his idea *over* to his audience clearly.	*express, convey*

However a topic is handled, its diction should be internally consistent as in the following:

Sign on a London bus:
> "Total abstinence from intoxicating drink
> promotes accuracy of skilled movements."

Sign along an American highway:
> "Drive carefully. The life you save may be your own."

CLICHÉ AND JARGON

A cliché is a hackneyed expression or expired metaphor that evokes a stereotyped image. Part of its unsatisfactoriness is that though one hears words, one does not see anything distinctly or individually— only the fuzz of human experience in general, about which it is impossible to have fresh feelings. A cliché is like an old coin, passed through so many millions of hands that its original effigy has become worn too smooth to be seen or felt distinctly. Certainly one cannot convey the uniqueness of an experience if one depends on secondhand language. Yet some clichés, actually more economical than unwieldy circumlocutions, are no doubt necessary, as Joseph Wood Krutch points out in a debate with Bergen Evans. Professor Krutch defends "Jack-of-all-trades" against "one who can turn his hand to any (or to many kinds of) work" or "rush in where angels fear to tread" against "hastily embark upon a course of action men wiser than ourselves would hesitate to enter upon without mature consideration."[4] One may not wish to dispense with "brass tacks," "pig in a poke," but it is possible to avoid expressions like the following:

the sands of time	good and ready
the road to success	in this day and age

---

4 "Great Cliché Debate (Cont.)," *The New York Times Magazine*, August 31, 1958, pp. 13, 32.

the pathway of life	greater and better goals
the hustle and bustle of civilization	few and far between
mother nature	goals and purposes
men of destiny	part and parcel of
fought long and hard	vitally necessary consideration

Clichés differ from **jargon,** words or expressions peculiar to a trade or profession. Descriptive linguists, for example, use technical terms like *phone, allophone, phoneme, morph, allomorph, morpheme,* which denote essential concepts in linguistics. Professional educators refer to "the whole child," "group processes," "child-centered approach to learning," "subject-matter areas," "sociometric considerations." For the general reader such concepts had better be expressed less technically.

Jargon in a less complimentary sense refers to polysyllabic words and unwieldy expressions often intended to impress the reader. Jargon in this sense is also known as gobbledygook, dressing simple thoughts in complex patterns that sound good but lack substance. Here are some examples with suggested revisions:

From a government bulletin:

But more adequate instruction will be realized to the full only when satisfactory teaching materials exist.

But more adequate instruction will be possible only with satisfactory teaching materials.

From a stockbroker's newsletter:

Although at the moment it would be the part of wisdom to maintain the cautious attitude we have recommended for several weeks, there are attractive investment opportunities in industries which appear favorably situated for the current year.

Although we continue to urge caution, there are attractive investment opportunities in selected industries.

From a brochure on an academic program:

By so integrating the development of communication skills with the subject matter in which the student is concerned, much of the ineffectiveness of the conventional composition or speech class should be rectified, and a living quality given to the student's activity in this respect.

By integrating communication skills with other subjects, speech and composition should become more meaningful to the student.

A program of studies and surveys, research and experimentation, and development of specialized instructional materials is a vitally necessary concomitant to an action program.

Research, as well as the preparation of instructional materials, is essential to a sound academic program. [In the first sentence "program" is ineptly used in different senses: to denote (1) a "plan" and (2) "academic offerings." "Action programs" is redundant. "Surveys" and "experimentation" are part of research.]

Clichés should be distinguished from proverbs, commonplace truths: "Waste not, want not," "A piece of pure liver won't choke a cat," or "Rome wasn't built in a day." Proverbs are avoided in exposition, because for every proverb in one direction, one of the opposite can usually be found: "Look before you leap," "He who hesitates is lost"; or "If at first you don't succeed, try again," and "A bird in the hand is worth two in the bush."

Proverbs, in turn, differ from epigrams, statements memorable for their wit and brilliance, like these by Oscar Wilde: "I can resist everything except temptation," "Consistency is the last refuge of the unimaginative."

EUPHEMISM

A **euphemism** is a word or expression designed to soften a harsh or unpleasant fact. Insurance agents speak of "not being in the picture" when they refer to death. Because our society is status-conscious, a "janitor" prefers to be known as a "building manager," a "salesman" as a "representative," a "beautician"—a euphemism itself for "hairdresser"—as a "cosmetologist." Euphemisms are often used in alluding to bodily functions, particularly those relating to sex. They are also common in referring to events associated with death, as the following excerpt from Jessica Mitford's *Atlantic* article "The Undertaker's Racket" (June 1963) shows. Miss Mitford cites terms recommended by morticians:

Mr., Mrs., Miss Blank, not corpse or body; preparation room, not morgue; casket, not coffin; funeral director or mortician, not undertaker; reposing room or slumber room, not laying-out room; display room, not showroom; baby or infant, not stillborn; deceased, not dead; autopsy or post-mortem, not post; casket coach, not hearse; shipping case, not shipping box; flower car, not flower truck; cremains or cremated remains, not ashes; clothing, dress, suit, etc., not shroud; drawing room, not parlor.

Euphemisms should be avoided in writing, because they impress the reader as coy. A more direct word or expression is usually available:

the fairer sex	ladies, women
lower extremities	legs
the great Bard	Shakespeare
in a family way	pregnant
inadequately motivated	lazy, dull (?)
social disease	syphilis
powder room	toilet

MALAPROPISM

The use of an inappropriate word, such as *illicit* for *elicit, immoral* for *immortal, doctorette* for *doctorate,* is known as a **malapropism,** a term derived from Mrs. Malaprop, a garrulous character in Richard Sheridan's eighteenth-century comedy *The Rivals,* noted for her verbal blunders. The remedy for this kind of embarrassing error is a dictionary, but advice to use a dictionary may be gratuitous, since those committing this blunder are seldom aware of it:

An *illusion* to Yeats is meaningless to a reader who has never read Yeats.
He was sentenced to the *eclectic* chair.
The accused was *arranged* before the judge.
The company refused to *budget* an inch.
Charlie proved to be an *amendable* friend.
Hitler's *anti-semantic* prejudice contributed toward his eventual defeat.

For a list of words sounding alike or nearly alike and sometimes confused in spelling, see pp. 279–281.

FIGURATIVE LANGUAGE

Metaphor

Metaphor (Greek: *meta,* "beyond"; *pherein,* "to bear"), the basis of figurative language, involves the transfer of meanings of words or phrases to contexts where these meanings do not normally apply. In the sentence "Miss Jane is a cat," for example, disagreeable characteristics often identified with cats are assigned to a person to imply that the lady is capricious and coquettish. Another context might require the sense of jazz addict, also a metaphor; and in rare instances the meaning might be purely literal, if the reference were to someone with a cat named "Miss Jane." Unless the literal meaning is intended, however, we certainly do not assume that Miss Jane walks on all fours. In figurative language, then, certain dominant characteristics associated with one thing are transferred to another, apparently unlike the first, but actually resembling it in significant ways. The writer gains because he can express himself more directly, and, in addition to the literal or referential sense of the transferred word or phrase, he introduces a new dimension of meaning: an appeal to the senses. He has a choice in saying that someone is cowardly or yellow, inexperienced or green, or that so and so is a dog, a rat, a wolf, or a tiger, rather than a rascal, sneak, flirt, or a lusty, virile male (or a powerful gasoline or sports car, as some advertisers would have us believe). No one has difficulty in grasping the sentence "He married a lemon" in its transferred sense, for as Bloomfield so aptly points out, "we know that men do not go through a marriage ceremony with a piece of fruit."[5]

In addition to making a statement, therefore, metaphor implies and suggests. We must not imagine, however, that it is a purely ornamental or decorative device, as some think, or that it is an exclusive feature of poetry. On the contrary, it is a means of economy and precision, for it can make the reader conscious of relationships not previously perceived. In its most subtle and perfected form, of course, it *is* poetry. In its most transient form it is slang, though even slang expressions sometimes endure and gain social status. Words like *highbrow, lowbrow, gimmick,* or *egghead* are used in serious writing without apology.

Analogy

Comparison, the essence of figurative language, requires ability to perceive significant similarities as well as differences. The writer brings his past experiences to bear—his knowledge of the world—to clarify, illuminate, or illustrate his meaning. Reporting on Colonel Glenn's orbital flight, *Time* (March 2, 1962, editorial) employs a sustained metaphor, called an **analogy**, for emphasis:

[5] Leonard Bloomfield, *Language* (New York: Holt, Rinehart & Winston, 1933), p. 149.

In his flight across the heavens, John Glenn was a latter-day Apollo, flashing through the unknown, sending his cool observations and random comments to the earth in radio thunderbolts, acting as though orbiting the earth were his everyday occupation.

The metaphor comparing Colonel Glenn's flight to that of the Greek god of the sun, of youth, of poetry and music suggests at once the daring, the extravagance, and the legendary reach of this human feat.

Irony

Another important type of comparison is **irony,** the deliberate discrepancy between literal and intended meaning. As a stylistic device, irony lets the writer withdraw behind a façade and assume an apparently detached point of view, when in truth he is deeply committed. The basic discrepancy of irony lies in the conflict between appearance and reality, between what seems and what is. The writer takes the reader into his confidence, provided the reader understands the rules: things are not really this way, and both writer and reader know better; but they pretend while the writer makes his statement. The student who thought that Jonathan Swift was a cannibal obviously missed the irony of *A Modest Proposal* (1729). In this satire the author presents a scheme for fattening and slaughtering Irish infants ostensibly to fill the pockets of English landlords—but actually to expose the indifference of the English government to the desperate conditions of Ireland. Irony is an index of intelligence and sophistication, and if the reader knows just when to suspend his disbelief, he and the writer can share a discovery or insight.

Irony may range from mild irreverence, as in the writings of James Thurber, to the savage indignation found in the last book of Jonathan Swift's *Gulliver's Travels* or in "A Modest Proposal." In the following passage from *The Thurber Carnival* the author pokes fun at the narrow fundamentalism in his childhood home:

The adults around me when I was in short pants . . . consisted mainly of eleven maternal great-aunts, all Methodists, who were staunch believers in physic, mustard plasters, and Scripture, and it was part of their dogma that artistic tendencies should be treated in the same way as hiccups or hysterics. None of them was an artist, unless you can count Aunt Lou, who wrote sixteen-stress verse, with hit-and-miss rhymes, in celebration of people's birthdays or on the occasion of great national disaster. It never

occurred to me to bite a bat in my aunts' presence or to throw stones at them. There was one escape, though: my secret world of idiom.
—JAMES THURBER, *The Thurber Carnival*

The classic example of sustained irony is found in "A Modest Proposal" where under the guise of his bizarre scheme to ameliorate the condition of Ireland the author rages against human callousness:

> I have been assured by a very knowing American of my acquaintance in London, that a young healthy child well nursed is at a year old a most delicious nourishing and wholesome food, whether stewed, roasted, baked, or boiled; and I make no doubt that it will equally serve in a fricassee, or a ragout.—JONATHAN SWIFT, "A Modest Proposal"

In the passage that follows, the irony is fractured: Swift's pity and anger join with savage passion, break through the ironical façade, and produce invective:

> I grant this food will be somewhat dear, and therefore very proper for landlords, who, as they have already devoured most of the parents, seem to have the best title to the children.

Irony, less grim than Swift's, is found in John Gunther's *Inside Africa* on the South African problem of apartheid:

> And after all the fact that almost a tenth of the total population is Colored shows that, for generations, a lively amount of holding hands must have occurred.

Forms of Irony

Gunther achieves irony through **understatement,** that is, by underplaying the contrast. **Mock-irony,** with its half-serious posture toward the object of ridicule, is found in Fred Grunfeld's description of the members of an orchestra:

> Confined to stuffy, windowless concert halls, they must bow and scrape on fiddles, or blow themselves breathless on horns that have not been substantially improved since the eighteenth century—and always subject to the whims and crotchets of an autocrat in evening clothes. Though they may muster majorities of a hundred to one, their very numbers condemn them to anonymity. And to play in an orchestra means sacrificing their childhood dreams, the hope they all cherished of becoming a soloist.
> —FRED GRUNFELD, *The Reporter*

Many other kinds of contrast fall into the inclusive category of irony. **Dramatic irony** refers to a statement, or statements, made by a character in a play (though it can also apply to situations in other genres) whose full intent or significance is perceived by the audience and certain other characters, but not by the speaker himself. The audience knows; the speaker does not. Drama thrives on this type of irony because of the pleasure it affords an audience in sharing a secret and participating in a character's gradual discovery of this secret. In a serious play, dramatic irony is called **tragic irony**, as in *Othello*, where the hero's unqualified trust in his lieutenant ("honest Iago") facilitates the deception practiced upon him and ultimately leads to disaster.

Socratic irony refers to a posture of ignorance assumed by the speaker or writer for the purpose of placing his opponent in an embarrassing and untenable position through the adept use of questions and answers. The technique, identified with the Greek philosopher Socrates, is widely employed in the Platonic dialogues.

Irony of fate has to do not so much with a form of expression as with a situation, though the basic contrast between appearance and reality obtains. One of the best-known examples is found in Sophocles' *Oedipus Rex* where Oedipus' search for the killer of Laius, former king of Thebes, gradually but irrevocably points toward himself as the evildoer, so that his determined and eloquent struggle to deliver Thebes of the plague ironically leads to his own destruction.

Allusion

A statement can be amplified by an indirect reference or comparison to a person, place, or event, actual or mythical. Such a comparison is called an **allusion.** As a device of communication, allusion can of course be effective only if the reader is familiar with the reference made by the writer. In the following, the allusions are unmistakable:

> Everyone has heard about Coventry if only because in the Middle Ages it originated the ultimate form of strip tease in the naked lady on horseback from whom all citizens turned their eyes except Peeping Tom.
> —LEWIS MUMFORD, *The New Yorker*

> For over a century, there have been protests against the use of slang and controversies on the relation of slang to the literary language or, as it is

now usually called, Standard English. Purists have risen in their wrath and conservatives in their dignity to defend the Bastille of linguistic purity against the revolutionary rabble.
—ERIC PARTRIDGE, *Here, There and Everywhere*

A more subtle allusion is found in a recent article whose author asserts that man will have to live with the threat of nuclear destruction as long as he knows how to create that threat:

To paraphrase the poet: it will be part of your shadow at morning striding behind you; you will see it in your shadow at evening rising to meet you; mankind will live in fear of a handful of dust.
—JOHN WHARTON, *Saturday Review*

The allusion, to T. S. Eliot's *The Waste Land* (I, 24–30), underlines the spiritual disorientation of modern man, the focus of the poem, and accounts for the scripturally inspired rhythm and metaphors that inform the quotation as well as the dimension of the poem.

Simile and Analogy

The purpose of a **simile**, a directly expressed comparison introduced by *like* or *as*, is to illuminate an idea or to create a sudden insight through an imaginative fusion of two essentially different things. The effectiveness of the comparison depends on the perception of a significant similarity between the elements compared. Most of us, for example, would probably be hard put to find a meaningful resemblance between a bathtub and a thesaurus, but the perception of such a resemblance enables the writer of this passage to make an amusing observation on certain attitudes held about Roget's *Thesaurus*:

In some quarters Roget's book is regarded somewhat like a bathtub: everybody likes to have it, few enjoy being seen using it.
—CHARLES POORE, *The New York Times Magazine*

Here are other examples:

Whatever whimsical gods there be, not the least of their ironies is this, that language, which is often durable as the granite-ribbed hills, is built with air.—CHARLTON LAIRD, *The Miracle of Language*

Although St. Sophia (as it is conventionally miscalled in the West) lacks the soaring grandeur of the Gothic cathedrals and today is rather shabby in its ornateness—like an overdressed dowager in decay—it remains a magnificent monument.—HERBERT J. MULLER, *The Uses of the Past*

An extended or systematically developed simile, also referred to as an *analogy*, is often used for explanation or clarification. It is especially suited therefore to expository writing. Paul Roberts employs this comparison to explain that each human voice is unique:

> Voices are like fingerprints. Some fingerprints are very much like others, but each one has some special loops and whorls. In the same way, some voices are very similar, but each one has its special personality.
> —PAUL ROBERTS, *Patterns of English*

The basic utility of simile—as of analogy and of other figures of speech—is that it allows us a device to assist in the task of describing the unfamiliar by comparing it with the familiar. In this function it is as useful to the scientist as to the poet or literary critic, for with the exception of formulas and other technical symbols, the scientist uses the same kind of prose as the rest of mankind. A physicist, for example, tells us that "very crudely, an atom or molecule may be considered as a tiny box that has electrons trapped inside it."[6] The writer of an organic chemistry text asks the reader to conceive of the polarization of light as

> a picket fence at which sticks are thrown in a random fashion, stipulating only that the sticks must hit the fence broadside and not end on. Obviously only those sticks will get through which happen to fly at the fence parallel to the pickets; these sticks will also get through two picket fences one behind the other. On the other hand, they will be stopped by a fence with horizontal pickets placed behind the first one.
> —ALEXANDER GERO, *Textbook of Organic Chemistry*

If none of these similes are really essential to the understanding of a scientific concept, neither are they purely decorative or ornamental. Their value lies somewhere in between: they illuminate difficult and abstract concepts by relating them to experiences most readers can readily grasp.

Dead and Mixed Metaphors

Skill in using figurative language, especially irony, is best cultivated from the writer's inner resources and experiences, for unless metaphors come spontaneously, they may seem wooden and manufactured.

---

[6] Jay Orear, *Fundamental Physics* (New York: Wiley, 1961), p. 266.

The beginner therefore should become alert to the possibilities of striking, imaginative comparisons, whatever the type. He must also exercise caution. The student who thought that "inventions sprouted and new means of transportation became available" was evidently unaware that inventions do not grow like potatoes. Certain figures of speech which the beginner finds attractive may actually be threadbare from overuse. Commonly referred to as **fading**, or **dead, metaphors**, they are seldom thought of in their figurative sense. Here are some examples of trite metaphors and similes, the kind that should be avoided:

blanket of snow	busy as a bee
clip [someone's] wings	lit up like a Christmas tree
mother nature	quick as lightning
rock bottom	smooth as silk
stand in [someone's] shoes	straight as an arrow
wolf in sheep's clothing	white as a lily

Or from student writing:

Love is the fruit of knowledge that falls from the tree of life.
His quick wit was the armor he put on when threatened by a flood of insults.

The last example mixes images from weaponry and natural disasters, and the reader wonders for an instant if the armor happened to be rust-resistant. A comparison shifted in the middle is called a **mixed metaphor.** Here are other examples:

Let us keep our ears to the ground and find out which way the wind is blowing.
When my pupils become loud, I want to find a nice niche and pull it over my head.

Whatever strength and economy might be gained from figurative language, mixed metaphors are embarrassing. Rightly used, however, figurative language can convey a rich complexity of meanings and give pleasure to the reader.

TONE

An elusive quality, **tone** defines the predominating characteristics of a piece of writing. It derives, in large measure, from the writer's attitude toward his subject, be it solemn, flippant, or cavalier. The writer's attitude, in turn, is largely conditioned by his notion of what his audience's attitude is. Depending on his intent, he will assume a stance that he knows is likely to appeal to his reader. Toward a campus controversy—whether or not student employees of the university food services should be permitted to wear beards—he may show thoughtful concern if he believes that the dispute is symptomatic of a larger discontent among the student body. Or his tone may be caustic if he perceives in the dispute an encroachment by the administration on the student's personal freedom. Finally he may wish a plague upon both houses if he thinks the matter altogether trivial.

The tone or prevailing mood of a piece of writing, then, helps create a rapport between writer and reader, much like the tacit understanding that exists in a class between instructor and students, each with certain expectations that make possible mutual respect and decorum and that provide the right atmosphere for learning. If these expectations are violated, rapport between teacher and students breaks down. Similarly, if the reader's expectations are violated after they have been painstakingly worked out, the rapport between writer and reader is impaired and communication seriously hampered.

Tone cannot be achieved by any single formula. It can be attained by deliberate strategy, of course, with sentence structure, rhythm, careful choice of words, figurative language, all contributing to the distinctive texture of a discourse. The buoyant, animated tone of the following passage, for example, derives largely from a string of coordinate clauses:

> Mah Jong was still popular during the winter of 1923–24—the winter when Calvin Coolidge was becoming accustomed to the White House, and the Bok Peace Prize was awarded, and the oil scandals broke, and Woodrow Wilson died, and General Dawes went overseas to preside over the reparations conference, and *So Big* outsold all the other novels, and people were tiring of "Yes, We Have No Bananas," and to the delight of every rotogravure editor the lid of the stone sarcophagus of King Tut-Ankh-Amen's tomb was raised at Luxor.—FREDERICK L. ALLEN, *Only Yesterday*

The next excerpt, from a "Talk of the Town" column written by James Thurber for *The New Yorker* shows how the italicized portions inserted by the editor of the magazine, Harold Ross, give the piece its casual tone, typical of *The New Yorker*. Thurber is reporting on his visit to the Metropolitan Museum of New York City:

For those who exclaim over armour, *a thing pretty rare with us*, the three new suits the museum has just come by will prove enthralling. One of them, a richly ornamented Spanish war harness, has more pieces of réchange, *or you might say accessories*, than any other battle suit in the world. . . . Among other prizes of the New Accession Room is the lid of an amphora, *but we never did find out what an amphora is*.
—JAMES THURBER, *The Years with Ross*

Comparison of the following versions of a brochure on two-year college courses shows how a change in point of view from the second to the third person eliminates the patronizing tone of the original, at the left:

Two-year terminal courses will give you special training for a vocation, and also a strong background of general education. General education is essential for promotion in almost any job that involves personal responsibilities and working with people. When you complete two years of study with a good record, you will receive a certificate showing that you have mastered a practical course of training in your chosen field. This certificate is valuable. The College Placement Bureau, which fits available jobs to trained students, reports that many employers ask for people trained in specialized areas not requiring a four-year college degree.

Most two-year terminal courses will give a student some special training for a vocation and also a strong background in general education. General education is essential for promotion in almost any position that involves personal responsibilities. Students completing two years of satisfactory work receive an appropriate certificate. The services of the College Placement Bureau are available to them in finding a position. In the past, many employers have requested persons with special training not requiring a four-year college degree.

The last excerpt shows how the clarity, balance, and restraint in Edith Hamilton's prose convey the author's deep respect for ancient Athens:

For a hundred years Athens was a city where the great spiritual forces that war in men's minds flowed along together in peace; law and freedom, truth and religion, beauty and goodness, the objective and the subjective— there was a truce to their eternal warfare, and the result was the balance and clarity, the harmony and completeness, the word Greek has come to stand for. They saw both sides of the paradox of truth, giving predominance

to neither, and in all Greek art there is an absence of struggle, a reconciling power, something of calm and serenity, the world has yet to see again.
——EDITH HAMILTON, *The Greek Way*

EXERCISES

1.   Improve faulty diction in the following sentences:

    1.   The hostess introduced the young guy as an official of the Swiss Embassy.

    2.   We visited two ancient seats of learning: Bologna University in Italy and Santo Tomas University in the Philippines.

    3.   Spilling out from his limousine into the Edgewood Hotel lobby, the Ambassador smiled broadly in spite of the curious eyes riveted to his foreign get-up.

    4.   We can certainly admit that an uninterested judge is always an impartial one.

    5.   All members of the buying public were asked to cooperate in the door-to-door interviews.

    6.   Despite his boasts, he had only one minor run-in with an officer of the law.

    7.   Though crisp, clear, and consummate in depicting the intrigues of high society, his novels obviously will never set the world on fire.

    8.   I would like to continue my studies because my thirst for knowledge has not been stilled by my high school diploma.

    9.   The entire class felicitated Winston Cleen on the occasion of his award of an exchange fellowship.

    10.   The Murdock Corporation's sales representative was requested to come again some other time.

    11.   The youth of today has a much greater sense of social awareness than its forebears.

    12.   A scientific study will be undertaken to ascertain the causes of insufficient motivation on the part of special students from the lower income brackets.

    13.   He used the attendance figures at football games as an example to show the declining interest in intercollegiate sports at his college.

    14.   Ungrammatical English is usually spoken by the underprivileged classes.

    15.   The following excerpt from the first draft of a radio address delivered by President Franklin D. Roosevelt was revised before delivery on April 14, 1938:

Today I sent a Message of far-reaching importance to the Congress. I want to read to you tonight certain passages from that Message, and to add certain observations by way of simplification and clarification.—PORTER G. PERRIN, *Writer's Guide and Index to English*, rev. ed. (Chicago: Scott, Foresman, 1950), p. 19.

Make whatever revisions you think appropriate.

2. Compare the treatment of a news item (such as a political gathering, an international incident, or a biographical account) in two newspapers or magazines, respectively, with special attention to diction. To what extent is the writer's purpose and attitude toward his subject and his reader reflected by his choice of words? Are all meanings overt?

   NOTE: If you select two newspapers, be sure that the two accounts originate from different wire services. A stimulating contrast is often provided by comparison of a story in a U.S. and a foreign newspaper or journal.

3. Select ten instances of connotative meanings in advertising, editorials, or political speeches (the *Congressional Record* is a fertile source for oratory) and discuss their use. Be sure you take context into account.

   SUGGESTION: Consider, for example, the consumer's dilemma in distinguishing "large-," "giant-," "king-," "family-," and "economy-size" tubes of toothpaste in a supermarket, or a "giant half pint" or "jumbo quart" from a "pint" or "quart," respectively.

4. Select ten instances of figurative language in expository writing (articles in weekly or monthly journals are a good source) and discuss their appropriateness and effectiveness. What precision, complexity, and/or simultaneity of statement has the author achieved through his use of figurative language? Has he afforded you any new insights through his use of metaphor?

25) Sentence Economy

Most of us write clumsy sentences more easily than clear and concise ones. The reason for this is that we transfer certain speech habits to the printed page. In our utterances we often make false starts, repeat ourselves unnecessarily, introduce parenthetical elements, and break our sentences off in the middle. President Eisenhower's policy to release verbatim quotations of his press conferences, a practice continued by the late President Kennedy, has produced sprawling sentences from both men that point up sharply the differences between a spoken utterance and a prepared statement. Here is President Eisenhower's reply at a news conference on June 17, 1959, to a question whether he favored a meeting of steel management and labor at the White House to reach agreement on a new contract:

> Well, I will tell you on that one: You have got historical incident—and I believe the outcome was an attempt to seize the steel plants—when exactly that kind of method was adopted.
>
> While I would urge again, personally and directly or indirectly and through press and press media, for each side to recognize the great dangers that come about in inflation and in price rises, I believe for the Government directly to go into this thing further, and in trying to apply political or other pressure, then we are getting inevitably into the beginning of a process that could be more hurtful than helpful.
>
> —*U.S. News and World Report*

The late President Kennedy made this statement on November 29, 1961:

> In answer to your first question, the reason I am answering it with some question is the "ties" at the present time, as you know, that East Germans and West Germans negotiate with regard to trade. So we have to decide— and those negotiations may continue and we will have a clearer idea of what form they will take if we get into a negotiation.—*Time*

Speech is interpersonal, employing vocal emphasis, gesture, eye contact, and context of situation to reinforce meaning. In writing, the meaning appears only as black marks on paper. But the writer has the advantage of examining and reshaping his work before it reaches the reader.

EFFECTIVE AND INEFFECTIVE REPETITION

A powerful rhetorical device for achieving emphasis is repetition. "Give me liberty or give me death," for example, is a more dynamic rendering than "let me die." The restatement of "it is" in the following excerpt from an editorial in the *Saturday Review* underlines an important idea:

> To most Africans . . . education is the most revolutionary part of a revolutionary age. It represents a flying leap from the tenth to the twentieth century. It is a road map out of feudalism. It is the tangible proof of liberation and the first fruit of freedom. It is a certificate of self-respect. It is a promise that fewer babies will die in infancy. It is an admission ticket to the office of a qualified doctor and a lifetime away from leprosy. It is emancipation from witch doctors. It is better crops and enough food. It is a whole host of great expectations that come with self-government. It is what people think about and talk about.—*Saturday Review*

A careful distinction should be made between effective repetition and its misuse, repetitiousness:

> He feels American art, music, and architecture have ceased to be great. He says literature has given up hope. He also asserts that education has declined. He uses the example of the American novel.

Perhaps this is what the student writer intended:

> He feels that American art, music, and architecture have ceased to be great, that literature, especially the novel, has yielded to despair, and that American education has gravely deteriorated.

Here is the same passage rewritten yet another time with more effective repetition:

He thinks that American art, music, and architecture have ceased to be great. He thinks that literature, especially the novel, has yielded to despair. And he thinks that American education has gravely deteriorated.

WORDINESS AND DEADWOOD

A writer is sometimes beset by the temptation to add words and phrases to his sentences to clarify his meaning. But when he examines later what he has written, he may find that he has added words which actually weaken his meaning, if not altogether stifle it. The use of unnecessary words to convey an idea is known as **wordiness,** or **redundancy.** Not exclusively confined to the apprentice writer, it is somewhat like a common cold in that it can hit us all and linger on, more of a nuisance and irritation than a fatal disease. Still, it weakens the bloodstream of a sentence and robs it of vigor.

The restoration of a tired sentence is best accomplished by a frontal assault on the well-worn, comfortable patterns of thought that tempt us to verbosity and redundancy, that replace directness and originality with stereotyped phrases, and more often than not, show a poverty of ideas. Best pursued with a red pencil, the assault demands a critical attitude toward one's imperfections, so that any excess verbiage that obstructs a sentence can be properly eliminated. But perhaps the best prevention against wordiness is an easy familiarity with, and confident control of, one's subject.

If the apprentice writer fears that the removal of wordy phrases and expressions reduces his efforts to a point where he cannot meet his instructor's requirements of length, he should remember that the exchange of a phrase for a word, or a clause for a phrase, results in a net gain of greater precision. And this surely is an advantage. The sophisticated writer does not "pursue a field of study"; he simply "studies." He is not "oriented in the direction of athletics," yet he may "favor athletics." And he does not "set goals of achievement out of possible reach," though he may "aim too high." "Problems in terms of individual differences" may simply mean "individual differences," and a "classroom situation" may refer to a "class" or a "problem"—one cannot be certain. "Teacher intern" is a more formal way of saying "student teacher," and "areas of knowledge" is not nearly as modest as "knowledge." Here are other examples of wordiness, together with suggested revisions:

> The program of study at WMU is divided into two parts. The first part is a program of study for the first and second years, while the second part is for the third and fourth years of undergraduate work in home economics.

REVISED: WMU offers two programs in home economics: one for the first two years and one for the last two years of undergraduate work.

> During the intense emotional experience that Nora subsequently goes through, she comes to a new realization regarding herself and her marriage.

REVISED: Her intense emotional experience brings Nora a new knowledge of herself and of her marriage.

> This type of community, which could be depicted as a "city with a country atmosphere," is usually predominantly residential, with commercial establishments only large enough to serve the immediate vicinity, and little or no industry. People are flocking to these areas in great numbers, striving to gain the peace and quiet that cannot be found in the city, and the conveniences of urban areas, which are lacking in the country. Unfortunately, along with these wonderful advantages come numerous disadvantages too, much to the chagrin of some suburbanites.

REVISED: The suburbs, "cities with a country atmosphere," are predominantly residential with little business or industry. City people flock to them to gain the peace and quiet of the country and the convenience of the city. But with all their merits, the suburbs offer a number of disadvantages, much to the chagrin of some suburbanites.

> As an example of emotional diction I would like to cite an excerpt from the Chicago *Tribune* (Sept. 29, 1960). It is an article by Victor W. Odin, head of engineering services for an aeronautical firm, in which he points out a lack of basic English grammar in their engineers.

REVISED: In an article in the Chicago *Tribune*, (Sept. 29, 1960), Victor W. Odin, head of engineering services for an aeronautical firm, criticizes the English of young engineers.

Excess verbal baggage, sometimes called **deadwood,** lengthens a sentence without adding anything to its meaning. It is an affliction to which after-dinner speakers and politicians are prone, but it looks especially impoverished on the printed page. Not only does it sap a sentence of vitality, but it often obscures its meaning as well. Here are some examples:

Briefly, to summarize the thoughts put forth in this paper . . .
In summary . . .

in the realm of the arts
in the arts

I had an interesting experience while visiting the world's fair. I shall try to relate it here.
[The last sentence is a filler. That the experience will be described is implied in the first sentence.]

Oedipus Rex by Sophocles and *Othello* by Shakespeare, though written in vastly different eras, have a striking similarity—their common theme of discovery.
Oedipus Rex and *Othello* have a striking similarity—their theme of discovery. [Authorship of these plays is common knowledge.]

Sometimes the meaning of a sentence is so remote that intelligent revision is almost impossible:

The constant movement toward adjusting oneself to suit others can only lead to a standstill in progress.
Constant adaptation to the needs of others can stultify one's personality. [?]

Intellectual subjects should be designed to help us appreciate the finer things in life. [Without knowing what the writer means by "intellectual subjects" and "the finer things in life," we cannot properly revise the sentence.]
A liberal education should make us more perceptive and imaginative. [?]

Tautology

A special kind of redundancy, **tautology,** refers to the use of two or more words to express a meaning that any one of them can convey alone. Here are some examples:

His writing was wordily redundant. [wordy *or* redundant.]
They were surrounded (on all sides).
He originated the idea (first).

They were (completely) annihilated.
He had an insurmountable problem (which he could not face).
He arrived at 4 A.M. (in the morning).
the settings in regard to the places the story
   took place [the settings of the story]

Tautologies, found in casual forms of speech, sometimes find their way into writing:

(basic) fundamentals
progress and develop [progress *or* develop]
She was (visibly) moved to tears.

TRIVIALITY

Wishing to be clear and explicit, the beginner sometimes confuses clarity and specificity with encyclopedic detail. He piles detail upon detail, unaware that he is offending his reader's intelligence by belaboring the obvious.

Time and *Newsweek*, which are magazines dedicated to the reporting of news . . .
   [That they are news magazines is generally known; whether they are "dedicated" to the reporting of news is a moot question. The relative clause should be omitted.]

The publication under discussion . . .
   [It is often better to repeat the name of a publication.]

While it is true that the major emphasis on listening will be made in the listening-lecture hours, there are ample opportunities for reinforcing and furthering such instruction by occasional classroom activities.
   [The sentence, from a manual for freshman English instructors at a mid-Western university, says that lectures are chiefly for listening—for what else?—but that listening may also be taught in the classroom. The writer evidently attempts to make a distinction between listening as a subject and as a means to assist in learning.]

Sentimentality is a thing which we all use. . . .
   [Whatever else it may be, sentimentality is not a thing; nor can it be "used."]

Mr. Jones wrote an interesting article instead of a scientific analysis.
   [A scientific analysis and an interesting article are not mutually exclusive. *Interesting*, moreover, is a weak adjective.]

PRETENTIOUSNESS AND FINE WRITING

The broad characteristics of an age are usually reflected by the arts. The sense of balance and order of the eighteenth century, for example, is present as much in the poetry of Alexander Pope as in the paintings of Gainsborough or Sir Joshua Reynolds. Our own society tends to be casual and informal. Present-day writing reflects these characteristics in its plainness, directness, and informality. Highly wrought, affected prose, as well as excessively sentimental writing, is therefore out of place:

A position of agreement can be taken with John Ford's statement.
I agree with John Ford that . . .

Although born in the charming country of Canada, residing in the metropolis of Detroit has been a most pleasurable experience for me during the past twenty years.

Although I was born in Canada, I have lived in Detroit for twenty years.

From "Program Notes" of a concert:

Although Mendelssohn was only twenty-four years old at the time he completed the "Italian" symphony, it may be said to have had the benefit of his full maturity. He was a musician who matured very early in life. His Octet for Strings and overture to the incidental music to "A Midsummer Night's Dream" were composed when he was seventeen and bear eloquent witness to his extraordinary precocity.
[Though not the worst prose one is likely to encounter in theater or concert notes, the passage is highly inflated and circuitous. The author seeks to impress more than to inform—or entertain. The first sentence simply says that the "Italian" Symphony, completed by Mendelssohn at twenty-four, reveals the composer's maturity.]

EXERCISES

1. Revise the following sentences, striving for sentence economy.

   1. The scene between her and Tony seems stilted now.
   2. It was Chekov's belief that one could never really know another person. His plays certainly serve to illustrate this belief.
   3. It was interesting to note that the total length of their services was 127 years.

4. The playwright creates a discussion period for his major characters to exchange their ideas and to act as mouthpieces for the author's political views.
5. The next point I wish to elaborate on rather fully is whether Americans take everything for granted.
6. He described the operation of the machine; then he told us how it works.
7. The end result the writer wished to attain was a scrupulous, careful, and complete assessment of the facts of the situation in Vietnam.
8. A native son of a remote fishing village in Quebec, I have resided in the metropolis of Detroit, which has been a most educational experience for me.
9. I had an unusual experience while visiting San Francisco. I shall spare no effort to describe it.
10. I have been away from learning situations too long to apply myself efficiently to a routine schedule.
11. So far as my experience in the field of selling is concerned, I have been connected with Lumber, Incorporated, for the past two years as a field representative.
12. In view of my earnest desire to join your company, I am taking the liberty of sending herewith my letter of application for the position of medical representative, advertised by your corporation in the Betterton *Times* of August 20, 1963.
13. Whatever qualities written prose may have, these qualities must be realized by means of grammatical patterns and styles.
14. A manuscript intended for others should display one's best efforts, because writing represents an irrevocable or nearly irrevocable commitment on the part of the writer.
15. Teachers of humanities, like their colleagues in the social and natural sciences, should reflect in their instruction the research being carried on in their field.
16. In his speech, delivered before his class, he attempted to discourse on planned obsolescence in the automobile industry.
17. *Death of a Salesman* is a play which is a criticism of modern American life.
18. I believe that unless something is done to replace the old methods of teaching a foreign language still resorted to by most teachers, it will be some time before we can expect students to speak, rather than merely to translate, another language.
19. I wish to take part in the constructive work for world peace through understanding, as well as to nurture and propagate the legacies handed down by our founding fathers.

20. A study was made in 1957 by the U.S. Office of Education, which describes the characteristics desired of home economics teachers.

2. The following excerpts are from a stenographic transcription of remarks made by members of a college committee on the admission and orientation of foreign students. Edit these remarks.

1. I have tried to react by my own reactions in the same situation. The fact is that there are a great number of graduate students, especially on the master's level, who are admitted, whose linguistic ability is very limited.

2. I would hate to see this committee work all fall and coming up with recommendations refuted easily. Whatever recommendations we do come out with should be for the long-range plan.

3. The student should successfully complete or pass a test geared to demonstrating his proficiency in English. Place him on the basis of his demonstration of proficiency. Remedial work for those not able might include direct, even intensive, English training, and registering in courses as a technique of gaining English training in the fields they are competent in.

4. I would like to see the committee discuss more the substance of orientation, to what we want to give the students, a definition of orientation, paying more attention to the academic program of the student and to all kinds of facilities to help him.

5. It is a very real academic responsibility of the entire faculty with the foreign student and his work; the whole matter of—I assume—so doing the job here for the foreign student that we don't give him the impression that we are trying to convert him to something or other, but that he returns to his own country with as fair an impression as possible, knowing full well that he will have some views strongly held about our academic program and our academic competence. The whole university is involved in this—all parts of it—involved while they are here and involved after they leave.

26) *Sentence Variety*

A popular record played over and over soon loses its novelty. Similarly, even the most exciting subject can be a bore if it is poorly presented. Monotonous sentence structure, the recurrence of the same pattern parts in the same position, of the same or nearly the same number of words in successive sentences producing the same singsong rhythm, these can easily put a reader to sleep. Variation and skillful blending of these elements—of sentence length, of sentence types, of coordination, subordination, parallel structure—*can* markedly strengthen a discourse.

But caution is indicated, for rearrangement of even a single word often affects the intent and meaning of a sentence:

Only I know the answer.
I *only* know the answer.
I know *only* the answer.
I know the *only* answer.
I know the answer *only*.

To be sure, the writer usually has a choice of patterns in rendering his meaning, yet one pattern almost always fits a particular context best. The following sentences are equally acceptable:

Sweden, with a population of 7 million, has nearly as many public libraries as the United States.

> With a population of 7 million, Sweden has nearly as many public libraries as the United States.
>
> Although it has only a population of 7 million, Sweden has nearly as many public libraries as the United States.

Given the context, it is clearly the first sentence that conveys the contrast between American and Swedish reading habits most emphatically:

> Child for child and man for man we read fewer books proportionately than almost any so-called cultured country in the world. Sweden, with a population of 7 million, has nearly as many public libraries as the United States.—CLAUDE M. FUESS, *Saturday Review*

SUBORDINATION

The inclusion of an insert sentence into a matrix sentence by means of a subordinator or a relative pronoun is known as **subordination.**[1] The term **subordinate** may indicate a variety of relationships between the included and the including clause, much as a subordinate or subplot bears clearly defined relationships to the main plot. Between plots the relationship is apparent in a number of ways—through character links, cross-triggers of action, and so on. Just so, an insert sentence, or included clause, has meaning precisely because of its relationship to the matrix sentence, or the including clause. If signaled by a subordinator the relationship may denote reason (*because, since, why*), purpose or result (*that, so that, so*), cause (*as, since*), manner (*as*), condition or doubt (*unless, if*), contrast (*while*), concession (*although, though*), alternatives (*whether*), time (*when, while*), or place (*where*). A relative clause, introduced by a relative like *who, which, that,* may qualify or restrict a noun or pronoun in the matrix sentence, or it may modify the matrix sentence as a whole.

Included clauses have been commonly called *dependent clauses,* and *including clauses, independent clauses.* These terms can be altogether misleading if one attaches anything but a grammatical or structural meaning to them, because they imply that a dependent clause contains less important ideas than an independent clause. This oversimplification has been responsible for much mischief, for a restrictive

[1] See Chapter 6.

clause, though dependent, is essential to the meaning of a sentence.[2]
"All students who took the test passed" is more specific than "All
students passed." But without subordination, the sentence with its
stated and implied meanings would have to be rephrased in four
separate constructions: "Some students took the test. They passed.
Others did not take the test. They did (or did not) pass." Such a
string lacks the economy which characterizes the language of intelligent adults.

Subordination, then, should be regarded as a grammatical require-
ment, but context and logic also play a role. As the opening statement
of a report on a sea rescue, the following sentence contains an
improperly subordinated clause:

> A navy helicopter, which rescued two seamen two days after the sinking
> of a destroyer, was part of a sea patrol.

The sentence is grammatical—and perhaps appropriate—in another
context, but not as an opening statement which should emphasize the
rescue mission instead of identifying the rescue instrument:

> A navy helicopter that was part of a sea patrol rescued two seamen after
> the sinking of a destroyer.

Wrong subordination makes the following sentence absurd:

> Man has no claws, large teeth, or hard skin to protect him, because he
> must use his intelligence to ward off enemies.

The absurdity is eliminated by subordinating the independent clause:

> Because man has no claws, large teeth, or hard skin to protect him, he
> must use his intelligence to ward off enemies.

Sometimes insufficient or excessive subordination impairs a sentence. For example:

> With only one semester of speech I decided to enter a forensic contest.
> For this contest I prepared a speech entitled "Our Asian Friend." It
> was about the Philippines.

[2] For an interesting discussion of this problem see James Sledd, "Coordination
(Faulty) and Subordination (Upside-Down)," *College Composition and Communication*, VII (December 1956), 181–187.

The string of sentences can be eliminated by proper subordination:

> After one semester of training, I decided to compete in a forensic contest by speaking on "Our Asian Friend," the Philippines.

Too much subordination obscures this sentence:

> Pastor Manders is so concerned with what society will think of him that he urges Mrs. Alving to decide against insuring the orphanage so that he cannot be criticized for his lack of faith in Divine Providence.

> Much concerned with what society will think of him, Pastor Manders urges Mrs. Alving to leave the orphanage uninsured so that he cannot be accused of lacking faith in Divine Providence.

Sentences beginning with *it is, there is (are), there was (were)* are often strengthened by removing the expletives:

> There is every indication that there is a need for adult education because of the prevalence of illiteracy in the rural areas.

> Widespread illiteracy in the rural areas indicates a need for adult education.
> *Or:* Widespread illiteracy in the rural areas makes adult education essential.

But an expletive is sometimes useful:

> The American homes as we find them today are of two kinds.
> *Better:* There are two kinds of American homes.
> *Still better:* American homes are of two kinds.

Certain subordinate clauses can be effectively reduced to phrases or words:

> He endangered the lives of others who were nearby.
> He endangered the lives of others nearby.

> There are certain components stated in F. L. Lucas's book *Style* that all good writing requires: clarity, readability, and brevity.
> In *Style* F. L. Lucas lists these requirements of good writing: clarity, readability, and brevity.

LOOSE AND PERIODIC SENTENCES

To achieve variety of sentence movement, the writer may construct a sentence whose full meaning is suspended until the end, or he may build a sentence that can be terminated at one or more points before the end. The first is called a **periodic sentence** and the second, a **loose sentence**. Of the two, the loose sentence is clearly the more common:

> An understudy is almost invariably a member of the cast who, if necessary, can play a larger role than the one he has, whereas a standby is a well-known actor in his own right who agrees to stay free of other engagements in order to remain on call.—"The Talk of the Town," *The New Yorker*

The quotation, an example of a loose sentence, could conceivably be terminated after *cast* or at other points before the end. The periodic sentence, on the other hand, suspends the full meaning as long as possible by placing its modifying elements before the main clause. It demands the reader's full attention until he reaches the end of the sentence. Its full effect can best be achieved by using it sparingly but deliberately, much like inversion, discussed in Part I.[3] For example:

> In Britain throughout the nineteenth century the Bank of England was able through the increase or decrease of the bank rate—in principle the rate of interest at which it stood ready to lend money to those who in turn were in the business of lending money—to have a measure of influence on the British banking and business life.
> —JOHN K. GALBRAITH, *The Affluent Society*

The more common sentence order would be as follows:

> In Britain throughout the nineteenth century the Bank of England was able to have a measure of influence on the British banking and business life through the increase or decrease of the bank rate—in principle the rate of interest at which it stood ready to lend money to those who in turn were in the business of lending money.

The full meaning of the Galbraith sentence is suspended by a long parenthetical phrase, but any kind of adjunct either at the beginning or immediately following the subject of the sentence delays predication and so constitutes a departure from normal sentence order:

> If language is intimately related to being human, then when we study language we are, to a remarkable degree, studying human nature.
> —CHARLTON LAIRD, *The Miracle of Language*

> If any one man was the American folk hero of the Twenties, unquestionably the man was the winner in the race for automobile millions, Henry Ford.—ERIC F. GOLDMAN, *Rendezvous with Destiny*

[3] See p. 45.

In the first quotation, two subordinate clauses and a parenthetical element that follows the grammatical subject "we" (in "we are . . . studying") suspend the meaning of the sentence until the end. In the second quotation, the subordinate clause points dramatically to the climax of the sentence, the identification of Henry Ford as "the winner in the race for automobile millions."

The proper distribution of both sentence types can contribute significantly to the overall effect the writer wishes to achieve. In the following excerpt loose and periodic sentences are evenly balanced, the first two being periodic and the last two, loose:

> The only philosophy that affords a theoretical justification of democracy, and that accords with democracy in its temper of mind, is empiricism. Locke, who may be regarded, so far as the modern world is concerned, as the founder of empiricism, makes it clear how closely this is connected with his views on liberty and toleration, and with his opposition to absolute monarchy. He is never tired of emphasizing the uncertainty of most of our knowledge, not with a skeptical intention such as Hume's, but with the intention of making men aware that they *may* be mistaken, and that they should take account of this possibility in all their dealings with men of opinions different from their own. He had seen the evils wrought, both by the "enthusiasm" of the sectaries, and by the dogma of the divine right of kings; to both he opposed a piecemeal and patchwork political doctrine, to be tested at each point by its success in practice.
> —BERTRAND RUSSELL, *Unpopular Essays*

More descriptive and personal than the preceding paragraph, which is primarily analytical, the following excerpt on Paris in the 1920's contains only two periodic sentences, the first and the last. The remaining seven sentences are loose:

> Paris was, it seemed to me, the center of the moral revolution. London and New York were not far behind, but Paris was in its usual position as the capital of Western taste, and its cosmopolitan youth influenced all the rest. More than three hundred thousand Americans used to come to Paris every year in the 1920's, the tide reaching its height in the years when the franc was low and the dollar high. Most of them were probably unaffected by anything they saw, but others remained long enough to realize that they liked the new ways better than the old. The same was true of the English. Englishmen still considered themselves licensed to greater freedoms of behaviour in Paris than at home, but a good number of them took their freedom home again. Prohibition may have made some

difference in America—increased the process in some measure by arousing instinctive rebellions—but the phenomenon was deeper and wider than anything within the scope of written laws. It was a general crumbling of middle-class morality throughout the West, starting in Paris (the logical center of Western taste) and reaching to the outposts of bourgeois culture. We can search the literature of the nineteenth century in all the Western countries in vain for any example of the kind of behaviour on view in 1929 at any party in Paris, London or New York. To our grandparents the ordinary manners, conversation, conduct and morals of educated and "respectable" people would have seemed suitable to the underworld.
—VINCENT SHEEAN, *Personal History*

Loose sentences tend to give an impression of casualness and informality; periodic sentences seem more formal and elaborate. A judicious blending of both types usually helps to insure variety.

PARALLELISM

Parallelism refers to the placing of similarly related elements in a sentence in similar grammatical constructions. These elements, which may consist of words, phrases, or clauses, are linked by a conjunction or joined in a series, with balanced constructions on both sides of the conjunction or in the series. A noun is paired with a noun (*truth and beauty*), a phrase with a phrase (*their claim of sovereignty and their policy of nonrecognition*), or a clause with a clause (*she left, but he continued his job*). The following violate these principles:

*He too admires someone, but his admiration is pure rather than lust. [An adjective and noun are improperly paired.]
He too admires someone, but his admiration is pure rather than lustful.

*You only see them when you need to borrow something or at church on Sundays. [A clause and a prepositional phrase are improperly paired.]
You only see them when you need to borrow something or when you attend church on Sundays.

*How the university is administered, the system of organizing its curriculum, and its offerings were discussed in detail. [A subordinate clause and a noun phrase are improperly paired.]
The administration of the university, the system of organizing its curriculum, and its offerings were discussed in detail.

Paired conjunctions, correlatives (see p. 86), require parallel constructions after each member. Correlatives like *neither . . . nor, either*

. . . or, not only . . . but, whether . . . or, not . . . but, as . . . as, both . . . and.

> The typical American playwright is encouraged to write, *not only* by the pull of literary ideals, *but* by the stimulus of successful Broadway plays. . . . —ROBERT BRUSTEIN, *Harper's Magazine*

The correlatives in Brustein's sentence are followed by prepositional phrases. The correlatives in the following example introduce clauses:

> *Just as* nature determined the location of commercial ports by the confluence of river and sea, *so* man is now directing future use and development of land by the location of interchanges on the new "limited access" freeways.—ROBERT AND LEONA RIENOW, *Harper's Magazine*

The internal structure of elements paired by correlatives need not be identical:

> Not only did he manage his brother's campaigns, but his principal legal experience has been as a partisan.—JOSEPH KRAFT, *Harper's Magazine*

Different basic patterns are paired by the correlatives in Kraft's sentence.

BALANCE AND ANTITHESIS

Balance refers to the use of similar or equivalent grammatical constructions in a sentence to underline or heighten meaning. Edith Hamilton's assessment of the Greek historian Herodotus in the following sentence, for example, gains strength and elegance from the three balanced clauses varied by the periodic arrangement of the last:

> He was born in an age of deep religious feeling, just after the Persian Wars; he lived on into the scepticism of the age of Pericles; and by virtue of his kindly tolerance and keen intellectual interest he was equally at home in both.—EDITH HAMILTON, *The Greek Way*

The following passage by Admiral Rickover derives much of its strength from the three balanced clauses in the second sentence, each defining an objective of European education. By implication, of course, the author censures American educational standards:

> European schools are neither social clubs nor finishing schools. Their objectives are limited and clearly defined: they seek to equip the child

with all the intellectual tools he can handle; they nourish his mind with as much general culture as he can absorb; and they give his body all the exercise it can take.—HYMAN G. RICKOVER, *Education and Freedom*

Antithesis refers to the use of contrast through similar or equivalent grammatical structures. It is characteristic of epigrams (see p. 317), and it is found in public utterances, as the following examples from the late President Kennedy's inaugural address show:

Let us never negotiate out of fear, but let us never fear to negotiate.
Ask not what your country will do for you; ask what you can do for your country.
United there is little we cannot do; divided there is little we can do.

And from a speech to the UN:

Mankind must put an end to war, or war will put an end to mankind.

Balance and antithesis are skillfully blended in the following editorial on predictions made by astrologists that the world would end in 1962:

What was most significant about the entire episode was that man's abode on earth was genuinely in danger but most people were looking in the wrong direction for the source of the trouble. The planets were not going berserk; it was man himself who was wandering precariously off course. And the eclipse of human intelligence, rather than the eclipse of the sun, was responsible for the long shadow obscuring man's future. A collision of nations was far more of a threat than any celestial accident. The universe showed no signs of withdrawing the conditions that made life possible; man himself, however, was showing every sign of rejecting this bounty.—NORMAN COUSINS, *Saturday Review*

Balance is achieved by the parallel development of the two major themes: the imaginary threats to the world from planetary disturbances and the real threats from man himself. The skillful contrast of these themes gives rise to antithesis.

EXERCISES

Discuss the style of each of the following excerpts. Consider such items as sentence movement and variety, favorite grammatical constructions, diction, figurative language, the use of special devices like inversion or ellipsis.

1.   Greek scientists in their century or two of life remade the universe. They leaped to the truth by an intuition, they saw a whole made up of related parts, and with the sweep of their vision the old world of hodgepodge and magic fell away and a world of order took its place. They could only begin the detailed investigation of the parts, but, ever since, Science has by an infinite labor confirmed their intuition of the whole. Greek artists found a disorganized world of human beings, a complex mass made up of units unrelated and disordered, and they too had an intuition of parts all belonging to a whole. They saw what is permanently important in a man and unites him to the rest.
—EDITH HAMILTON, *The Greek Way*

2.   Everyone knows the popular conception of Florence Nightingale. The saintly, self-sacrificing woman, the delicate maiden of high degree who threw aside the pleasure of a life of ease to succour the afflicted, the Lady with the Lamp, gliding through the horrors of the hospital at Scutari, and consecrating with the radiance of her goodness the dying soldier's couch—the vision is familiar to all. But the truth was different. The Miss Nightingale of fact was not as facile fancy painted her. She worked in another fashion, and towards another end; she moved under the stress of an impetus which finds no place in the popular imagination. A Demon possessed her. Now demons, whatever else they may be, are full of interest. And so it happens that in the real Miss Nightingale there was more that was interesting than in the legendary one; there was also less that was agreeable.
—LYTTON STRACHEY, *Eminent Victorians*

3.   Every year swallows are drawn to Capistrano, lemmings pour suicidally into the sea, and waves of young ladies wash into New York City to go on the stage. They hurl themselves through and over walls of discouragement built of legends, statistics, and the lyrics of wry popular songs. If they are more understandably driven than the lemmings, they are proportionately more touching and more awesome. For they deliberately elect to hunt employment in a profession which has never heard of the five-day week, takes pride in devouring the young, and boasts of a way of life into which no nice young lady should enter.—
HENRY BUTLER, "To Be a Bernhardt," *Harper's Magazine*, August 1963

4.   *The New Yorker's* overuse of commas, originating in Ross's[4] clarification complex, has become notorious the world over among literary people. In Paris, in 1955, an English journalist said to me one night, "The

---

[4] Harold W. Ross, founder and editor of the magazine from 1925 to 1951.

biography of Ross should be called *The Century of the Comma Man*."
A professor of English somewhere in England wrote me ten years ago
a long, itemized complaint about the *New Yorker* comma, objecting to,
among other things, its use after "moreover" and "furthermore," in
which, he said the comma is implicit. He picked out this sentence in a
New Yorker casual of mine: "After dinner, the men went into the
living room," and he wanted to know why I, or the editors, had put in
the comma. I could explain that one all right. I wrote back that this
particular comma was Ross's way of giving the men time to push back
their chairs and stand up.—JAMES THURBER, *The Years with Ross*

5. For the last twenty years the American Santa Claus has been almost
foolishly generous to "creative" writers. (These are usually defined as
the producers of fiction, plays, and poetry, although sometimes the
ground rules are stretched to include criticism.) So many foundations
now offer them subsidies that practically anyone with a hint of talent
can pick up some kind of grant or traveling fellowship. Some two
hundred medals and prizes are awarded every year to celebrate their
output. Artistic game preserves such as the MacDowell Colony provide
them food and lodging in pleasant surroundings so that they can cultivate
their genius without distraction or anxiety. Innumerable colleges offer
courses in Creative Writing, plus semi-sinecures for resident poets and
novelists. So if the United States is not yet producing literary masterpieces by the cord, it certainly isn't for lack of final encouragement.
—JOHN FISCHER, "Helping Hand for a Literary Upstart," *Harper's
Magazine*, September 1963

Index

Index